Vision and Reality, Market and State

By the same author

Overcentralization in Economic Administration, 1959
Mathematical Planning of Structural Decisions, 1967
Anti-Equilibrium, 1971
Rush versus Harmonic Growth, 1972
Economics of Shortage, 1980
Non-Price Control, ed. (with B. Martos), 1981
Growth, Shortage and Efficiency, 1981
Contradictions and Dilemmas, 1985–86

Vision and Reality, Market and State

Contradictions and Dilemmas Revisited

János Kornai

ROUTLEDGE
NEW YORK

First published in the USA in 1990 by
Routledge
an Imprint of Routledge. Chapman and Hall, Inc.
29 W. 35th Street
New York, NY 10001

Printed in Hungary

Library of Congress Cataloging-in-Publication Data

Kornai, János,
    Vision and reality, market and state.

    Continues: Contradictions and dilemmas.
    Includes bibliographical references.
    1. Hungary—Economic policy—1968–   .
2. China—Economic policy—1976–   .
3. Communist countries–Economic policy.
I. Kornai, János. Ellentmondások és dilemmák.
II. Title.
HC300.28.K674 1990   330.9172'4   89–24285

ISBN 0–415–90285–1

Contents

List of Figures

List of Tables

Preface to the English edition

As indicated by its subtitle, 'Contradictions and Dilemmas Revisited', this book is a continuation of my earlier collection of essays, published under the title *Contradictions and Dilemmas*. The essays confront the visions and hopes of reformers with the reality of the transformation process of socialist countries, which exhibits a particular blend of coordination by the state and the market.

The essays were written during the period 1983 to 1988.[1] Some were addressed to an audience or readership of experts. Yet I hope that the bulk of this volume or perhaps the whole text will be useful to any educated reader, including not only economists but political scientists, sociologists, philosophers, journalists, people involved in politics and government, and anyone seriously interested in the affairs of the socialist world. I also expect that some of the papers could be used as background material in the teaching of comparative economic systems and socialist economy.

Although most of the essays deal with *positive* description and analysis, there are one or two exceptions. For example, a previously unpublished memorandum provides the author's comments on prices and inflation, and an excerpt from a book (written with Á. Matits) summarizes the authors' position on the firms' taxation, subsidies, profit and price determination. It is now clear that these two studies were futile attempts to influence policy-makers who, not surprisingly, did not listen.

Some of the essays discuss topics on a rather general level, or focus on a country other than Hungary, such as the one (written with Zs. Dániel) on the Chinese reform. Even though most of the papers tend to concentrate on Hungary, the issues discussed are fairly general and of relevance to the study of other socialist countries. On the cover of the Hungarian edition of my earlier book *Contradictions and Dilemmas* there was a photo collage in which a map of Hungary appeared inside a laboratory test tube. And indeed, Hungary can be regarded as a laboratory in which experiments on the transformation of a Stalinist regime into something else are conducted. Of course, it is doubtful that Hungarian citizens enjoy their role of guinea pigs. There have been blood and tragedies, euphoric phases alternating with disappointment. There have been waves of optimism and pessimism, the simple joy of the first refrigerator or the first car, and the first shocking experiences with accelerating inflation and with unemployment.

While writing this preface, Hungary's future is unpredictable. One can imagine various scenarios. A relatively peaceful transition to a genuine multi-party democracy and a genuine mixed economy can be regarded as a realistic expectation. But the economic situation is disastrous; millions feel depressed and betrayed by broken promises, and they suffer from the deterioration of the standard of living and accelerating inflation. Given these circumstances, an explosion, something like the uprising of 1956, may occur, followed either by the stabilization of a new regime or a brutal restoration of the old one. The brutal repression of the Chinese freedom movement is a traumatic warning in this respect. But there is another vision of the future: prolonged frustration, despair and unresolved contradictions, a strange 'equilibrium', where all the countervailing forces are too weak to get the upper hand and exert true leadership. Analysts agree that these are among the main scenarios, allowing, of course, for variations and combinations, while opinions differ on the subjective probabilities attached to each expectation.

This book does not join in the speculation. However, I hope that whatever course history may take, a book like this will serve a modest but useful purpose for both Hungarians and non-Hungarians. It is an eye-witness's report, describing from the inside what is going on in the laboratory experiments. The essays may influence prevailing thought; promote the erosion of old dogmas and open the mind to new ideas. And such an impact on public opinion may become more important in the long term than any direct influence on the current decisions taken by the ruling bureaucracy of socialist countries.

These days the tone of the debate in Hungary, but also to some extent in Poland, Yugoslavia and the USSR, is highly emotional, filled with accusations and counter-accusations, rage and impatience. In this sense, this book is out of tune; its essays are written in a deliberately calm style, striving towards scholarly impartiality and fair balance. The essays try to eliminate false hopes and naiveté and at the same time to strengthen the commitment to a consistent transformation.

Finally, although most of the essays deal with down-to-earth economic topics, such as decentralization, the abolition of the command system, soft and hard budget constraints, inflation and so on, I sincerely hope that they convey an underlying moral and political philosophy, which reflects the desire of many Hungarians (and I am convinced, also of many people from other socialist countries) to establish as the ultimate outcome of the present painful transformation process a society with strong guarantees for individual freedom, autonomy, and for national self-determination.

Budapest and Cambridge, Massachusetts,
February 1989   János Kornai

NOTE

1. I wish to express my thanks to all those who participated in the translation and the publication of these essays: Magda Benczédi, Robert Bolick, Mária Kovács, Carla Krüger, Ilona Lukács, Brian McLean, Shailendra Raj Mehta, Anna Seleny, Miklós Uszkay and Judit Vári. I am very grateful for their attention and care. Further acknowledgements will be added in the notes following each chapter.

1 Bureaucratic and Market Coordination*

This paper has two objectives. Firstly, to raise a few theoretical ideas and outline an analytical framework that can be used for investigating related problems. Secondly, to make a contribution to the discussion of economic reform from the viewpoint of bureaucratic and market coordination. The paper is a partial product of a longer research.[1] Owing to a shortage of space, I shall be forced to discuss great and complicated issues briefly: they will be explained in detail in later publications.

1.1 THE FOUR MECHANISMS OF COORDINATION

In the paper different *coordination mechanisms* will be confronted with each other. Coordination in the present paper is defined as the regulation of two or several mutually interacting individuals or organizations. Not only the control of the production and trade of economic goods in the everyday sense are included, but also the regulation of every kind of social transformation and transaction process. Thus, not only coordination of the production and sales of iron or textiles, but also of automobile transport and the health service are included.

---

* The author's inaugural address on Apr. 16, 1983 at the Hungarian Academy of Sciences.
The author gratefully acknowledges the support of the Institute of Economics, Hungarian Academy of Sciences and the Alexander von Humboldt-Stiftung, German Federal Republic.

The term *allocation mechanism* may be used as a synonym. Co-ordination includes the allocation of the inputs and outputs of the activities.

For the purpose of abstract analysis, four pure types will be distinguished.

To distinguish the basic forms of coordination three main characteristics of each will be stressed.

I.I.I Bureaucratic coordination[2]

a. There is a vertical relationship, sub- and superordination, between the coordinating individual or organization and the coordinated individuals or organizations. Above the direct bureaucratic control of the microprocesses, there is usually a multi-level hierarchy of sub- and superordinations, which indirectly participate in the coordination.

b. The individuals and organizations are motivated to accept the orders and prohibitions of the coordinator through administrative coercion supported by legal sanctions. The vertical relationship is lasting and institutionalized; it is mutually acknowledged both 'above' and 'below'.

c. The transactions are not necessarily monetarized. But if they are, the subordinated individual or organization is financially dependent on its superior.

I.I.2 Market coordination

a. There is a horizontal relationship between the buyer and seller individual or organization; the two participants are equal from the legal point of view.

b. The individuals or organizations are motivated by the intention to make profit in terms of money. In its pure form market coordination takes place at free prices based on an agreement between buyer and seller; at prices which it pays for both parties to sell and buy.

c. The transactions are monetarized. This is the only form of coordination which is necessarily monetarized.

I.I.3 Ethical coordination

a. As with market coordination, a horizontal relationship exists between individual organizations.

b. The actors are not motivated by administrative coercion or by the intention of making profit in terms of money. Coordination may be based on reciprocity, on the expectation of mutual help, but it may also be one-sidedly altruistic. On the level of abstract discussion the question of by what moral principles individuals or organizations are motivated will be left open. For a lasting prevalence of this form of coordination it is necessary that it should be fixed by custom or tradition and the underlying principles be raised to morally obligatory norms for the participants.

c. The transactions are, as a rule, not monetarized (though there may be exceptions; one of their possible forms is a present of money).

1.1.4 Aggressive coordination

a. There exists a vertical relationship between a superordinated and one or several subordinated individual(s), organization(s). To this extent it resembles 1.1.1

b. The motivation is established by force on the part of the superordinated towards the subordinated in order to achieve the desired transformation or transaction. This is a wilful force — not acknowledged by law and morality. This is precisely what distinguishes it from 1.1.1: coercion is not institutionalized. For this reason it is mostly not lasting but of occasional nature.

c. The transactions may be either monetarized or not.

I will quote two examples to illustrate the four basic forms. One example is coordination of *land use.* Bureaucratic coordination: the state authority allocates the land for the users. Market coordination: the ownership of land or the right to use it is sold and bought for money. Ethical coordination: the occupants of free land voluntarily agree which land will be used by whom; or the owner gives the land as a present. Aggressive coordination: the land is robbed from the earlier possessor.

The other example is coordination of the *traffic of passenger cars,* that is, allocation of the right to use the road. Bureaucratic coordination: official prescriptions of behaviour on the roads, the observance of which is monitored and enforced by the police. Market coordination: the setting of parking fees or the collection of tolls for the use of the roads. Ethical coordination: the voluntary attention and consideration of drivers towards other drivers. Aggressive coordination: the driver wilfully restricts or infringes upon the rights of other drivers: overtaking them by forcing them to sudden braking, 'pushing' them from behind, etc.

I would add some general remarks to the above classification.

- A considerable part of the literature on the problem classifies the *organizations* according to various criteria and then examines the behaviour of some characteristic type of organization (e. g. the 'bureau' or the 'enterprise'). In contrast, we are studying *control processes*. Such a coordination mechanism may cover a very wide scope of activities. (E.g. control of all kinds of production and trading activities of the state-owned enterprise in the framework of the mechanism of directive planning.) But it may be narrow, covering some partial area such as the coordination of passenger car traffic previously mentioned.
- In our analysis we are discussing not only objects or physical actions and processes, but more importantly relationships between people, that is, social relationships.
- The research task to be performed is to elaborate the *political economy of coordination*.
- Our discipline is only beginning to cope with this task.
- I have made efforts to provide a *complete classification*[3] with the four basic forms reviewed.
- The classification is complete in the sense that the direct control of every microprocess is performed by one of the basic forms or by some of their combination.[4]
- Never in history has a society existed in which every activity was coordinated exclusively by one of the four basic forms. The most ancient forms are 1.1.4 and 1.1.3, but also the basic forms 1.1.1 and 1.1.2 look back on a long historical past.

In reality the different basic forms operate side by side. Their scope is partly disjunct, but partly they assert themselves more or less closely intertwined. History has already brought about a huge variety of combinations and, parallel to the existing ones, new combinations are continuously coming about.

Historical transitions from one basic form to another also took place frequently. 1.1.3 may change into 1.1.1: the ethical norms become institutionalized as legal norms, their observance is no longer left to conscience, but is forced by sanctions and, together with this change, the bureaucratic machinery of coercion also ap-

pears. There further exists another kind of historical transformation: the ethical coordination becomes 'commercialized', that is,
1.1.3 turns into form 1.1.2. Thus, the activity is increasingly motivated by financial gain instead of by moral command. Or, again,
another kind of historical transition: 1.1.4 changes into form 1.1.1.
The openly wilful force becomes institutionalized, it turns into
legally sanctioned bureaucratic coercion. But the reverse exists, when
the legally regulated bureaucratic coordination operating in a lawful
framework degenerates into open wilfulness. Coordination changes
from basic form 1.1.1 into 1.1.4.

An important direction of further research is the *historical* and
the related *causal* analysis. It has to be clarified which basic form
of coordination comes to the fore in which historical situation and
under what social conditions together with the proportions, and
relative weights with which the basic forms participate in the
combinations. The present study does not undertake this historical
and causal examination. Instead, we shall restrict ourselves to asking much narrower and more modest questions.

1.2 THE TENACITY OF BUREAUCRACY

The first question to which I should like to find an answer is whether
the role of the bureaucratic mechanism is growing, stagnating or
diminishing in the social coordination of Hungary today. Owing to
the spatial limitations of this paper, I will not engage in the discussion of the *relative* proportions, and weights of the various mechanisms. I shall restrict myself to examining the *dynamics* of the
bureaucratic mechanism.

The scope of bureaucracy is difficult to measure. In Table 1.1
we make an attempt at characterizing the expansion of bureaucratic coordination with the aid of a few indicators. I make no comments on the individual development of the six kinds of time series.
There is some fluctuation. Expansion and restriction do not occur
uniformly with the various indicators. Yet it may be established,
with global picture presented by the table, that *the series of data
shows a rather high stability. Nowhere do we find a declining trend;
either stagnation or growth can be experienced. This shows the extreme tenacity of bureaucratic coordination in a historical situation*

Table 1.1: Some indicators of the expansion of bureaucratic coordination

Indicators	Unit of meas- urement	1970	1971	1972
1 Number of legal orders	pieces		319	364
2 Staff of central organs	heads	10,245	10,791	10,892
3 Administrative expenses of budgetary organs (at constant prices)	million Ft	3,098	3,268	3,462
4 Centralized part of net income	per cent	71.5	73.6	73.4
5 Ratio of central government contribution to the own funds in the development fund of the county councils	per cent	427.9	432.9	489.1
6 The ratio of profit-deflection caused[2] by redistribution in state-[3]owned enterprises	per cent			

Explanation and source of the data: The data in row 1 were compiled in the Ministry for Justice. See also the article by Á. Kováts. — The data in row 2 include only the staff of the central organs, but excludes those of the councils. Nor do they include the armed forces. The data were compiled in the Ministry of Finance. — The data in row 3 include the administrative expenses of the central organs, plus those of the councils of the capital and of the counties as well as those of the councils of larger cities of county rank. They do not comprise the administrative expenses of the smaller communities (district and town councils, etc.), the expenditure on defence, law and justice, nor those spent on social and economic purposes, etc. The data at current prices were taken from the budget estimates: the actual figures differ little from these. The source is the budget act on the years in question. The data at current prices were converted to constant prices with the aid of a series of prince index numbers received from the Central Statistical Office. It was the series relating to 'public consumption' that was used for the purpose. — The source of the data in row 4 is the book by Kupa (1980) and the data for the last years were compiled by him (Institute for Finance Research). — The data in row 5 compare the two sources of receipts of the councils of the capital, the counties and cities of county rank: the central government contribution is divided by the own sources of the councils and expressed in percentages. The source of the data is the budget acts. — The data in row 6 were taken from the material of a research project, conducted by a group of researchers directed by the author. (See the study by Kornai—Matits—Ferge; We determined what the profit of a state-owned enterprise would be if no taxes were levied on it and no state subsidies under any title would be received. This we called 'original profit'. The data in the table are a quotient: original profit less actually accounted profit per original profit. The indicator shows approximately the relative weight of income redistribution implemented in the scope of state-owned enterprises.

1973	1974	1975	1976	1977	1978	1979	1980	1981
307	382	371	399	386	332	406	431	433
10,719	10,721	10,806	11,046	11,012	10,993	10,750	10,699	10,069
3,587	3,995	4,221	4,156	4,220	4,369	4,517	4,789	5,049
70.4	69.0	69.6	70.2	69.0	70.0	70.9	70.3	
489.1	522.9	519.7	736.8	631.9	677.7	666.7	614.1	660.8
		70.2	59.3	53.7	56.4	63.0	65.8	

when, as a matter of fact, a deep decentralizing reform process took place.

I separately stress row 3 of Table 1.1, which shows the expenditure on bureaucracy, at unchanged prices, thus eliminating the inflationary effect. Let us confront this with the dynamics of production. The main data are comprised in Table 1.2. We divided the period for which the data on administrative expenses were available into two subperiods: the years between 1970–1978, before the braking of production, and the years of restriction between 1979–1981.

We all know Parkinson's book (1958)[5] in which he shows that while the British colonial empire was dwindling the central colonial bureaucracy increased. Table 1.2 seems to present some kind of Hungarian Parkinson's law: While the growth of production radically slowed down, the growth of expenditure on the bureaucratic

Table 1.2: The growth rates of output and of administrative expenses in per cent

Period	GDP	Administrative expenses
1970–1978	5.9	4.4
1979–1981	1.4	5.6

Source: The GDP-data were taken from the Statistical Year-books.
For the source of data on administrative expenses see the explanation of row 3 in Table 1. Both series of data were compiled at unchanged prices.

machinery continued to increase, it even accelerated somewhat. What caused this tenacity? What is the explanation for the fact that the growth of bureaucracy is an almost irreversible process? Without a claim to completeness, I would stress four explanatory factors.

1.2.1 The inclination of bureaucratic coordination to self-accomplishment

Bureaucracy spans a network of rules in the flow of some social microprocess. If the net is too thin, every kind of irregularity slips through it. The solution is to make the network thicker. We may call this the *'inclination to self-accomplishment' of bureaucracy: it is inclined to complement the general regulation again and again with more concrete and detailed rules.*

I will quote two examples, the first from the field of price and profit regulation. In 1979 the Ministry of Home Trade issued an order on the so-called 'price-risk fund'[6]. The idea was suggested by the practice of the market mechanism. If the conditions of sale demanded it, the trading firm should be in a position to grant a price reduction. The enterprise should form a separate fund from its receipts in order to compensate for the receipts lost in consequence of price reduction. The idea is rational, but now comes the bureaucratic regulation of the affair. 'What is allowed, is compulsory...' The formation of the price-risk fund is not only allowed, but even prescribed by order. In fact, it is determined to the minutest detail how much the enterprise is to place into fund — in percentage of the price receipts. The Trial (trading in toys) 0.8 per cent, the Amfora (glassware) 0.7 per cent, the Piért (paperware) 0.2 per cent, the Ecclesia cooperative (candles, books and painting, etc., related to the practice of the Catholic religion) 0.6 per cent, and so forth. Should the fund prove to be too big, it cannot be used to increase profits, but should it be too small, it has to be refilled from profits.

My other example concerns the financial stimulation of managers. In 1980 the Ministry of Home Trade regulated, by order, the financial incentives of enterprise managers.[7] The order emphasized all kinds of 'viewpoints' which should be taken into account in allocating bonuses. Among them we find several concrete 'tasks' from the implementation of energy saving regulations to satisfy demands of families with many children and of retired people to the reduction of stocks. The order meticulously determined the lower and upper limits of the bonus coefficients, taking care that the upper limit of 4.0 should be in the 'trade in miscellaneous articles', while in the commodity leasing enterprises and in the travel agencies it should be only 3.5.

We examined the regulations and orders of several years and can quote dozens of similar examples.

1.2.2 Extension of bureaucracy to earlier little-regulated fields

In the preceding section we spoke about the intensive growth of bureaucracy, we shall now pass to its extensive growth. *When the role of bureaucracy is pushed back in some area, its point of emphasis frequently shifts to another field.* The phenomenon resembles the surgeon removing a cancerous tumour at one place in an organism, but in the meantime a metastasis has developed and the proliferation of cancer cells has started elsewhere.

The problem became clear after 1968. The mechanism of bureaucratic instruction was eliminated from the direct control of production. True, it steals back again and again. But, and this is even more important, a metastasis has developed in the regulation of enterprise income. The Ministry of Finance carried out a study on the regulators affecting profit.[8] Accordingly, profit is affected by 228 kinds of so-called regulatory elements (i.e. bureaucratic interference). A dozen state organs claim the right to give or take, that is, actively interfere with the formation of profit.

1.2.3 Shortage and administrative allocation

In the case of shortage, when market coordination cannot fulfil its function, the mutual adjustment of demand and supply, either the mechanism 1.1.4 steps in (might is right...) or bureaucratic coordination becomes indispensable.

A vicious circle begins.[9] The bureaucratic regulation unavoidably leads to excessive claims, because the claimants believe they will improve their bargaining positions in this manner. Rationing leads to hoarding, i. e. to the swelling of users' stocks. Demand becomes almost limitless — and shortage becomes permanent, if only on this account. In this lasting shortage situation the administrative system of allocation becomes unavoidable — and so forth.

Many examples could be quoted, beginning with the administrative allocation of state-owned flats to some still existing material quotas. A fresh example is the intensification of the shortage of foreign exchange. The bureaucratic regulation of imports from the West and of the use of convertible currencies has suddenly revived and is booming: exports are forced through administrative pressure.

1.2.4 Interest in doing away with bureaucracy

In Hungary everybody is against bureaucracy — and yet this cannot develop into some kind of mass movement. Why not?

It is firstly the bureaucrat in charge of a certain area that is mainly interested in maintaining bureaucratic coordination in the field under his supervision. This provides power and prestige, and it rarely occurs that people voluntarily and gladly renounce them. But also, those, who are beneficiaries of its redistributive effect or may expect such effect in the future, are interested in maintaining bureaucratic coordination. Let us consider the example already mentioned, the regulation of enterprise income. Several state organs are in a position of great power in that they can provide income to the enterprise or can draw away income from it. Also the enterprises which to some extent draw advantages from the present redistribution or expect to enjoy such favours later are interested in preserving this influence.

There are many advocates of further decentralization and of further increasing the role of market coordination in the circles of economic leadership. However, many of them are adhering to this reform process in such a way, that they advocate the preservation of bureaucratic position *in their own sphere of power only — as an exception* to the general rule. As every economic executive has its own sphere of power, every bureaucratic position has a strong defendant. In addition, those defending their positions can count on a mass background of supporters, in the sphere of the actual or prospective beneficiaries of their own reallocation activity. *This is the paradox in the fight for suppressing bureaucracy: in spite of the general anti-bureaucratic feeling great powers are fighting for the preservation of every single bureaucratic position.*

1.3 DISPUTE WITH THREE VIEWS

Although, as is apparent from the preceding section, the scope of bureaucracy has proved to be stable up to now, there are many — myself included — who believe that we must fight to reduce its role. But opinions are divided as to *how* to fight. I should like to challenge three views.

1.3.1 Neither bureaucracy, nor market?

After a scientific discussion a young woman sociologist fulminated: 'I hate bureaucracy and I hate the market'. I assume she does not like aggressive coordination either. It logically follows that she is of the opinion that the 1.1.3, i.e. ethical coordination, should become dominant.

This is not an exceptional standpoint. In my opinion it is unacceptable in this extreme form. In pre-industrial societies — particularly in the primitive ones — the scope of 1.1.3 was still much wider. Then the coordination of activities was a much simpler task. Society did not move for a long time, it was stationary, and under such conditions custom, the routine-like repetition of the same activities, and the influence of tradition obtained a greater role. Society was morally much more homogeneous than in recent times.

Now that has all been changed. Owing to technical progress and the much more differentiated division of labour, coordination has become much more complicated. The economy and society are undergoing constant and rapid changes, custom and tradition can become less stable. There are deep conflicts between the moral concepts of various social strata and groups. It is not a matter of faith or hope whether under such conditions 1.1.3 can play a dominating role. The proposition can be empirically proven that *moral coordination does not — and cannot – play a dominating role in any modern socio-economic system.*

In our age the 1.1.3 seems to be rather unstable and transient. In several fields where ethical coordination takes place sooner or later 'commercialization' occurs (1.1.3→1.1.2) or it becomes institutionalized and bureaucratic (1.1.3→1.1.1), and in the worst case it is ousted by aggressive coordination (1.1.3→1.1.4). *There is no vacuum in coordination!* Where there is no strong and tough mechanism 1.1.1 and/or 1.1.2, and where 1.1.3 proves to be weak, 1.1.4 will break in.

In my opinion the role of ethical coordination may be restricted to the following:

• It may regulate processes in which neither bureaucracy nor the market plays — perhaps even cannot play — the main role. For example, the choosing of a partner (in marriage) is a coordination and allocation process. In our age this is basically regulated by an ethical coordination mechanism, and the other mechanisms perform at most complementary functions. (Obviously, this was not always so in the course of history.)

• It may appear also in combinations, as complementary to 1.1.1 and 1.1.2 as main coordinators. In the best case, it may achieve that bureaucracy or the market should be 'honest'.

As long as not more is expected of the ethical coordination, it deserves the warmest support. It is essential that the family, the school and the media should invoke unselfishness, voluntary adjustment and attention to our fellow-beings.[10] It deserves, however, quite different judgement, if somebody expects more than that and believes — and makes others believe — that the control of production can be based, massively and generally, on ethical coordination. This is naive Don-Quixotism, which is usually associated with a nostalgic desire for past 'more ethical', 'more community-minded' ages. In the final analysis these naive views may even have harmful effects, because they prevent people from facing the true dilemma: what role to give to 1.1.1 and 1.1.2, to bureaucracy and to the market. These and only these are the really strong and weighty alternatives.[11]

1.3.2 Complete elimination of bureaucracy?

As a representative of the second view I shall quote from an article of mine published 34 years ago under the title 'Let us uproot bureaucracy'.[12] Many support this view even today. This, too, is an extreme and naive view. As for myself, I am now of the opinion that it does not hold water.

The great virtues of the market are well-known. It provides a sensitive information system. And stimulation is automatically linked to information: not only positive stimulation rewarding success, but also a negative one punishing poor performance. Who does not adjust, and does not economize, will be eliminated sooner or later on the market, the producer and the seller are forced to heed the demand of the buyer.

All that notwithstanding, the market coordination also has great deficiencies. There are several such functions of coordination in which the market fails. These are commonly known, and, precisely, on this account there is a social demand for the elimination of market failures. Together with that, *there also exists a social demand for applying bureaucratic coordination.* This social demand, too, keeps bureaucracy alive, not merely the tenacious clinging of bureaucrats themselves to their own influence. This is so in the capitalist market economy and this social demand asserts itself even more in the socialist socio-economic system. Without claiming a complete analysis I shall emphasize three issues in this context.

The first is *the deficiencies of the market in performing economic coordination.* Some activities may have detrimental qualities which the market does not account among the costs, and others produce social benefits which are not accounted among the receipts. This is the well-known problem of *externalities.* In such cases interference through bureaucratic control is mostly unavoidable. Prohibitive administrative regulations or officially levied deterring taxes are needed in order that the participants in economic life restrict their activities entailing unfavourable external effects. Similarly, actions entailing favourable external effects can be stimulated by officially regulated financial advantages, e.g. tax rebates.

A related problem is that of *transaction costs.* The coordination of the use of highways might be solved, as a matter of course, by taking tolls at every corner from those actually using that road. But this 'pure' market solution would be very inconvenient and expensive. In this case the bureaucratic solution is more advantageous: the owners of cars pay taxes and the maintenance of the road network is covered from tax income as a free service. The market solution is also circumstantial in several other cases and involves prohibitive transaction costs, while the bureaucratic solution may prove to be cheaper.

Another important issue: *the deficiencies of the market in securing a fair distribution of income.* The market differentiates incomes in a manner that necessarily infringes upon the moral principles relating to just distribution of income. It may bring about an extent of inequality which is no longer necessary for stimulation to better performance. Such high incomes emerge from unsatisfactory socially useful performance, merely good fortune, inheritance, etc. And conversely, low incomes exist which cannot be attributed to the lack of industry, but to inherited unfavourable conditions or other misfortunes.

To develop more just income proportions, taxes, subsidies, welfare payments and other interferences serving redistribution are necessary and for their implementation a bureaucratic machinery is necessary. The stronger the claim on redistribution, the greater the role of the bureaucratic machinery will be.

Finally, a third issue is related to *the monopolies*. Development of the productive forces entails the specialization and concentration of production and this unavoidably leads to the emergence of monopolies. An accompanying phenomenon of this historical process is the appearance of social demand for the restriction of monopolistic power. Bureaucratic organizations evolve for the purpose of controlling the monopolies or they are nationalized, or their functions are taken over by bureaucratic institutions.[13]

To sum up: *bureaucracy cannot be uprooted because – above a certain level of development of productive forces – its roots are found in social existence itself.* The troubles with the other coordination mechanisms make the appearance of bureaucracy unavoidable by themselves. To remain with the example of the 'tree and the wood', we have to remain satisfied with more modest aims: the tree of bureaucracy should not grow to the skies, it should not proliferate like a jungle.

1.3.3 A harmonious symbiosis of the market and bureaucracy?
The third view I should like to challenge is a simplification of the symbiosis of market and bureaucracy. The advocates of this view are usually satisfied with such stereotypes as: let the 'government-regulated market' or the 'planned regulated market' function. But this is easier to wish, to proclaim as a slogan in fully general terms than to actually implement.

The market and bureaucracy are not a gin and tonic that can be mixed in any proportion wanted. There may be a certain level of bureaucratic market restrictions which still allows breath for the market. But beyond a critical limit bureaucratic restriction cools down the live forces of the market, kills them — and only the appearance of a market remains. And there exists a combination of market and bureaucracy which unites, as it were, only the disadvantages of the two, while the separately existing advantages of both are lost.

As an example I should like to quote the prices adjusting to world market prices, the so-called 'competitive price system' introduced in Hungary. The basic order was issued in November, 1979. Since then, until April 1983, 14 orders have been issued which complement, modify or interpret the original, that is, one every 2 or 3 months. But, so it seems there always remains something requiring new regulation. Let us have a look at a concrete order, that of April, 1981.[14] On a real market it depends on the horizontal relationship between seller and buyer and is determined by the relation of supply to demand, to which buyer the seller will sell the commodity and at what price. Against that, the order quoted interferes with this process in a vertical manner. The original order wished to adjust the price that can be charged on the domestic market to the external market price. The modification provides exemption from this rule under definite conditions. It establishes that the producer needs to reduce the price level of domestic sales even if the profitability or price level of the non-rouble exports diminished, insofar as the following conditions are met:

- the ratio of non-rouble exports is 5–12 per cent of domestic sales and non-rouble exports have grown by 10 per cent, or
- the ratio of non-rouble exports is 12–15 per cent of domestic sales and non-rouble exports have grown by 8 per cent, or
- the ratio of non-rouble exports exceeds 25 per cent and non-rouble exports have grown by 6 per cent.

It seems that these ratios have not stood the test. A few months later a modification of the modification was issued.[15] The earlier critical values of 10–8–6 per cent have been now replaced by 8–6–4 per cent. Why exactly 8–6–4 per cent? Why not double or half these values? And has the sales price on the domestic market nothing to do with the state of the domestic market at any time?

These two orders are typical examples of bureaucratic market restriction. The price system adjusting to world market prices is usually characterized by its advocates by saying that in this case it is the office that simulates the market. The situation rather reminds me of female impersonators. The superficial viewer may have the first impression that he sees a woman, while in reality the one he sees is not a woman exactly in the most distinctive characteristics. This alleged simulation of the market differs from the real market in the most important and most advantageous feature of the latter: that the seller depends on the buyer (and not on the office).

The example we have reviewed is not simply a vicious circle in the relationship of the market and bureaucracy. More aptly, we may speak about a whirlpool, the *whirlpool of bureaucratic market restrictions*. The more frequent, clumsy and mechanical the interference, the poorer the operation of the market. Thus, the authority increasingly feels it has to intervene more frequently and in greater detail — in response to which the market will operate even more poorly and so forth. The bureaucratic restriction of the market deepens and, in the final analysis, the market becomes atrophied.

From what has been said two normative viewpoints follow. One is that in several fields it is more expedient to separate than to mingle the roles of the market and of bureaucracy. In many cases it can be clearly and unambiguously separated so that the control of some processes should only be performed by 1.1.1, and that of another one by 1.1.2. The other normative viewpoint: if a combination becomes unavoidable, the two mechanisms should be 'let together' with caution. In most cases, a 50–50 proportion is not necessarily an ideal compromise. One of the forms should remain dominating, and the other should correct and complement.

1.4 CONCLUDING REMARKS

Having reached the end of this paper, I should like to make a few rather personal remarks. Bureaucracy is a popular topic, and is suited for declarations with strong emotional content. As far as possible, I have made efforts to remain objective.

I should like to join the ranks of those who wish to reduce substantially the scope of bureaucracy — but I join the fight without overheated expectations. On the one hand, the chances are not too heartening. I have discussed in detail how tenacious bureaucracy is, and how strong the resistance is to the pulling down of power positions. In spite of this, the effort is not in vain. At any rate, I do not want to make my own standpoint dependent on the chances of either acceptance or of success. On the other hand, we cannot have illusions that the market, the only serious rival of bureaucratic coordination, could perfectly regulate the socio-economic processes.

In spite of all this, I am of the opinion that there are many fields in which the market mechanism could provide more advantages than disadvantages. This is why it is necessary and worthwhile to work on the substantial suppression of bureaucratic coordination and on the expansion of market coordination.

NOTES

1. I should like to express my thanks here to K. Balog, M. Nagy and L. Horváth for their valuable help in the research. I read an earlier version of the paper at the László Rajk college. I am grateful for the remarks and advice of the audience which I exploited in formulating this later version.
2. There is a vast literature on the scientific investigation of bureaucracy. I only stress a few works which form most of the literary background of the present paper: M. Weber (1967), H. Simon (1976) and W. A. Niskanen (1971), and from the Hungarian literature the works of A. Hegedűs (1970) and K. Kulcsár (1982).
3. In working out the classification I was inspired by the well-known 'integration schemes' of K. Polányi (1968). But the classification given here differs from that of Polányi in several essential respects. I only stress the most important deviations: What Polányi calls 'redistribution' is mostly related to what I call — in agreement with many other researchers — 'bureaucratic coordination'. Redistribution may take place in the framework of bureaucratic coordination, but this is not the only, not even the most important activity of this form of coordination, but also distorts its evaluation. In several of his readers — and particularly in the 'Polányist' believers — the impression is left that, against the 'unjust' market, the 'redistribution' secures a more just redistribution. It may be observed that with the adherents of Polányi we find an antipathy towards the market and a sympathy for 'redistribution'. Also Polányi's 'reciprocity' is a too narrow concept: this is one of the particular — but certainly not general — cases of the basic 1.1.3 of ethical coordination.
4. In order to avoid misunderstandings, this does not mean that the many-sided description of some concrete social system or subsystem would be exhausted by telling which basic form of coordination or what combination of these performs the direct control of the micro-processes.
5. Parkinson, C. N. (1958). *Parkinson's Law or the Pursuit of Progress*, London: Murray.
6. Order No. 24/1979 (XII. 30) BkM on the price-risk fund.
7. Order No. 12/1980 (VII. 15) BkM on the system of financial incentives of higher enterprise executives.
8. See Pénzügyminisztérium (1982).
9. On this subject see the book by the author: 'Economics of Shortage', (1980), particularly Chapters 5 and 17.
10. This is what, among other things, E. Hankiss (1982) has had in mind in his study when he calls attention to the importance of 'behavioural culture'.
11. This point came up also in the disputes with the New Left in the West. See A. Lindbeck's (1971) well-known book.

12. See Kornai (1956).
13. In a socialist economy this kind of tendency to bureaucratization is further strengthened by the artificial creation of monopolistic enterprises (through amalgamation of enterprises, elimination of overlap in 'production-profiles', making some enterprises fully responsible for the supply of certain goods, etc.). In an officially created and protected monopolistic situation also the behaviour of the enterprise develops accordingly: it behaves as if it were an 'authority'; it dictates its partners, distributes administrative allocations and so forth.
14. Order No. 13/1981 (IV. 18) ÁH of the chairman of the National Office for Materials and Prices, on the modification of the Order No. 6/1979 (XI. 1) ÁH on the price formation adjusting to foreign economic prices.
15. Order No. 24/1981 (XI. 26) ÁH of the chairman of the National Office for Materials and Prices on the modification of the Order No. 6/1979 (XI.1) ÁH about the price formation adjusting to foreign trade prices.

REFERENCES

Hankiss, E. (1982) 'Viselkedéskultúránk torzulásai' (Distortions of our Behavioural Culture), in: E. Hankiss: *Diagnózisok* (Diagnoses), Budapest: Magvető, pp. 15–63.

Hegedűs, A. (1966) 'Bürokratikus viszony és szocializmus' (Bureaucratic Relationship and Socialism), *Kortárs*, No. 8.

Hegedűs, A. (1970) 'A bürokratizmus, mint a szakigazgatás szociálpatológiája' (Bureaucracy as the Social Pathology of Specialized Administration), *Kortárs*, No. 7.

Kornai, J. (1956) 'Gyökerestül irtsuk ki a bürokráciát' (Let Us Uproot Bureaucracy), *Szabad Nép*, Vol. 14. October 14. Kornai, J. (1980) *Economics of Shortage*, Amsterdam: North-Holland.

Kornai, J., Matits, Á., Ferge, Zs. (1983) *Az állami vállalatok jövedelmének redisztribuciója – Első beszámoló* (Redistribution of the Income of State Enterprises – First Report), mimeographed, Budapest: Ipari Minisztérium (Ministry of Industry).

Kováts, Á. (1978) 'Jogszabálytervezetek véleményezése, koordináció a Minisztertanács Tanácsi Hivatalában' (Report on and Coordination of Draft Legal Rules in the Council Office of the Council of Ministers), *Állam és Igazgatás*, Vol. 28, pp. 1082–1090.

Kulcsár, K. (1982) 'A bürokratizmus társadalmi összefüggései' (The Social Interrelations of Bureaucracy), in K. Kulcsár, *Gazdaság, társadalom, jog* (Economy, Society, Law), Budapest: Közgazdasági és Jogi Könyvkiadó, pp. 235–254.

Kupa, M. (1980) *Jövedelemelosztás — költségvetés — gazdasági folyamatok* (Income Distribution — Budget — Economic Processes), Budapest: Közgazdasági és Jogi Könyvkiadó.

Lindbeck, A. (1971) *The Political Economy of the New Left*. New York: Harper & Row.

Market and State 19

Niskanen, W. (1971) 'Bureaucrats and Politicians', *Journal of Law and Economics,* Vol. 18, pp. 617–643.

Pénzügyminisztérium Ellenőrzési Főigazgatóság (1982) (Auditing Directorate of the Ministry of Finance): *A normativitással kapcsolatos értelmezések és kísérlet a normativitás érvényesülésének körvonalazására* (Interpretations Related to Normativity and an Attempt at Outlining the Assertion of Normativity), mimeographed, Budapest.

Polányi, K. (1968) *Primitive, Archaic and Modern Economies,* (ed. G. Dalton), New York: Doubleday.

Simon, H. (1976) *Administrative Behaviour,* New York: Macmillan.

Weber, M. (1967) *Gazdaság és társadalom* (Economy and Society), Budapest: Közgazdasági és Jogi Könyvkiadó.

2 The Soft Budget Constraint*

In many segments of contemporary economies a remarkable trend can be observed: the budget constraint of economic units becomes 'soft'. The phenomenon appears in mixed economies and it is conspicuously apparent in socialist systems. The 'soft budget constraint' syndrome is usually associated with the paternalistic role of the state towards economic organizations, that is towards state-owned and private firms, non-profit institutions and households.

The organization of the present chapter is as follows. The purpose of Section 2.1 is conceptual clarification. I introduced the concept of the soft budget constraint in my book *Economics of Shortage* (1980) and in the expository paper (1979) summarizing the theory of chronic shortage in socialist economies. Since then the concept has been widely discussed, and I have received many written and oral comments.[1] Here a reformulation will be presented, which partly overlaps and partly departs from the original definitions and interpretations.[2]

Section 2.2 surveys how 'softening' of the budget constraint affects the conduct of the firm. Sections 2.3 and 2.4 describe empirical observations in three socialist economies, Hungary, Yugoslavia and China, and in mixed, non-socialist economies.

---

* The chapter is the product of research during the period, when the author was a member of the Institute for Advanced Study in Princeton in 1983–84 and F. W. Taussig Research Professor of Economics at Harvard in 1984–85. The support of both institutions is gratefully acknowledged. The chapter was originally a paper presented at the Ninth Annual Marion O'Kellie McKay Lecture at the University of Pittsburgh in 1985.

2.1 CONCEPTUAL CLARIFICATION

The term 'budget constraint' is, of course, taken over from micro-theory of the household. The assumption that the decision-maker has a budget constraint is equivalent to the assumption that Say's principle prevails.[3] In agreement with Clower (1965) the budget constraint is not a book-keeping identity nor a technical relation, but a rational planning postulate. Two important properties must be underlined. First, the budget constraint refers to a behavioural characteristic of the decision-maker: he is used to cover his expenses from the income generated by selling his output and/or by earning return on his assets. Therefore, he adjusts his expenditures to his financial resources. Second, the budget constraint is a constraint on *ex ante* variables and first of all on demand; it is based on expectations concerning his future financial situation when the actual expenditure will occur.

The 'softening' of the budget constraint appears when the strict relationship between expenditure and earnings has been relaxed, because excess expenditure over earnings will be paid by some other institution, typically by the state. A further condition of 'softening' is that the decision-maker expects such external financial assistance with high probability and this probability is firmly built into his behaviour. Figure 2.1 is a simplistic illustration of the case.

We see the usual commodity space for two commodities A and B and the original budget line. The economic unit has a cost overrun: actual expenditure P_1 exceeds the original budget line. The excess, however, will be covered by some external financial support. Perhaps in the next period with the same internal financial resources actual expenditure P_2 will be even larger, but the excess will be covered again. The budget constraint visualized usually as a strictly determined line becomes 'expendable'. (That is represented on Figure 2.1 by the dotted strip.) Another way to express this idea is to use probabilistic terms: external assistance is a random variable. The decision-maker has a subjective perception of the probability distribution of this random variable. The higher the subjective probability that excess expenditure will be covered by external assistance, the softer the budget constraint.[4]

After some general clarification of the concept, the remaining part of this section and the next one will analyse the case of the firm only, both the public and the private firm. Section 2.3 and 2.4 will be more

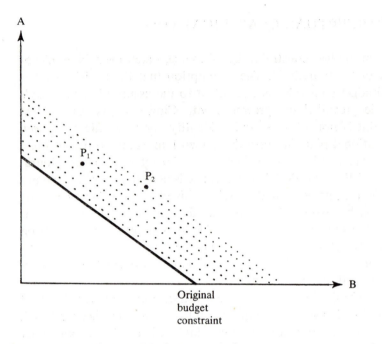

Fig. 2.1: The 'softening' of the budget constraint.

general again, discussing — besides the firm — the budget constraint of state organs, local governments, and non-profit institutions as well.

There are different ways and means to soften the budget constraint of the firm.

2.1.1. *Soft subsidies* granted by national or local governments. The subsidy is soft if it is negotiable, subject to bargaining, lobbying, etc. The subsidy is adjusted to past, present or future cost overruns.

2.1.2. *Soft taxation.* The attribute soft does not refer to the rate of taxation. Even with a low tax rate the taxation system can be hard, if rules are uniform, fixed for a long period and the payment of taxes rigorously enforced. In contrast, taxation is soft, even with a high tax rate, if the rules are negotiable, subject to bargaining, political pressures. The tax rates are not uniform, but almost tailor-made according to the financial situation of different sectors or different regions or different forms of ownership. The fulfilment of tax obligations is not strictly enforced; there are leaks, *ad hoc* exemptions, postponements, etc.

2.1.3. *Soft credit.* Again, softness does not refer to the magnitude of the interest rate. The credit system can be hard even with a low interest rate (provided that the credit market generates a low rate), if the fulfilment of credit contracts is strictly enforced. The creditor lends money expecting discipline in debt service and not for the sake of assistance to an ailing firm which will not be able to service its debt. Enforcement of the credit contract continues to the bitter end: harsh sanction in case of insolvency, including receivership, bankruptcy, forced merger, sellout or other similar legal means. By contrast, the credit system can be soft even with high interest rates, if the fulfilment of a credit contract is not enforced, unreliable debt service is tolerated, and postponement and rescheduling are in order. Soft credit is used to assist firms in great and chronic financial trouble, without real hope of repayment of the debt.

2.1.4. *Soft administrative prices.* This can be applied in the case when the price is not set by a free contract between seller and buyer, but by some bureaucratic institution. The administrative price is hard if, once set, it restricts expenditure and does not automatically adjust to cost increases. An administrative price is soft if it is set according to some permissive 'cost plus' principle, that almost automatically adjusts the price to costs.

These four means of softening the budget constraint are not mutually exclusive; they can be applied simultaneously or successively. The list is not exhaustive, there are other means as well.

A few qualifications and explanatory comments should be added to the general description.

Figure 2.1 presents a static picture. In real life the issue is a dynamic one. All four means of softening the budget constraint of the firm refer to dynamic processes: assistance fills up the gap between the flow of expenditures and the flow of sales-generated revenues of the firm.

It is meaningless to talk about the softness or hardness of the budget constraint of one individual firm, looking at the history of that firm. As mentioned in the general definitions, the subjective probability distribution of external assistance will depend on collective experience. The decisive question in this respect is this:

what was the regular experience of a larger number of firms over a longer period in the past? And can it be expected that similar experiences will occur in the future?

'Hard' and 'soft' are two extreme positions on a scale of stringency. In a deterministic maximizing model an upper constraint either holds or does not hold. But here we are facing a stochastic problem: subjective expectations concerning external assistance and the enforcement of financial discipline. Therefore, intermediate positions between a strictly binding and a totally redundant constraint may exist. Consider the speed limit on highways[5]. Some people will observe it, some others not, exceeding the permitted limit more or less frequently, to a larger or smaller extent. The distribution of violations will depend on the enforcement of the limit. But even with soft enforcement, the mere fact that there is a limit may have some influence on speed. That is, the constraint is not completely redundant.

There is one more reason to think in terms of a stringency-scale rather than in a 'yes or no' framework, in which a completely binding or a completely ineffective budget constraint are mutually exclusive possibilities. External assistance is usually not granted automatically, as some effort is needed to obtain it. The firm's managers (and in the case of a private firm, also the owners) must resort to political pressure groups and lobbies, or to personal connections. Explicit bribery might be frequent or rare, with experience varying from country to country. Some hidden corruption in the form of reciprocal favours is more wide-spread. All these efforts resemble the rent-seeking behaviour described in A. O. Krueger (1974). She discusses mainly efforts for the sake of less negative interventions, and here we talk about efforts for the sake of more positive interventions. In any case, rent-seeking and budget-constraint-softening is not without costs. Therefore, even if it might be softened, the budget constraint has at least some influence on the behaviour of the firm or of other microunits.

Hardness of the budget constraint is not a synonym for profit-maximization. A profit-maximizing firm, if it is in the red, will try to cut its losses. A hard budget constraint means that even if the firm tries hard to cut its losses, the environment will not tolerate a protracted deficit. The emphasis is on punishment. The budget constraint is hard, if persistent loss is a matter of life and death; the more the loss-maker is spared from tragic consequences, the softer is the constraint. What is really important is the psychological effect of the constraint: with a hard budget constraint, a deficit causes fear, because it may lead to extremely serious consequences. Profit-maximization refers to the internal goal-setting of the decision-maker in the firm; the softness-hardness of the budget constraint refers to the external tolerance-limits to losses.[6]

It follows from this line of reasoning that the stringency of the budget constraint is not simply a financial matter. It reflects in a financial form a deeper socio-economic phenomenon. Using a Marxian term: it reflects a certain social relationship between the state and the economic microorganization. Clower and Due (1972) wrote about Say's principle (and accordingly about the hard budget constraint) that it 'constitutes an implicit definition of the concept of a transactor as distinguished from the concept of a thief or a philanthropist'.

In the case of a soft budget constraint, the state and firm are neither merely transactors, nor is the firm a thief or the state a philanthropist. We are faced with a new kind of relationship. Different analogies come to mind: the state as a protective father and the firm as a child, the state as patron and the firm as client, the state as an insurance company and the firm as the insured party. The soft budget constraint syndrome is the manifestation of the paternalistic role of the modern state.

The economic theory of the market concentrates on the horizontal relationship between seller and market. The sociological theory of bureaucracy, from its beginning with Max Weber up to now studies the vertical relationship of superiors and subordinates within a hierarchy. The firm with a soft budget constraint is an issue at the intersection of these two disciplines. Our firm has horizontal relationships with his customers and suppliers, and at the same time a very special vertical relationship with the state.

One last word on conceptual clarification. This paper deliberately refrains from an overtly pedantic definition. I refer to the conventional term 'budget constraint' to awaken certain associations with microtheory. The concept, however, must not be interpreted too literally, but more as a metaphor.[7] The notion of the soft budget constraint refers to a trend in modern society: the relaxation of financial discipline, the weakening of the feeling that spending, survival, expansion depend on earning capability and not on external assistance.

2.2 THE IMPACT ON THE FIRM'S CONDUCT

The trend toward the softening of budget constraint has many interrelated consequences. Here only three of them will be surveyed: the impact on price responsiveness, on efficiency and on the creation of excess demand. As in the second half of the previous section we still focus on the behaviour of the firm.

The first issue is the effect of prices on the decision-making of the firm. The trivial case of a downward sloping demand curve by the firm for its inputs presupposes the existence of a hard budget constraint. The softer the budget constraint, the weaker the compulsion to adjust demand to relative prices. In the extreme position of a perfectly soft budget constraint the own-price elasticity of demand is zero, the demand curve is vertical, i.e. determined by other explanatory variables and not by the price. As a glimpse at Figure 2.1 makes clear, the exact slope of the original budget line does not matter too much if cost increases can easily be compensated by external assistance, so that the strict budget line is replaced by a broad fuzzy strip.

The softness of the budget constraint decreases the elasticity of demand of all alternative inputs, of all factors; diminishes the firm's sensitivity toward the interest rate, exchange rate and so on. Similarly, the multi-product firm will be less sensitive to changes in relative output prices. To sum up: the general price responsiveness of the firm declines.[8]

A large part of the literature on disequilibrium or non-equilibrium states of the market is concerned with the rigidity of prices, wages, interest rates, exchange rates and so on. As important as these issues might be, they are preceded by an even more fundamental one: does the price have an effect at all? And if so, is this effect strong or rather weak? The non-Walrasian state of the market is in many systems explained not so much by the rigidity in price formation but rather by the weakness of price responsiveness and the latter attribute of the system depends to a large extent on the softness of the budget constraint.

A second issue worthy of attention is the impact on efficiency of the trend toward a softer budget constraint. Allocative efficiency cannot be achieved when input-output combinations do not adjust to price signals. Within the firm there is not sufficiently strong stimulus to maximum efforts: weaker performance is tolerated[9]. The attention of the firm's leaders is distracted from the shop floor and from the market to the offices of the bureaucracy where they may apply for help in case of financial trouble.

The most important issue is dynamic adjustment. If the budget constraint is hard, the firm has no other option but to adjust to unfavourable external circumstances by improving quality, cutting costs, introducing new products or new processes, i.e. it must behave in an entrepreneurial manner. If, however, the budget constraint is soft, such productive efforts are no longer imperative. Instead, the firm is likely to seek external assistance asking compensation for unfavourable external circumstances. The state is acting like an overall insurance company taking over all the moral hazards with the usual well-known consequences: the insured will be less careful in protecting his wealth.[10] Schumpeter (1911) emphasized the significance of 'constructive destruction': the elimination of old products, technologies, organizations which were surpassed by the more efficient new ones. The soft budget constraint protects the old production line, the inefficient firm against constructive destruction and thus impedes innovation and development.

A third consequence of the soft budget constraint syndrome may show up in the formation of excess demand. Whatever goals the managers of the firm have (maximizing short- or long-term profits, sales, growth of sales, size of the firm, discretion and power) these objectives or any combination of them will be associated with expansion. And whatever specific input-output combinations may serve expansion, the drive to achieve the goals listed above generates an ever-increasing demand for at least some inputs over time. If the budget constraint is hard, this demand is constrained. Expenditure on purchasing inputs is conditional on past, present and future revenues generated by the sale of output, which again is constrained by the demand for the firm's output. If, however, the budget constraint of many firms is soft, their demand for inputs becomes unconstrained (or at least unconstrained from the point of view of financing). Runaway demand will appear. These firms feel that when they cannot pay the bills, someone else will step in and bail them out. Therefore there is no compulsory limit on demand for inputs, and particularly, on investment.[11] If the share of economic units with a soft budget constraint and a tendency to runaway demand for inputs is large enough to have a strong effect on total demand, the system becomes a 'shortage economy'.

Here we arrive at some theoretical conclusions. As emphasized before, the existence of a (hard) budget constraint is equivalent to Say's principle being in force. If, however, the budget constraint is soft in sufficiently large segments of the economy, then Say's principle does not hold and as a consequence, Walras's law does not hold either. Consider a large firm, planning an investment project. Say's principle assumes that the firm is ready to start the project only if it seriously believes that the flow of revenues from the sale of output generated by the new project will cover the flow of expenditures needed to accomplish the project. True, in a world of uncertainty different decision-makers might exhibit different degrees of risk-aversion. But given the distribution of risk-aversion over all investment decision-makers, total demand for investment resources (investment credits, investment goods, etc.) will be constrained, because of genuine fear of a financial failure, that is because the budget constraint is hard. There will be self-restraint in the capital formation decision. This symmetric relationship between demand for investment resources and the supply generated by the same investment resources underlies the idea of Walras's law, i. e. the sum of the (positive and negative) values of excess demands will be zero.

This kind of symmetry gets lost in the case of a sufficiently large number of decision-makers with soft budget constraints. The symmetry breaks down if financial support can appear like manna. The firm can start a project even though it may have the subconscious suspicion that the cost will be more than planned and the revenue less. In case of financial failure it will be bailed out. Under such circumstances there is no self-restraint in investment intentions; the demand is not counterbalanced by a 'dead serious' consideration of revenues and ultimately of supply.

There are identities in all economies: stock-flow balances of real inputs and outputs and of money. These identities self-evidently hold also in economy with soft budget constraints. But Walras's law is not an identity but a certain relationship between buying and selling intentions. Intentions can be inconsistent. In case of a soft budget constraint they *are* inconsistent. Subsidies, soft tax-exemptions, soft credits, etc. will be financed through the redistribution of income via taxation or inflation. There are expected burdens (the usual tax, the usual expected inflation rate, etc.). Everyone takes into account the usual tax burden, inflation rate and so on, when planning his finances. The expectation that the firm can spend more than its 'earnings' because in case of failure it will be bailed out, comes on top of that. Here is the source of asymmetry: the possibility of run-away demand of the firm with soft budget constraints. The individual expectations can be incompatible with each other. The softening of the budget constraint is an inducement to such incompatibility: the softer the budget constraint and the larger the sphere of the economy where the syndrome prevails, the more incompatibility appears.

Another important aspect is the effectiveness of monetary policy. A monetary ceiling[12] is a necessary condition of financial disci pline, but it is not sufficient to ensure it. See Hicks (1983). The transmission between a tighter monetary policy and the micro-response becomes unreliable in case of a soft budget constraint. The latter is like a cogwheel made of putty in this transmission. The microunit will not react to monetary restraint by restricting its demands when it is not convinced of the dangers of financial failure. In the sphere of microunits with a soft budget constraint money is more or less 'passive', see Brus (1961) and Grossman (1965). Demand management works only if it is associated with sufficiently hard budget constraints. This is one of the important relationships between macro- and microeconomics.

2.3 EXPERIENCES IN SOCIALIST ECONOMIES: HUNGARY, YUGOSLAVIA AND CHINA

We now turn to empirical observations, first to socialist economies. The case of 'classical socialism', i.e. the highly-centralized pre-reform command economy, is rather straightforward. It is officially acknowledged that profitability must not play a decisive role: entry, exit, expansion and contraction of the firm does not depend on profitability but is decided by the higher authorities applying other criteria. A loss-making firm or a whole sector can survive indefinitely, provided that the higher organs of the state want it.

It is more challenging to study what is happening in Yugoslavia, in Hungary and China which were the pioneering countries in introducing decentralization reforms associated with a larger role of profit incentives. If we observe — as is the case — that the budget constraint in these three economies is still rather soft, then a similar proposition concerning the pre-reform 'classical socialism' is *a fortiori* true.

In all three countries the reform process has gone on for several decades and has produced impressive results. This is not, however, the place for a general assessment of the balance between success and failures[13]. We want to concentrate on a single issue: the stringency of the budget constraint in the three countries.

In Hungary a research team is studying the financial situation of all state-owned enterprises (1,755 firms in 1982) which produce the bulk of total output[14]. The balance sheets of all these firms have been processed and several special indicators have been computed for cross-sectional and dynamic analysis. Here only a few examples of the numerical results can be presented.

Some explanation of terminology is needed (for more detailed definitions see the sources mentioned in note 14). We distinguish four categories of profit.

2.3.1. *Original profit*. This is a hypothetical number: profit before receiving any kind of subsidies from the state and before paying any kind of taxes to the state. The word 'before' does not refer to temporal order in real calendar time, but to the abstract logical order of the complex fiscal redistribution of profits.

Computing 'original profit' (and similarly in the course of the whole research project) we take existing prices as given. We do not calculate shadow-prices and then compute shadow-profits of the firm. Accordingly, 'original profit' is not a profit which would occur under the imaginary conditions of a competitive market associated with genuine market-clearing prices.

2.3.2. *Corrected original profit*. This is original profit plus subsidies granted for the sake of keeping certain consumer prices down, minus turnover taxes levied for the sake of keeping certain consumer prices up. The rationale for this correction is as follows. We want to filter out the component of fiscal redistribution which aims at subsidizing or taxing the consumer households, and not the producer firms.

2.3.3. *Reported profit*. This is the profit reported in the balance sheets and later on, in all sectoral and national statistics on profits. They reflect already a very large degree of fiscal redistribution: most of the subsidies are added and most of the taxes are subtracted from original profit at this stage.

2.3.4. *Final profit.* After the reported profit is determined, a few more subsidies are added and a few more taxes are subtracted.

In some computations we use a fraction instead of the volume of profit, where the numerator is one of the four profit indicators and the denominator is the value of the physical assets (structures, equipment and inventories), i.e. 'physical capital'. We call this kind of indicator 'profitability' and use it to facilitate cross-sectional and dynamic comparisons.

The first observation is that the size of fiscal redistribution is very large. This is shown in Table 2.1.

Table 2.1: Relative size of fiscal redistribution in Hungary

	Total subsidies per total original profit	Total taxes per total original profit
1980	1.09	1.28
1982	0.91	1.27

The state-owned sector as a whole is a net tax-payer. But the final net outcome is preceded by a far-reaching reshuffling of profits criss-crossing among all individual firms. The state takes away money from a firm with one hand — and then gives money to another firm (or perhaps to the same firm, but with another 'entitlement') with its other hand. Or more precisely, the state has not only two hands but it is a Shiva with many more hands: there are in total 276 types of taxes and subsidies used by different tax-levying or subsidy-granting authorities (see Falubíró [1983]).

Table 2.2 presents correlation coefficients between the different profitability indicators over the whole population of state-owned firms and over the state-owned firms in manufacturing.

The most telling parts of Table 2.2 are the two upper right corners, which show that there is no substantial correlation between pre-redistribution and post-redistribution profitability. Even if we filter out the effect of consumer price policy *via* subsidies and taxes implied in consumer prices, still the correlation between indicators 2 and 4 is very weak, especially in manufacturing.

At this point a word of caution is in order. We do not suggest

Table 2.2: Correlation coefficients between profitability indicators in Hungary in 1982

	Profitability indicators			
	1	2	3	4
All state-owned firms				
1. Original profitability	1	0.63	0.42	0.09
2. Corrected original profitability		1	0.64	0.15
3. Reported profitability			1	0.39
4. Final profitability				1
State-owned manufacturing firms				
1. Original profitability	1	0.63	0.33	0.04
2. Corrected original profitability		1	0.47	0.05
3. Reported profitability			1	0.42
4. Final profitability				1

that profitability No. 1 should be the indicator of genuine efficiency. With the given distorted relative price system that cannot be the case. Therefore it is not legitimate to draw the simple normative conclusion to stop differentiated financial redistribution, and apply a kind of flat tax while maintaining the present price structure. We do not want to draw any normative conclusion here, only to point out the characteristic feature of the present situation. When fiscal redistributions are so wide-spread and so complex, then 'profitability' does not have and cannot have any reasonable meaning. Reported and final profitability depend at least as much on the generosity or tight-fistedness of different subsidy-granting or tax-levying authorities, as they depend on success or failure in production and on the market.

The fiscal redistribution of profits shows a conspicuous tendency to give financial assistance to the losers. We computed the following indicator: the total subsidy given to a firm over total taxes paid by the same firm. We call it the 'ratio of redistribution'. The correlation coefficients between original profitability and the ratio of redistribution for the whole population of state-owned firms is − 0.99 for 1980, − 0.97 for 1981, and − 0.92 for 1982. The very strong negative correlation demonstrates that the lower is original profitability, the higher is the probability of getting a larger subsidy and paying a smaller tax.

Table 2.3: Transition probabilities due to fiscal redistribution in Hungary in 1982

To: Final profitability From: Original profitability	Loss-maker	Low profitability	Medium profitability	High profitability
Loss-maker	0.11	0.77	0.06	0.06
Low profitability	0.03	0.93	0.04	0
Medium profitability	0	0.84	0.13	0.03
High profitability	0	0.46	0.43	0.11

The redistribution pattern, therefore, is to redistribute profits from winners to losers. For the sake of demonstration firms are classified in four categories: 'loss-making' means profitability less than −2 per cent ; 'low profitability' is between −2 per cent and + 6 per cent; 'medium profitability' is between +6 per cent and +20 per cent; and 'high profitability' is more than +20 per cent. Table 2.3 presents the transition probabilities from one category to the other due to fiscal redistribution for all state-owned firms.

Firms with high original profitability have only an 11 per cent chance of ending up in the same category after redistribution; almost every second one will be down-graded to low profitability. In contrast 9 out of 10 loss-making firms will be upgraded. This is a rather paradoxical form of 'egalitarian' redistribution: profit incentives dampened by the levelling of profits.

Every year a few Hungarian state-owned firms go out of business. They are liquidated or merged into a larger firm. Our analysis as well as other studies,[15] have shown that exit is not related to profitability. The relationship between profitability and the growth of the firm is also worthy of attention. For the sake of cross-sectional and dynamic comparison we defined an indicator of 'investment activity': expenditure on real capital formation divided by the value of physical assets. Table 2.4 examines the potential lagged effect of profitability on investment activity. The table clearly demonstrates that investment activity is not correlated with profitability at all.

The research on fiscal redistribution over Hungarian firms is continuing. The findings up to now support the observation that in spite of decentralization measures, the budget constraint of the state-owned firm is still rather soft. The financial dependency of the firm on the state remains very strong.

Table 2.4: Correlation between profitability and investment activity in Hungary

Correlation with investment activity in later years	1976	1977	1978	1979	1980
Profitability in the year indicated below					
Original profitability					
1975	−0.03	−0.03	−0.04	−0.04	−0.02
1976		−0.03	−0.07	−0.04	−0.08
1977			−0.04	−0.01	−0.07
1978				−0.03	−0.11
1979					−0.08
Reported profitability					
1975	−0.07	−0.07	−0.03	−0.03	−0.03
1976		−0.07	−0.04	−0.03	−0.01
1977			−0.04	−0.03	−0.01
1978				−0.04	0
1979					0

In Yugoslavia the bulk of total output is produced by firms in social ownership. (Since the top management of the firm is elected by the workers and not appointed by state authorities, this form of non-private property cannot be regarded as 'state-ownership'.) The economic unit is called in Yugoslav terminology 'Basic Organization of Associated Labour') (BOAL); larger enterprises can be composed of several BOALs.

Table 2.5 shows that a large number of economic units are making losses.

Table 2.5: Loss-making and rehabilitation in Yugoslavia in 1980–1981

	Number of BOALs	Number of workers involved (thousands)
Total (end of 1981)	13,667	4,848
Units with uncovered loss on 1980 annual financial report	1,303	277
Units where rehabilitation is in process	178	51
Units where bankruptcy procedure has been initiated	20	2

Source: Knight (1984), pp. 5 and 80.

Most of the units in deep financial trouble survive. 'Rehabilitation' implies many forms of external assistance: partly non-reimbursable subsidies, partly credits. There is a large variety of financial sources available for the loss-maker; banks (which are actually controlled by the BOALs themselves), local, regional and federal organs participate in the process of bailing out the firm.

A remarkable way of 'solving' liquidity troubles is wide-spread interfirm credit created outside the banking system. Interfirm claims have been growing at twice the rate of inflation in the late seventies, see Knight (1984). The interfirm credit is frequently forced upon the supplier of the good: the purchaser firm does not pay from his funds, but issues a promissory note. Liquidity troubles are passed on from one firm to the other, and the spill-over effects lead to more general liquidity crises.[16]

The situation is aptly characterized by two quotations from Yugoslav sources. 'In Yugoslavia anybody could order goods, invest, distribute, and consume, without paying for it. The guilty persons were not punished by being deprived, through bankruptcy, of the right to manage social property.' The quotation is from one of the leading newspapers, *Ekonomska Politika* in 1969[17]. As Table 2.5 shows, not much has changed since then. A. Bajt, the renowned Yugoslav economist, wrote: 'Obligations are undertaken without the intention to keep them; sanctions for violations are lax or non-existent, which allows the unchecked growth of transaction without payment.'[18]

The widely shared consensus of analysts[19] and the conclusion of the above cited facts is this: the Yugoslav economic unit in social ownership exhibits all the attributes of a rather soft budget constraint.

As for China, overall statistics reflecting the stringency of the budget constraint of state-owned firms are not yet available. The analyst must rely on the study of governmental resolutions regulating profit-retention and taxation, furthermore on reports describing the experiences in various sectors and regions published in the Chinese daily press and in professional journals. At first a profit-retention scheme has been introduced in 1978, which evolved into a 'profit-contract system' in the early 1980s. The latter means a negotiated agreement between the owner, i.e. the central or local government, and the firm concerning mandatory profit delivery to the state. The profit earned above the delivery can be retained by the firm. 'Bargaining over profit became one of the main activities of the industrial hierarchy, replacing bargaining over plan targets', writes Naughton (1985, p. 238). The latest stage is called 'tax-for-profit' system. It substitutes the payment of taxes for the former negotiated 'profit delivery'. There are various taxes; one of them is called 'adjustment tax' with the explicit purpose of levelling off the burden between different enterprises with more or less favourable operating costs. The determination of the actual rate of adjustment tax is based on case-by-case negotiations. We quote Naughton (1985) for an overall appraisal: 'Currently, it is absolutely unquestionable that the Chinese enterprises face a soft budget constraint: Numerous avenues exist for enterprises to escape the consequences of misguided decisions in investment or production. The operation of the profit-contract system practically exemplifies the meaning of a soft budget constraint, and Chinese economists describe the same phenomenon when they say that enterprises are "responsible for profits, but not for losses". While the tax-for-profit system may effect some marginal changes in this situation, it is unlikely to alter things fundamentally in the foreseeable future' (p. 248). Similar conclusions are drawn by Riskin (1985) and Wong (1985).

2.4 EXPERIENCE IN MIXED ECONOMIES

Socialist economies exhibit a rather extreme degree of budget constraint softness. To a lesser degree and in more restricted segments of the system similar phenomena can be observed in mixed economies as well.

It is impossible to make definite general propositions concerning the degree of softness or hardness of the budget constraint in mixed economies. The variance is large; there are great differences between countries and within a particular country the situation may change as parties and political currents in power change. What we can offer is only a classification and a systematic survey of the different types of organizations where the soft budget constraint syndrome appears:

(i) There are non-private firms in many mixed economies, owned either by the central or by local government. Usually they do not have a privileged legal status, but are treated as business firms which are supposed to make profit. Nevertheless quite a few make losses for extended periods and are kept alive with the aid of subsidies and/or other 'softening' methods.[20] In some instances the true motive behind nationalization is in fact to let the state (i.e. ultimately the taxpayer) pay for the persistent deficit of ailing private firms. In some other cases the deficit of the state-owned firm is the direct consequence of a governmental price policy that keeps the price of certain goods or services produced by the firm artificially low.

In the case of many public utilities which have a monopoly or almost-monopoly in supplying certain goods or services, some sort of administrative price regulation is unavoidable. It is rather common that the administrative price is 'soft', and some kind of 'cost-plus' principle is applied. The administrative price adjusts to actual costs whatever the reason for cost increases. This again is a typical soft budget constraint phenomenon.

(ii) Related to type (i) is the public investment project. After completion it might be operated by a public organization or handed over to private business. Expenditures are financed totally or partially through governmental sources. A rather frequent course of events is this: at first, overly optimistic cost estimates are made; then, the cost overrun is finally covered from public sources. This is clearly a case of a soft budget constraint. The downward bias of the *ex ante* estimate is induced by the rather safe expectation that on the one hand this may improve the chances of the proposal being accepted, while on the other hand the public will pay the excess costs.

(iii) In many countries the national or local governments are willing to give regular assistance over long periods to private business which would otherwise be in financial trouble. Such support is granted in some cases to large firms or whole sectors (steel, shipbuilding, etc.) composed of large firms. In some other cases assistance goes to small-scale producers (e.g. farmers).

It would be a grave mistake to overrate the similarities between socialist and non-socialist economies in this respect. The bail-out of Chrysler does not mean that the budget constraint of the large corporations in the United States is soft. Chrysler was obliged to pay back all financial assistance soon and it *did*. The Chrysler case was an exception to the rule, attaining great national attention. In Hungary we are witnessing the first bankruptcy of a state-owned firm. There the bankruptcy is the exception and the bail-out is the normal routine. The reader must be reminded that the budget constraint becomes soft when the decision-maker can expect with high subjective probability that he will get external assistance. There *are* segments in many modern mixed economies where this is the case, but it is not the general situation for the majority of private firms.

(iv) Privately owned commercial banks have a special position. In most countries they are subject to special governmental control. The public is assured that the government and/or other central institutions (typically the Central Bank) guarantees the safety of deposits. Since the shocking experiences of the Great Depression, the backing of the private banking sector became more explicit in most countries. This leads to the softening of the budget constraints of private banks: they are less wary of making risky loans since they are sure that they will be bailed out.

(v) There is a large variety of non-profit institutions offering different services to the public. Some are single organizational units (e.g. a university), others are huge multi-level organizations (for example a nation-wide health service or a pension fund, public broadcasting and so on). Their legal status is different from the branches of the government; they are not part of the civil service. At the same time, many are not independent from the government: they get privileges, but they are also subject to some governmental control. And what is most important from our point of view, they rely to some extent on governmental financial support. 'Non-profit' means, strictly speaking, that they cannot accept money from private investors and pay dividends for this private investment. Otherwise they are supposed to be self-sufficient, financing expenditures out of contributions of members, donations and of the returns of their assets. In many cases however they run into financial trouble and must turn to the government for assistance. Or they are established at the outset in such a way that a part of their regular income comes from governmental sources. This of course undermines autonomy. At the same time, it brings about the common soft budget constraint phenomena: bargaining for assistance, and inefficiencies and cost overruns tolerated in the hope that deficits will be covered from public sources.

An outstanding — and in many aspects a very special — example is health care. Not only may nationalized health service show the usual symptoms of the soft budget constraint syndrome, but the very same symptoms can appear also in a private individualistic health system, based on voluntary medical insurance. The provider of health care, the physician, or the clinic is not very careful in spending because whatever the costs they are not paid directly out of the pocket of the patient. The bills are presented to impersonal institutions, which can pass the cost increase along in small quantums to the large number of insured individuals. This is even more true if the large, bureaucratic health care and insurance institution is not a private business firm, but some kind of non-profit institution that can turn for financial assistance to the state.

(vi) In many countries local governments have more or less financial autonomy and they are supposed to be self-sufficient, i.e. to cover expenditures from taxes and other revenues they are able to raise. If a local government gets additional funds from a higher-level governmental budget, then a soft budget constraint situation may evolve. External assistance depends on bargaining. If the local government runs into deficits, it can hope that it will be bailed out by the higher-level authorities. The chances are rather good that even careless spending does not lead to a financial catastrophe.

(vii) In paragraph (vi) we looked at multi-level governmental structures in the spatial-regional dimension. Somewhat similar situations can be observed if we look at the functional dimension, namely at the position of different departments, or ministries working side-by-side at the same level of government. A department or ministry is not expected to be self-sufficient, since it gets all financial resources from the common budget. The allocation of the budget over departments or ministries is the outcome of a complex negotiation and bargaining process, both on the bureaucratic and on the political planes. Top administrators must 'fight' to get more funds for their own area. Again, some features of the soft budget constraint syndrome will usually appear. There is no sufficient inducement to save, after the budget has been allocated already, because unutilized appropriations can lead to cuts in future budgets. In fact, some overspending is helpful in future manoeuvring, because it demonstrates that the sum allocated the previous time was not sufficient. The more powerful and prestigious the department or ministry (a typical case is a department in charge of defence), the more intensive the soft budget constraint syndrome. There is no strong motivation to minimize costs. Large cost overruns never lead to the termination of a project, as financial sources are adjusted to the increasing costs.[21]

After the survey of organizations which may have a less hard or perhaps a rather soft budget constraint, a few words must be said about the forces which create the phenomenon.[22] As a first approximation we consider the arguments of the organizations which are asking for and expecting external assistance. The variety of specific arguments is, of course, very large, but we can try to find out their most important common ingredients.

(a) The most frequently quoted reason for external help is the protection of jobs. In a system of perfectly hard budget constraints of firms and households all adaptation — both cyclical macroadjustments and structural microadjustments — would be associated with large lay-offs and with wages fluctuating in both directions according to the situation on the labour market. Exit of the firm hurts owners, managers and employees; they try to get state assistance to avoid shut-downs. During recessions the demand for state intervention is supported by great masses. But also in upswings there are sectors or single firms which are still ailing. The employees feel that it is not fair that they are left out of the benefits of growth.

(b) Another rather frequent argument is the protection of domestic production against foreign competition. This frequently coincides with issue (a), i.e. with defending jobs. Not all protectionist measures imply the softening of the budget constraint, but quite a few have such implications. The most important measures in this respect are the subsidies to firms or whole sectors which — because of high domestic costs — have troubles in competition with foreign firms selling at lower prices.

(c) In many instances the softening of the budget constraint is related to redistributive policies in favour of the poor, the handicapped, the sick, the elderly. This may lay behind many of the cases discussed in paragraphs (iv)–(vii) above. Redistributive objectives in the name of fairness, social justice and solidarity can motivate non-profit institutions, local governments or certain branches of the national governments in their demands for additional financial assistance.

(d) An important argument, closely related to (a) and (c) in favour of softening the budget constraint, is the demand for security and stability: to protect the individual and ultimately the society as a whole against fluctuations and uncertainties. We already used the analogy of the state as a general insurance company. This desire for security and stability is the motivation for impeding the 'natural selection' executed by the market, for guaranteeing the survival of malfunctioning banks and producing firms.

(e) Each organization serves — almost by definition — a certain purpose; an important argument is to refer to the social importance of that particular purpose when arguing for external additional support. As mentioned before the leaders of an organization 'fight' for the survival and for the expansion of their unit, usually supported by their staff. In this fight, military leaders will refer to the importance of national defence, the top administrators of the police to the importance of public security, the top administrators of the health system to the importance of health care, and so on. All these requirements and claims are, of course plausible and legitimate. Since they serve objectives which have no 'market value', it is unavoidable that their relative valuation is determined by a political process.

Ultimately, the soft budget constraint phenomenon is a joint outcome of two closely interrelated socio-political trends. First, the increasing, and often overloading demand of society on the state to become a 'protector', responsible for welfare, growth and the national economic interest,[23] and second, the self-reinforcing tendency of bureaucratization. The softening of the budget constraint is an indicator of the fact that many basic allocative and selective processes are not left to the market, but are highly influenced or taken over by bureaucracies and by political forces. This trend proceeds with uneven speed in different countries; there are also reversals for some time. In any case, there is no contemporary mixed economy where the paternalistic role of the state and of political forces is not much stronger than, say, half a century ago.

A final remark on political and ethical implications. There will surely be readers who draw extreme conservative conclusions from the ideas outlined here. This is far from the intentions of the paper, which does not suggest that the hard budget constraint is 'good' and the soft is 'bad'.

A system based on a perfectly hard budget constraint for every decision-making unit is a terribly cruel one. The symbol of such a system are the debtor's prison, the bailiff bringing under the hammer the home and the household goods of the insolvent family, mass lay-offs in bankrupt firms and so on. All changes departing from these brutal extremes contain some elements of a softer budget constraint. It can be hardly denied that the majority of the population in all countries wanted to move away from that extreme point.

Careful case-by-case considerations are needed if we turn to policy suggestions. Sometimes these are relatively easy. The budget constraint can be hardened for the sake of efficiency without (or with little) painful human consequences. In many other cases, however, the choice is much more difficult. There can be a trade-off between the two kinds of consequences of softening or hardening the budget constraints: the impact on efficiency and the impact on human well-being and suffering. The hardness of the budget constraint is based on fear of a financial catastrophe, the softness eliminates this fear. A hard budget constraint induces competition: the winner gains, the loser will be ruined. A soft constraint has mercy on the loser. It is not the purpose of this paper to 'solve' the ethical dilemmas. There is no general solution; one has to search for acceptable compromises in each case. Here we want to emphasize only that there *is* a deep dilemma. Efficiency and security-solidarity are to a large extent conflicting goals.

NOTES

1. I have benefited from many stimulating remarks at a large number of seminars and conferences and in the reviews on my book (1980). I am particularly indebted for the suggestions of A. Bergson, K. Farkas, S. Gomulka, A. O. Hirschman, A. Leijonhufvud, Á. Matits, D.N. McCloskey, F. Seaton, J. D. Sachs, A. K. Soós and J. W. Weibull.
2. I do not want to bore the reader with a meticulous comparison of the original (1980) and the revised formulation. As far as they are different, this paper represents my present thinking on the subject.
3. See Clower (1965) and Clower–Leijonhufvud (1983).

4. For a formalization of the probabilistic framework of paternalistic financial assistance see Kornai–Weibull (1983).
5. The analogy has been suggested by A. O. Hirschman.
6. The concept of a hard or soft budget constraint can be used also if an objective other than profits, e. g. sales or output is maximized, or if the behaviour of the firm is described in a non-maximizing framework such as satisfying behaviour.
7. Of course the rigorously defined concept of a budget constraint in the microtheory of the household is also a metaphor, like all other models of economics. (See McCloskey's [1983] paper on the rhetoric of economics.)
8. An indicator of the general price responsiveness of the firm could be a weighted average of demand elasticities for different inputs; another indicator could be a similar weighted average of supply elasticities for different outputs. The value of such indicators is zero in case of total lack of responsiveness.
9. In Leibenstein's (1966) terminology, this leads to a loss in X-efficiency.
10. Jackall (1983) characterized the attitude of the manager under bureaucratic control this way: socialize risks and privatize benefits.
11. Hungarian literature calls this almost insatiable demand for investment resources 'investment hunger'.
12. I am indebted to A. Leijonhufvud who drew my attention to this relationship with Hicks's ideas on monetary ceilings.
13. For an overall description and appraisal of the reforms see Antal (1979), Balassa (1983), Hare (1983), Hewett (1981) and Nyers—Tardos (1980) concerning Hungary; Bergson (1982), Burkett (1983), Horvat (1976) and Tyson (1980) concerning Yugoslavia, Perry—Wong (1985) concerning China.
14. The study is directed by the author and by Á. Matits. The main findings of the first report (Kornai–Matits–Ferge[1983]) have been summarized in English in Kornai—Matits (1983). More recent results are in the second report: Matits (1984). The source of all data in Tables 2.1—2.4 are these two reports.
15. See Laki (1982).
16. See Tyson (1977).
17. Quoted in Havrylyshyn (1984).
18. Bajt (1971), quoted in Soós (1984).
19. For example L. Tyson (1983) refers to 'the continued softness' of enterprise budget constraints that reduced enterprise sensitivity to changing financial and monetary conditions. P. Knight (1984) observes that 'the interlocking system of banks, enterprise and socio-political communities has produced a very soft budget constraint.' Similar statements can be found in Burkett (1984) and in Havrylyshyn (1984).
20. Goal-setting and performance in public firms is discussed in Aharoni (1981) and Borcherding, Pommerehne and Schneider (1982).
21. There is resemblance to the soft budget constraint syndrome in the situation of many governments' domestic budgets: increasing deficit covered by ever-expanding credits. This situation frequently has similar consequences to the soft budget constraint of the firm: less care in spending because the gov-

ernment cannot go 'bankrupt'. I feel, however, that including this issue in our list (i)—(vii) would stretch the concept of the soft budget constraint too far. A substantial component of the definition given in Section 2.1 is this: the soft budget constraint reflects a social relationship between a paternalistic patron and a patronized organization. This component of the definition cannot be maintained without artificial reinterpretation for the case of the domestic governmental budget.

22. Section 2.4 discusses observations in mixed economies. Most of these situations can be observed *mutatis mutandi* also in socialist economies. Section 2.3 analysed only the soft budget constraint of firms in non-private ownership, that is category (i) in the above list. There is no space in the present study to run over categories (ii)—(vii) again with special reference to socialist systems.

23. See Crozier—Huntington—Watanuki (1975).

REFERENCES

Aharoni, Y. (1981) 'Performance Evaluation of State-Owned Enterprise's *Management Science,* November, pp. 1340–1347.

Antal, L. (1979) 'Development with Some Digression—The Hungarian Economic Mechanism in the Seventies', *Acta Oeconomica,* July *23,* pp. 257–273.

Bajt, A. (1971) 'Ekonomisti. Koreni Inflacije' (Economists. The Roots of Inflation), *Ekonomska Politika,* December 6.

Balassa, B. (1983) 'Reforming the New Economic Mechanism in Hungary', *Journal of Comparative Economics,* September 1, pp. 253–276.

Bergson, A. (1982) 'Entrepreneurship under Labour Participation: The Yugoslav Case', in: J. Ronen (ed.), *Entrepreneurship,* Lexington: Lexington Books.

Borcherding, T. E., Pommerehne, W. W. and Schneider, F. (1982) 'Comparing the Efficiency of Private and Public Production: The Evidence from Five Countries', *Zeitschrift für Nationalökonomie,* Supplementum 2. pp. 127–156.

Brus, W. (1972) *Ogólne Problemy Funkcjonowania Gospodarki Soocjalistycznej* (General Problems of the Functioning of the Socialist Economy), Warszawa, PWN, 1961. English edition: *The Market in a Socialist Economy,* London: Routledge & Kegan Paul.

Burkett, J. P. (1983) *The Effects of Economic Reform in Yugoslavia,* Berkley. Institute of International Studies, University of California.

Burkett, J. P. (1984) *Stabilization Measures in Yugoslavia: An Assessment of the Proposals of Yugoslavia's Commission for Problems of Economic Stabilization,* mimeographed, Kingston: University of Rhode Island.

Clower, R. W. (1965) 'The Keynesian Counter-Revolution: A Theoretical Appraisal', in: F. H. Hahn and F. Brechling (eds.), *The Theory of Interest Rates,* London: Macmillan.

Clower, R. W. and Due, J. F. (1972) *Microeconomics,* Homewood: Irwin.

Clower, R. W. and Leijonhufvud, A. (1983) 'Say's Principle, What It Means and Doesn't Mean', in: A. Leijonhufvud, *Information and Coordination.* New York/Oxford: Oxford University Press.

Crozier, M. J.; Huntington, S. P. and Watanuki, J. (1975) *The Crisis of Democracy*, New York: New York University Press.

Falubíró, V. (1983) 'Szabályozás és vállalati magatartás 1968-tól napjainkig' (Control and Firms' Behaviour from 1968 up to Now), *Gazdaság*, October, *16*, pp. 31–49.

Grossman, G. (1965) 'Gold and the Sword: Money in the Soviet Command Economy', In: Rosowsky, H. (ed.), *Industrialization in Two Systems*, New York: Wiley.

Hare, P. G. (1983) 'The Beginnings of Institutional Reform in Hungary'. *Soviet Studies*, July, *35*, pp. 313–330.

Havrylyshyn, P. (1984) *Yugoslav Trade Liberalization: An Economic Background*, mimeographed, Washington, D. C.: George Washington University.

Hewett, E. A. (1981) 'The Hungarian Economy: Lessons of the 1970's and' Prospects for the 1980's' in: *East European Economic Assessment, Part I, Country Studies, 1980, A Compendium of Papers Submitted to the Joint Economic Committee, Congress of the United States*, Washington, DC: USGPO.

Hicks, Sir J. (1983) 'Are there Economic Cycles', in: *Money, Interests and Wages: Collected Essays on Economic Theory*, Vol. II, Oxford: Blackwell.

Horváth, B. (1976) *The Yugoslav Economic System*, White Plains: International Arts and Science Press.

Jackall, R. (1983) 'Moral Mazes: Bureaucracy and Managerial Work', *Harvard Business Review*, September—October, *61*, pp. 118–130.

Knight, P. T. (1984) 'Financial Discipline and Structural Adjustment in Yugoslavia: Rehabilitation and Bankruptcy of Loss-Making Enterprises', *World Bank Staff Working Papers*, No. 705.

Kornai, J. (1979) 'Resource-Constrained *versus* Demand-Constrained Systems', *Econometrica*, July, *47*, pp. 802–820.

Kornai, J. (1980) *Economics of Shortage*, Amsterdam: North-Holland.

Kornai, J.; Matits, Á. and Ferge, Zs (1983) *Az állami vállalatok jövedelmének redisztribuciója: első beszámoló* (Redistribution of the Income of State-Owned Firms. First Report), mimeographed, Budapest: Ministry of Industry.

Kornai, J. and Matits, Á. (1983) 'A költségvetési korlát puhaságáról vállalati adatok alapján' (About the Softness of the Budget Constraint Based on Enterprise Data), *Gazdaság*, October, *16*, pp. 3–30.

Kornai, J. and Weibull, J. W. (1983) 'Paternalism, Buyers' and Sellers' Market', *Mathematical Social Sciences*, *6*, pp. 153–169.

Krueger, A. O. (1974) 'The Political Economy of the Rent-Seeking Society', *American Economic Review*, March, *64*, pp. 291–303.

Laki, M. (1982) 'Liquidation and Merger in the Hungarian Industry', *Acta Oeconomica*, January, *28*, pp. 87–108.

Leibenstein, H. (1966) 'Allocative Efficiency *vs.* X—Efficiency', *American Economic Review*, June, *21*, pp. 392–415.

Matits, Á. (1984) *A redisztribució szerepe az állami vállalatok jövedelmezőségének alakulásában: második beszámoló* (The Role of Redistribution in Determining the Profitability of State-Owned Firms: Second Report), mimeographed, Budapest: Ministry of Industry.

McCloskey, D. N. (1983) 'The Rhetoric of Economics', *Journal of Economic Literature*, June, *21*, pp. 481–517.

Naughton, B. (1985) 'False Starts and Second Wind: Financial Reforms in China's Industrial System', in: E. J. Perry and C. Wong (eds), *The Political Economy of Reform in Post-Mao China*, Cambridge, MA: Harvard University Press, pp. 223–252.

Nyers, R. and Tardos, M. (1980) 'Enterprises in Hungary Before and After the Economic Reform', in: W. Baumol (ed.), *Public and Private Enterprise in a Mixed Economy*, London: Macmillan.

Perry, E. J. and Wong, C. (eds.) (1985) *The Political Economy of Reform in Post-Mao China*, Cambridge, MA: Harvard University Press.

Riskin, C. (1985) *Political Economy of Chinese Development since 1949*, mimeographed, New York: Columbia.

Soós, K. A. (1984) 'A reformok utáni magyar és jugoszláv gazdasági mechanizmus néhány fontos közös sajátossága' (Some Important Common Properties of the Hungarian and Yugoslav Post-Reform Economic Mechanism), *Társadalomkutatás*, April, 2, pp. 71–86.

Schumpeter, J. A. (1934) 'Theorie der wirtschaftlichen Entwicklung,' 1911, *The Theory of Economic Development*, Cambridge: Harvard University Press.

Tyson, L. D. (1977) 'Liquidity Crises in the Yugoslav Economy: An Alternative to Bankruptcy?', *Soviet Studies*, April, *29*, pp. 284–295.

Tyson, L. D. (1980) *The Yugoslav Economic System and Its Performance in the 1970s*, Berkeley: Institute of International Studies, University of California.

Tyson, L. D. (1983) 'Investment Allocation. A Comparison of the Reform Experiences of Hungary and Yugoslavia', *Journal of Comparative Economics*, September, 7, pp. 288–303.

Wong, C. (1985) *The Economics of Shortage and the Problems of Industrial Reform in Post-Mao China*, mimeographed, Berkeley: University of California.

3 Memorandum on Prices and Inflation

Hereunder follows the author's unaltered letter, addressed to László Ballai, head of the Economic Policy Department of the Central Committee of the Hungarian Socialist Workers' Party, dated June 9, 1986. The Memorandum comments on documents prepared with reference to producer prices, but it can be followed without difficulty by anyone not acquainted with the documents.

***

I wish to thank you for the invitation to participate in the joint session of June 6 of the Economic Workteam and the Consultative Committee to discuss the documents presenting a comprehensive evaluation of the producer price system and elaborating on future tasks.

Let me make one remark in advance.

Prices and inflation represent the most controversial issues of economic theory. No one can claim to know exactly the cause of the problem or the one and only feasible way to solve it. I am fully aware that all the comments I make hereunder are controversial. But the decision-makers obviously wish to weigh the different positions against one another, and as a party to the dispute, I see fit to say what I have to say directly, without adding qualifications and cautionary remarks to each sentence.

I shall comment mainly on the *Recommendation* and on its Chapter III in the first place containing the proposals firstly, since the rest of the material is centred around these. I shall not follow the order of the pieces received, but discuss seven points altogether.

1. My starting point is the relation between market and prices. In my view, one can speak of a 'market mechanism' if and *only* if the price is formed by demand and supply, and prices exercise a fundamental influence on demand and supply. I do not assert that other factors cannot at all affect prices, demand, and supply. This much is to be stressed, however: if the interaction between price, demand and supply is not duly asserted, the market can be no more than a 'pseudo-market', and the price does not fulfil its principal function.

However well-known this fact may be, the problems of the Hungarian economic mechanism lie exactly here, especially in the state-owned sector. My memorandum is practically concerned with that sphere only, where the system of relative prices, or price proportions, does not reflect the relation between demand and supply and only slightly affects demand and supply.

The descriptive analyses of the documents, however, do not highlight this problem, which in my opinion should be the starting point of the discussion. They do not analyse the firms' price- and cost-responsiveness, nor do they provide information on how much the disproportions of demand and supply or the slacks and shortages are reflected in the relative prices. They also fail to examine the dynamics of a crucial triple relationship: if the relation between demand and supply changes, is it reflected in the shift of relative prices? And conversely, if relative prices change, does it affect the relation between demand and supply?

This interaction is almost totally neglected in the proposals. Ideally, however, it should be at their core, for if it is not asserted, the market will not function.

To this, the following must be added, and I shall refer to it again: prices constitute a closely linked system. If one part of the price system is arbitrary and does not reflect the relation between demand and supply and relative scarcities, the *entire* price system is arbitrary. What is arbitrary and distorted in the price system affects the rest of the prices because, either as a cost element it is part of their formation, or because it affects the cost of living and thereby wages, and in the final result, costs again. I do not wish to put this comment in an extreme form. If, on well-considered grounds, exceptions are made to this principle in the case of a few products and services, it will not spoil the entire price system. Such exceptions, however, must remain extremely rare.

2. A close relationship exists between the relative price system on the one hand, and taxes and subsidies on the other. This is a perfect example of the classic question: 'What came first, the chicken or the egg?' The original cause and effect cannot be clearly distinguished. On the one hand: if the price is arbitrary and distorted, the profit does not reflect efficiency. This compels the state to compensate the loss-maker through a subsidy, and to tax away 'unduly high' profits. But taxes and subsidies become fixed and get built into the cost and price system, thus conserving the wrong relative prices. The process may, however, start from the other end. There are certain taxes and subsidies which were once based on a valid consideration but remain in place after the original consideration has long since lost its validity; but the cost and price system is still adjusted to them. The intricate fiscal system consisting of a hundred different channels of taxes and subsidies, and the distorted relative price system, are two aspects of a single phenomenon.

I think that the prepared documents do not reveal this problem with sufficient clarity. Also, the part setting forth the proposals does not expand on the point that the price and fiscal systems should be readjusted jointly and simultaneously. This is a 'vicious circle' which can *only* be, and *must* be broken in a single stroke. Otherwise, the system of subsidies and taxes will again drive the price system towards distortions, and conversely, distortions of the price system will again bring out a hundred different kinds of taxes and subsidies.

3. The documents presented treat inflation as a kind of impersonal spontaneous process which must be slowed down through anti-inflationary policy. It is my conviction that this is the wrong approach. In both capitalist and socialist countries, the creation of money is ultimately in the hands of the fiscal and monetary authorities. Inflation prevails where the government creates inflation and, in Hungary, an inflationary process has emerged because the government pursues an inflationary policy. As long as the Hungarian government does not change its policy, inflation will not disappear.

Inflation is only secondarily a problem of the price control office. I do not claim that price policy in general, and the price control office's activities specifically, are without effect. They can have an influence, especially on the distribution of the average rate of inflation among different goods and services. This is, however, only a secondary influence. The price level cannot generally rise if there is no one to buy goods at excessively high prices.

In this respect, neither the analysis, nor the proposal is clear enough; they do not state exactly and unambiguously the determinants of the future inflationary process, and its speed. In my opinion, the process will not depend on the percentage of inflation rate 'prescribed' or 'permitted' by the plan, or the political resolution adopted prior to the plan.

4. What I have said in paragraph 3 is not to suggest that the price policy cannot contribute to the acceleration of the inflationary process. As I see it, it has indeed done so — for at least twenty years now — through its repeated attempts at improving the relative price structure through *partial* price adjustments. The prices of products belonging to group 'A' are raised, on the premise that they are too low in comparison with those of groups 'B', 'C', etc., but the price increase for 'A' pushes up the costs of 'B', 'C', etc., or, if consumer articles are involved, the cost of living. Sooner or later, the costs of the groups of products 'B', 'C', etc., will outpace their prices, which will then have to be raised, just as the rise in the cost of living will provoke a rise in nominal wages, which in turn will push up the cost level. The series of partial price adjustments inevitably engenders a cost-price-wage spiral thus diminishing the change in relative prices initially pursued through partial increases. At the date of the increase, the price of the group of products 'A' rose, say, by 30 per cent relative to groups 'B' and 'C', whereas in three to five years' time the prices of the products 'B' and 'C' will also have been raised to the same level by the inflationary process. While engendering an inflationary spiral, the series of partial price adjustments does not and cannot drive the price system towards the proper proportions. This process, prolonged over several decades, will not converge within a reasonable time toward the desired state of the price system. During the process, the relations between costs, demand and supply will also be constantly shifting, and disproportions will be reproduced. Although the Hungarian case provides clear evidence of this fact, the documents in question do not even attempt to prove the opposite, namely, that we are coming closer to a reasonable and practicable relative price system that harmonizes demand and supply.

As a matter of fact, the part of the *Recommendation* that submits the proposal also promises to continue the policy of partial adjustments over a prolonged period of time. This, I think, rather than help find the solution, will spur the inflationary spiral.

The problem can be solved only through a *general and comprehensive* price reform which places the entire price system on a market basis in a relatively short time. I am convinced that from the economic point of view, the solution must be applied in such a way that it resembles a single big shock. Anything else amounts to putting off the problem. I am not competent to judge whether the political-social conditions for such a general solution are given; or if the leaders and the population of this country are prepared to accept the idea. But if they are not, I am afraid that all the existing problems will remain.

5. The key to slowing down inflation is to have a hold on macrodemand, and although this is not discussed in detail in the proposal concerning prices, it ought to be accentuated. Control over macrodemand, not bureaucratic intervention in the market price formation, will be the determinant.

To me, however, the wording seems to be unclear in the proposal's repeated references to an 'excessive allocation' of resources. Presumably, this refers to the socio-economic mechanisms that reproduce shortage, excess demand, and runaway purchasing power. But then, there is need for a thorough analysis, since open inflation, repressed inflation, and shortage cannot be eliminated without elimination of excessive resource allocation.

Of course, it is not enough to restrict the market on the demand side only. It is no less important to adopt an economic mechanism which would compel the supply side to adjust to market signals. This can be accomplished through an apt combination of incentive and economic compulsion. On the one hand, market competition rewards with profit those who properly adjust, and the state does not neutralize the high profit by taxing it away. On the other hand, the state does not compensate the losses of those who fail to adjust. Naturally, transitional credits could be granted to firms suffering under the initial shocks of the general price adjustment. But such credits should be repaid and, like any one-time subsidies that were granted, should have a clearly defined expiration date. After that, let the winners be the true winners and the losers true losers.

This train of thought also suggests that the general assertion of market prices, radical and thorough revision of the monetary and the fiscal policy, and the creation of the equilibrium between demand and supply constitute an inseparable set of tasks, to be carried out simultaneously.

6. The documents repeatedly discuss the linkage between the price system and foreign trade. Together with many fellow economists, I mistrust the 'simulation' methods so far recommended for replacement of a market approach to foreign trade. The market cannot be simulated, and attempts to do so only lead to the proliferation of bureaucratic interventions, as in the past.

Within the framework of today's distorted price system and of the accompanying chaotic system of taxation and subsidization, neither the domestic costs of export transactions, nor the economic gains of import transactions are known. Thus, the most elementary information necessary for deciding on whether it is worth substituting a domestic product for an imported item is missing. For this reason, no one can assert the numerical value of the exchange rate that would properly orient exports and imports. To me, it is obvious that a marginal exchange rate is needed, and I am entirely unable to follow the logic of the arguments raised up against it[1]. Yet I cannot say — because of the otherwise arbitrary price system — what the numerical value of a reasonable marginal exchange rate would be. It is regrettable that the document does not discuss the exchange rate, thus creating the impression that this is a problem that has been solved when in fact no genuine progress has been made.

7. The parts of the Memorandum concerned with 'indecent price' and 'abuse of superiority', and its suggestions for the use of administrative sanctions in these affairs do not convince me, either. My impression is that the writers of the documents themselves are hesitating, they are not sure what can be expected from such sanctions in an economic situation in which it is not the buyer's but the seller's market that predominates.

In my opinion, it is mistaken as well as illusory to expect the police or the courts to compel the seller not to take unfair advantage of his superiority in a shortage market. It is clear that it is correct to take action against cheating, deceiving and misleading the buyer. Here, legal protection of the buyer is called for. But when demand exceeds supply and prices go up, it is not a case of 'profiteering' or 'abuse of superiority'; it is simply the first normal response to shortage. And it ought to be followed by the second response: increase of supply, decrease of demand, and in the final result, elimination of shortage. It is a poor prospect to base our expectations, *instead* of a normally functioning market, on bureaucratic market supervision, or on the application of Act IV/1984 (a law against dishonest business).

Although several other questions need to be addressed, I content myself with the seven problems mentioned. To finish, I wish to stress the following: it appears from the *Recommendation* and the documents that the authors sincerely wish to promote the reform process. Nevertheless, I am worried; the proposals seem to me too timid, and do not formulate the energetic measures that should be taken for the sake of the development of the Hungarian national economy.

NOTE

1. For an explanation of the notion 'marginal exchange rate' see footnote 18 in the next chapter.

4 The Bureaucratic Redistribution of the Firm's Profit*

Co-author: Ágnes Matits

4.1 SUBJECT OF THE RESEARCH

One of the leading principles of the Hungarian economic reform was to make profit a central element of the incentive system for firms. Has it been a successful effort, or is it still just an illusion? How much does the firm's profit depend on proceeds from sales in the market and on expenditure on inputs, and how much does it depend on central intervention and on the bureaucratic redistribution of profits? To what extent and in which way does the state intervene in the formation of profit? We have sought to answer these vitally important questions which are intriguing from the theoretical as well as from the economic policy viewpoint.

---

* The text published in the present volume has been taken from the book *A vállalatok nyereségének bürokratikus újraelosztása (The Bureaucratic Redistribution of the Firm's Profit)* by János Kornai and Ágnes Matits. Changes have been made only inasmuch as was necessary to compose a smoothly readable unit from the passages selected.

The book sets forth the results of extensive research carried out under the guidance of the two authors, with the contribution of numerous participants. All the state-owned firms' balance sheets of the years 1975–82, or to be more precise, various data from these sheets, were fed into a computer. For each year and for each firm, 101 different indicators were composed. These indicators formed the basis of the mathematical-statistical analysis and of the economic conclusions to be drawn therefrom.

The original book concentrates on the analysis of data with some comments added. The emphasis is shifted in the present excerpt which, according to the character of this book, focuses on more general comments and conclusions.

Our attention is centred on the firm's profit, which the state affects directly through various prerogatives: it taxes away some of the firms' income for the benefit of the state budget, or it adds to the firms' income by debiting the budget. The total process of taxation and subsidization affecting profit or the spending of profit is called *fiscal redistribution,* as it takes place in the *firms'* sphere.[1] For the sake of brevity, the attributes 'the firms'' and 'fiscal' will not always be used hereafter. However, whenever reference is made to redistribution, it is meant in this strictly defined and limited sense.

In the final analysis, our examination is concerned with the question, *in what manner does fiscal redistribution affect the firms' profit and thereby their behaviour?* Although this question is already far narrower than the wider problem area formulated above, it can be answered only partially. A more complete answer requires that numerous details be clarified.[2]

4.2 PROFIT INCENTIVE IN THE CAPITALIST ECONOMY

Before embarking on an analysis of Hungarian economic problems, we shall do an overview of today's capitalist market economy and of the thought process it repeatedly evokes openly or tacitly in Hungarian economists dealing with reform. The capitalist economy, it is usually recognized, yields excellent results in technical development, innovation, fast adjustment to needs, reduction of production costs. But can these results be achieved in a reformed socialist economy, in which public ownership will not be given up for private ownership?

From the outset, we wish to avoid any misunderstanding or misinterpretation of our analysis. It is not our purpose to set up the modern capitalist economy as an example to be followed by Hungarian reformers. The combination of different political, ethical, social, and economic considerations will inevitably affect any decision on what can indeed be borrowed from the practice of the capitalist market economy by Hungary; and these considerations lie beyond the scope of our present endeavour. Still, we cannot seriously consider the matter of reform without carefully and objectively studying the functioning of modern capitalism.

The portraits of capitalism are as varied as the many extant schools of economics. The one that we will sketch here is not intended as a synthesis, nor does it reflect a consensus on the part of these different schools; rather, it constitutes the authors' subjective picture, and it is restricted to the areas that are essentially germane to the subject at hand. In short, our picture is a sketchy one: only a few features of the market economy based on private ownership have been drawn up.

The modern capitalist economy is not a homogeneous phenomenon: it looks different in the more individualistic USA than in the Scandinavian welfare states or Japan, and it is different again in the newly industrialized countries that are fast emerging from a backward state, such as South Korea and Brazil. Great differences exist between the individual countries regarding the role played by central economic policy. For our purpose, and precisely with a view to highlight the contrast, we shall investigate the characteristics of those economies in which state intervention is the least marked. Also, while countless small firms, as well as other legal formations, do populate these economies, our theme can be effectively developed by concentrating on the small private firm and the joint stock company, especially on large ones.

A private firm may be owned by an individual, a family, or a group of strangers. The owner bears unlimited responsibility for repayment of the firms' debts, and his interest in profit is unambiguous: the greater the profit, the more the firm can grow, and by direct consequence, the owner's personal wealth. Furthermore, it is up to the owner to decide how his wealth will be divided between consumption, reinvestment in the firm, and savings. If, however, the firm is continually incurring net losses, the owner will, sooner or later, be compelled to give up the undertaking, since his private means may well be depleted in the process of covering losses and repaying debts. Indeed, bankruptcy and liquidation are frequent events among small firms in private ownership, and their property, or the firms themselves, then have to be sold to new owners. Small firms live and die — some are ephemeral, others long-lived.

The development of the share-holding company was inspired, among other things, by the wish to protect the owner's private wealth, and this was accomplished by rendering him responsible for the firm's liabilities, but only up to the amount of his investment. Accordingly, in the worst of cases, his entire invested capital could be lost and the value of the shares reduced to nothing, but beyond that, the owner — i.e., the shareholder — could not be held responsible for the firms' debts. It is interesting to note, however, that even such limited responsibility generates a strong proprietary interest: whether the amount of capital invested is considerable or not, the owner is not indifferent to its fate.

A familiar argument regarding the large capitalist corporations is that its owners have virtually no effective power, since it is not the shareholders who make the decisions, but the managers. The latter, it is further argued, are the real rulers of the company, even though they are no more than salaried employees at the head of a large bureaucratic apparatus. Taking this argument to its ultimate logical conclusion, it could even be asserted that the managers' position is not significantly different from that of their counterparts in, say, a large Hungarian firm.

In our opinion, this reasoning is wrong. Not infrequently, the manager himself holds shares in the company he works for. But this is not the point, for even if he does not have any direct interest connected with ownership, he is forced to serve the 'proprietary interest.' The manager, even if shareholding is dispersed and the right to vote at the corporation's meetings is merely a formality, must bear in mind that the owner or shareholder exerts his power primarily through the stock market, where he 'votes with his feet'. If, on the one hand, the owner loses confidence in the company, he will 'walk away' by getting rid of his shares and investing his money elsewhere, thus causing the value of the share to diminish. If, on the other hand, confidence in the company grows, its shares will be in demand and their value will increase.

It is also important to remember that not only is the corporation under obligation to inform the public about its financial situation, but independent auditors control the accuracy of the balance sheets and cheating carries legal penalties. Thus, difficulties may be concealed for shorter or longer periods, but not permanently: stock market experts are bound to find out about the deteriorating financial situation of a corporation, as well as its poor business prospects.[3] Furthermore, although the individual interested in buying shares does not make a choice on his own, a broker or a financial commission agency specialized in the field will act upon his global instructions. The profit of the brokers or agencies, in turn, will depend on whether they make felicitous choices on their mandator's behalf: whether they buy or sell the shares of a given company at the appropriate time. Clearly then, it is in their own interest to keep a sharp eye on the financial situation of firms.

Of course, mistakes are made in the process, pieces of information are at times deliberately distorted, panic can set in, and reckless measures are not uncommon. Most errors, however, will be redeemed sooner or later, since the actors in this market are keenly interested in obtaining accurate information. The more transparent, the better organized, and the more mature the capital market, the less distorted the pieces of information on the situation and prospects of firms will be.

It is clearly in the manager's best interest that the firm's shares gain rather than lose in value, and therefore that the firm's financial position be strong, its credibility beyond doubt, and its net worth on the rise. The manager's direct financial interests usually coincide with this proposition in the long term: if the business prospers, the managers are paid sizeable premiums, and more importantly, their professional careers become firmly established. If the manager improves the firm's finances, he may be promoted within the firm, or he may be invited by another firm to assume a higher position. If, however, the firm's finances deteriorate under his management, his reputation will suffer, and he may be dismissed, or his chance to get a higher post with another firm might be diminished.

Of course, loss-making in a given year is not the only factor taken into consideration. After all, loss can result from exogenous factors, such as a general recession, or a downturn in a particular industry. But if the firm's market share and financial position have deteriorated in comparison with those of its competitors, and if this relative loss of ground turns out to be a persistent trend, then the manager will, justifiably, be held accountable. This may lead to failure, i.e., to the irreversible decline of his career — a permanent damage which can be only partially counterbalanced by the usually high compensations stipulated in managers' contracts. For managers, the stakes are very high: they have a great deal to gain or lose in the course of their careers.

It has already been mentioned and is now particularly emphasized that one single year's profit-flow, or the attached profit rate, is not the decisive criterion in judging a firm's situation.[4] A temporary loss may be overcome by various means, including resort to credit and the sale of loss-making units, and these, in turn, are reflected in the corresponding stock indicator: falling net worth. The key criterion in appraising a firm, however, remains the same: its future prospects. Is there hope that it will recover and increase its net worth again? Thus, even though the current profit is not the decisive factor, it is quite obvious that a very close connection exists between past, present, and future profit-flow, on the one hand, and the dynamics of net worth on the other. This claim is easy to prove theoretically and to support empirically. The greater and the more presistent the loss-flow, the higher the probability that the firm's net worth will continue to deteriorate.

In certain cases, small, medium, or even large companies become insolvent and go bankrupt. There are, however, other forms of failure. If the property is concentrated to a sufficient degree, or if the shareholders are able to take concerted action, they may relentlessly fire the managers. Or, the entire shareholding company (or as many shares of it as make a quorum) is purchased by another company. For example, in the case of aggressive takeovers, the group that is to buy the company openly declares that as soon as the transaction is settled, previous management will be replaced. The managers may try to ward off the offensive, but the poorer the business results, and the more the shares have lost in value prior to the takeover attempt, the less hope there is for successful resistance. A common outcome is that the weak firm is simply merged into the strong one.

Let us sum up what has been said thus far. With the privately owned small firm, causal relationships between profit, on the one hand, and survival, growth, and increase of wealth on the other, are direct and transparent. The same causality exists in the case of the large company, but it is more indirect. Permanent loss may lead to failure with a lag, or none at all, and failure is not necessarily manifested in bankruptcy. Yet the causal relationship does exist and exerts considerable influence. The capital market for the shares, the labour market for the managers, and the keen competition between firms combine to enforce such a relationship: the manager is compelled to do his best to increase profit.

The performance of modern capitalism mentioned at the beginning of this chapter cannot be explained by the mere fact that the market coordinates the relationship between buyer and seller. An equally important explanatory factor is the extremely strong profit incentive of the economic units. Put in another way, if only the role of market relations is emphasized and that of the profit incentive is neglected, then one cannot explain why the producer-seller makes efforts to win over buyers from competitors, develops technology, puts out new products, tries to reduce costs, and adjusts to the prevailing situation.

Of course, in today's capitalist economy the growth of profit is not the only motive, and the economic system does not consist solely of firms working for profit. Among other things, a state bureaucracy exists, and it is propelled by motives of its own to interfere in the economy. Its role will be discussed in a subsequent section. Also, another point must be made with regard to the theoretical-historical background of the problem. When both Marxist political economy and neoclassic economic theory make it their starting point that the behaviour of the firm in capitalist ownership is characterized by profit maximization, they somewhat simplify the question of motivation. Owners as well as managers are motivated by various factors and the term itself, 'profit maximization', is not an unambiguous decision criterion. The behaviour of the profit-maximizing decision-makers depends also on which specific indicator is used to measure profit; the time horizon under consideration; and the way risk is calculated (whether lower but more secure profit is preferred over larger, but less secure profit).

However, even though the matter is in fact somewhat simplified, it is admissible for the purpose of a theoretical examination. It seems realistic to start from the point, in a general analysis of the modern capitalist market economy, that the firm's decision-makers strive to earn the highest possible profit.[5]

4.3 THE INTENTION AT THE START OF THE HUNGARIAN REFORM TO CREATE PROFIT INCENTIVE

After this cursory view of capitalism, let us now direct our attention to the Hungarian economy. One of the fundamental ideas of the 1968 reform was to create profit incentive for the state-owned firms. The programme of the reform initiators is summed up in the following:

1. After the command economy is eliminated and plans are broken down to fit the individual firms, profitability should become the primary numerical criterion in the appraisal of firms.

2. Managers and workers of the firms must be made directly interested in increasing profitability.

We shall prove with a few quotations that such intentions were indeed expressed at the beginning of the reform. We begin by quoting from Rezső Nyers's address made at the Central Committee meeting of November 18–20, 1965, of the Hungarian Socialist Workers' Party (H.S.W.P., 1965), which was subsequently passed by the Central Committee. (Rezső Nyers was the Secretary of the Party in charge of economic affairs at that time.)

'Two tasks are to be centrally specified as the common objective' of the firms' activities: 1. to satisfy consumers' needs as well as possible in regard to quantity, quality, and time; 2. to continuously increase profitability... What will take place in practice is that the existing administrative constraints will be replaced by economic regulatory instruments, which will then drive and even force firms to take the correct actions. Economic instruments such as central taxation, foreign exchange restrictions, price and wage policy, and credit policy are in fact to convey the national economic plan's objectives to the firms.' (p. 24)

'...it will be expedient to develop a system in which managers' personal income, and to some extent also the employees' income, depend on the firm's [net] income (profit).[6] If they can increase [net] income, firms ought to be able to provide higher profit shares for their employees and, from permanent and secure additional income, also raise wages, within proper limits.' (p. 25)

'A price system ought to be developed which — by virtue of relative prices and profitability — can better orient producers and consumers than the existing one.' (p. 26)

A second source of quotations is Rezső Nyers's book: *25 Questions and Answers on Economic Policy,* published in 1969, which means it was written in consideration of the first year's experience of the reform.

'Although the content of the firms' long-term plans varies according to sector, they must concentrate on long-term profit optimization, and on the stable foundation of technical development.' (p. 20)

'To start with, I wish to state that the principle of profit incentive has been proved correct in practice during the last one and a half years. As the primary yardstick of the firm's performance, it offers complex information on economic efficiency... May I recall that, in elaborating the reform, it was still under dispute if the socialist firms were to be made interested in increasing profit, or gross income. This dispute (it was very good that we had that dispute!) led us at the time, in 1965–6, to the principle of profit incentive.' (p. 81)

The passages quoted clearly show that profit incentive was a leading idea of the reform, and today we are still of the opinion that it was the proper decision to concentrate to such an extent on the principle of profit incentive. Our research, however, as well as other studies, have found that this conception, although the proper one, has not been consistently put into practice.

One of the main causes of the inconsistency lies in the bureaucratic redistribution of profit, and from this point of view, the 1968 conceptions were already fraught with inner contradictions. On the one hand, the reform leaders wished to give way to the selective effect of competition, but on the other, they wished to reassure economic actors that the reform did not threaten their jobs and activities. In addition, they stressed the necessity of reducing subsidies, but they also reassured the firms that the bulk of subsidies would remain, that 'protectionism' was needed in the face of foreign competition, and so on. Further quotations follow hereunder, from Rezső Nyers's book, published in 1969.

'What matters is that we see clearly the difference between the momentary and transitory financial difficulties of a firm, and chronic inviability... For myself, I think that in the socialist planned economy we need not fear massive closure of firms, which cannot happen, but rather the longevity of clearly non-viable firms.' (p. 29)

'... Central subsidies are distributed over-profusely. This is what matters. As I have mentioned, we do not intend to fully abandon protectionism, or the government's financial policy of subsidizing socialist firms. However, in order to improve the production structure, subsidies will have to be gradually decreased, or more efficiently spent.' (p. 157)

'...in principle, protectionism consists of two elements. One is permanent, which means that firms need not fear that all the financial sources which are provided by the state today will dry up, leaving them without central subsidy. The other element of central protectionism is composed of certain temporary means of assistance, provided by the state during some brief, transitory period when the firm is supposed to transform its production structure so as to produce more profitably and in greater conformity with market demands.' (pp. 156–7)

'...central subsidy is exaggerated (price subsidy, overall subsidy, foreign trade reimbursement, tax-exemption), and levels the economic results of firms of high, medium, or low efficiency. Too many firms do not have to struggle for profit.' (p. 203)

'Subsidies of exports and of consumer prices, as well as other allowances, render profitability all too sure for firms. These subsidies, in the extent to which they are currently granted, have been made necessary by the need to stimulate continuous growth of production, yet they are to be gradually reduced in the future. This reduction is made possible by the fact that the allowances in question were meant to apply only for a definite period. The government can modify and restrict its financial policy within the framework of the five-year plans, and this will indeed be necessary.' (pp. 209–210)

It is remarkable that the problem area we are concentrating on in our research and in the present study was so clearly seen in 1969. Already at that time, Rezső Nyers saw government interference in the formation of profit as exaggerated; and he expressed his concern by claiming that it would deaden profit sensitivity, and weaken encouragement for increased profitability.[7] However, in retrospect, it also becomes quite clear that the reform leaders of the time did not perceive the inconsistency of the requirements they formulated. It is not possible to intensify the profit incentive and at the same time accept its weakening, the latter being something which is bound to occur if the system of subsidies and redistribution is maintained, even if at a reduced rate.

Official pronouncements made in the early period of the reform not only stressed that the survival of non-viable firms was not to be allowed, but also condemned 'exaggerated' financial subsidies and promised 'restriction' of the financial policy. Indeed, all of these seemed to point towards a hardening of the budget constraint. And yet, the hope of softening was from the outset held to firms and the bureaucratic organization. This was manifested in the references made to 'protectionism' and to the further granting of various kinds of subsidies; as well as in the reassurance that there was no need to fear the drying up of all central financial sources. In short, ambivalence about the hardness or softness of the budget constraint was present right at the pronouncement of the reform objectives.

So far, we have covered various issues in different ways, but in fact we have been trying to outline the same group of questions all along. In a market economy, based on private ownership, profit is earned in the market and it strongly affects economic agents. But what is going on in the reformed Hungarian state-owned sector? Where is the magnitude of profit determined? In the market, or on the desks of bureaucrats? To what extent does profit affect the economic agents' behaviour? To what degree have the 1968 reformers' original intentions been implemented in this respect? Has the tendency to soften the firms' budget constraint been successfully stopped?

Let us now turn to a numerical examination.

4.4 DERAILING THE PROFIT

In our analysis, an important role is played by a concept we have introduced: *original profit*. Let us assume — hypothetically — that in a given year, the state does not carry out any profit redistribution. That is to say, the firms' total annual proceeds and expenditures are accounted at the prevailing prices, there is no taxing away, and the firm is to be reimbursed for payments to the state budget made during the year. Conversely, the state does not give the firm any money, and it will demand repayment of all grants and exemptions extended during the year. What remains after all these conditions are put into effect is the original profit.

Note, however, that in calculating original profit, all the effects of fiscal redistribution are not eliminated. Namely, no hypothetical price system free from fiscal redistribution has been built, which means that the total redistributive effect latent in the costs of products is not eliminated. Only those elements of redistribution which actually appear in the profit account of the firm under examination are corrected for. Thus, a category of profit is established, one which the firm would attain — assuming a functioning price system and market — if the state were to cease all interference with the formation of profits realized through prices. Furthermore, it is to be stressed that the concern here is not with redistribution in general, but with redistribution of profit earned by the state-owned firms and realized by the particular firm under examination.

Also, before proceeding with our analysis, we would like to make it clear that no value judgement is attached to the concept of original profit. For instance, we do not at all mean to suggest that it should be an indicator in the sound appraisal of the efficiency of production. In fact, the question is not even to be raised once the prevailing price system is simply considered as a given condition. It should be pointed out, however, that the economic content of the concept of original profit would be obvious in a market economy: it is the gross profit realized at the prevailing prices.

Hungarian firms do not report original profit in their balance sheet. What is more, they do not even calculate the value of original profit. Firms and the superior authorities are interested in profit *after* distribution, that is, after adding taxes and deducting subsidies. Therefore it was a highly unusual undertaking to calculate original profit in the framework of our research project.

The following remark is often heard in the course of discussions about our research project: 'original profit' is a fictitious category. We do not agree with this assessment, since the firm's customers do not pay fictitious prices for the firm's output, but real ones, the firm does not pay fictitious prices for its inputs, but real ones, and the difference between the actual proceeds from outputs and the actual expenditure on inputs is also an economic reality. The latter magnitude is called (pre-tax, gross) profit in the language of economics. And, important as it may be, the question of whether these input and output prices are rational, is irrelevant here. It is our conviction that a vast amount of economically unjustifiable arbitrariness weighs on the price system. And yet these are genuine prices, and therefore the difference between the proceeds from outputs and the expenditure on inputs is not a 'fictitious' category. True, it is of an economically unjustifiable and arbitrary magnitude, since it reflects the unjustifiable and arbitrary nature of the price system. This arbitrariness, however, is only aggravated by the arbitrariness of redistribution. But here, we are jumping ahead to a point that will be discussed in greater detail later on.

Fiscal redistribution taxes away from and adds to the original profit in a series of steps to arrive at the various degrees of the *'actual profit'* (accounted profit, post-redistribution profit, final profit). In our computations, the original profit and the actual profit are contrasted in many different ways. Similarly, both indicators are divided by the value of assets, so that original profitability and actual profitability can be contrasted. As a result of fiscal redistribution, the firms' actual profit differs from original profit. The extent of the deviation of actual profit from the original one reflects what is in fact the state's role in influencing the firms' profitability.

The extent of redistribution can be described, on the one hand, by the magnitude of the deviation of actual profit from original profit ('profit diversion' for short) and on the other hand, by the magnitudes of the elements of redistribution: taxes and subsidies. Namely, the same total extent of profit diversion, that is, the same measure of the joint effect of redistribution, may result from widely different magnitudes of subsidies and allowances, and of the firms' payments made upon various grounds.

Let us see, therefore, what can be said of the extent of redistribution among the Hungarian state-owned firms.

PROPOSITION 1. The redistribution of profit is very large: first, in the course of redistribution, a wide profit diversion is effected; second, the amount of profit shifted through subsidies and taxes is vast.[8]

The relative values of taxes and subsidies determined for each branch and sector are shown in Table 4.1. In respect of the total number of state-owned firms, as well as a number of branches and sectors, the following observation can be made: the amount of taxes exceeds the amount of total profit originating within the group of firms in question. (The value of the ratio tax/original profit is

Table 4.1: Relative size of taxes and subsidies in 1982

Group of firms	Tax/ original profit	Subsidy/ original profit	Subsidy/ tax
Engineering industry	0.83	0.32	0.39
Light industry	1.03	0.57	0.55
Food processing	2.10	2.02	0.96
Industry (except food processing)	0.93	0.69	0.74
Industry (total)	1.10	0.87	0.80
Construction industry	0.82	0.21	0.25
Agriculture	1.05	1.61	1.54
Trade	1.73	1.00	0.58
Services	1.30	0.59	0.45
State-owned firms: Total	1.27	0.91	0.72

Note: The sectoral indicator is the average of the firms' indicators weighed by the denominator.

higher than 1.) This is possible only in the case of multiple redistribution, that is, if the state first grants with one hand what it subsequently takes away with the other. That is to say, the net profit tax burden reaching 30 per cent on average is levied through repeated reshuffling of a vast amount of profit.

It is an important fact to be mentioned that practically no change was found in this field in the period under examination. The 'centralization' of the firms' profit is also reflected by the unweighted average of the firms' tax/original profit indicators. With respect to the totality of state-owned firms, this value is 0.92, which is to say that, on average, 92 per cent of the total of original profit originating in these firms is centralized.

PROPOSITION 2. As a consequence of redistribution, the firms' actual profit deviates widely from the original profit.

The wider apart the firms' original and actual profitability, the greater the role of redistribution in shaping profitability.

Among many other computations, correlation analysis was carried out with profitability indicators (the ratio of profits and the value of assets). Table 4.2 presents the correlation coefficients determined for 1982 for the total number of state-owned firms, and for the industrial firms. The low values of the correlation coefficients show the deviation of the original profitability indicator from the other profitability indicators. Similar results were shown by the correlation calculations made with other samples.

Table 4.2: Correlation coefficients between the profitability indicators

Indicators	2	3
1. Original profitability	0.39 0.44	0.18 0.18
2. Profitability according to balance sheet		0.55 0.50
3. Final profitability		

Note: The results come from 1982 data. The upper figure contains the computations covering the industry, the lower one contains those covering the total number of state-owned firms.

4.5 THE REDISTRIBUTION OF PROFIT
AND THE ILLUSION OF REGULATION

We shall resort to an analogy in order to throw light on the problem. We begin by assuming that every student of a higher-grade school originally received the same basic scholarship to cover the cost of living. However, it is decided later that scholarships will be increased for students who achieve excellent results in the major subjects, and that they will be reduced for poor performers. As long as this is the only criterion of redistribution, it can presumably stimulate improved performance in the major subjects. But later, yet another kind of redistribution is introduced: outstanding performance in sports is to be awarded with another scholarship, and poor performance is to be punished through reduction of previous assistance. This change will weaken the original stimulus, since poor academic performance now can be counterbalanced by excellent sportsmanship. And then a third kind of redistribution is adopted: active participation in the agendas of political and mass organizations to be awarded with increments to the original scholarship, whereas apathy is to be punished by reductions. A fourth redistribution will follow, meant to encourage participation in the choir, orchestra, art circle, etc. And a fifth redistribution whose criterion in social inequality will take place: the children of poor families will receive additional scholarship whereas those of well-to-do children will be reduced.

Each redistributor can feel that he holds an instrument — financial incentive — with which to influence the students' behaviour or counterbalance their disadvantaged position. But in fact, each new redistribution weakens the effect of the preceding one.

Let us now leave our analogy and turn our attention to the redistribution of profit. The original profit of each firm is given and it is precisely what will be redistributed through different entitlements. It is true that each kind of redistribution changes only a part of the total amount of profits, and serves a presumably useful and specific purpose. In short, each has a marked 'character' which can be described by the criteria and specific proportions of that particular redistribution.

The more different kinds of redistribution that are implemented and the more these differ in character — putting in place a whole system of criteria — the higher the rate of the total amount of original profit that is shifted, and the less effective a particular redistribution will be, since its stimulating or compensating effect will be mitigated by the redistributions of many different objectives.

László Antal's (1979) paper introduced an apt term: a *regulation illusion* persuades the leaders of the economic mechanism and those who intend to regulate, that they can achieve their purpose through intervention. Both our theoretical train of thought and the practical experience of profit redistribution indicate that *over*-regulation ultimately makes regulation illusory. If only one or two market diversions from the original profit were applied, it might be effective. But a combination of a thousand different considerations is ineffective. If social psychologists and economists joined forces, they might find out, through practical observations or experiments, where the *stimulus threshold* of redistribution lies. If only a few redistributions took place, each one might surpass the stimulus threshold and exert its influence. Yet the change caused by a fragmentary part of total redistribution is surely below that threshold.

What is more, this imperceptibility is further enhanced by endless change. It is not enough simply to register the consequences of one or another distribution. The actor has to be able to react to them, and his reaction should then be integrated into the permanent attitude of the firm. Yet by the time this can occur, the other kinds of redistributions are again introduced.

The innumerable and perpetually changing redistributions together indicate that the final profit is unpredictable: it depends on luck, or on the caprice of regulators. And if this is so, it is better to influence the regulators through lobbying, bargaining, and other similar means.

Here, just as in every aspect of the functioning of the Hungarian economic mechanism, market and bureaucracy coexist. The firm's profit depends on both. In the final analysis, however, according to the experience reflected in Propositions 1 and 2, the larger force is that of bureaucratic redistribution: the firm's profit depends first and foremost on this factor.

All this has effects on the profit incentive. If the actual profit retained by the firm is not heavily dependent on the proceeds earned in the market and on the expenses paid out in the market, it is not worthwhile to strive for higher proceeds and lower expenses. Under such circumstances, the profit incentive is bound to diminish, thus undermining the very basis of the conception of 'regulation through economic instruments'. And if the incentive of profitability cannot intensively assert itself, the so-called regulators are bound to remain powerless and ineffective.

4.6 LEVELLING

So far we have seen how the great number of separate redistributions, each guided by different intentions and purposes, make the deviation of the actual profit from the original profit practically unpredictable. On closer examination, however, this in practice turns out not to be the whole truth. There are a few strongly influential tendencies which penetrate the complex redistribution process and ultimately endow it with certain regularities and special but universally valid features. Those special features are described in Propositions 3 and 4.

PROPOSITION 3. The original profitability fundamentally influences the nature of redistribution. That is, loss-making clearly increases the chances of receiving subsidies, whereas rising profitability results in higher taxes.

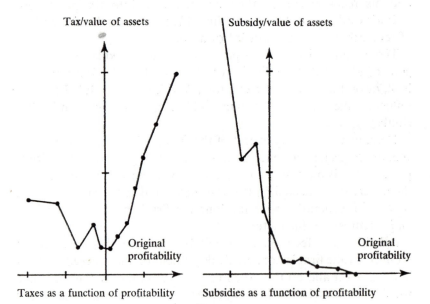

Fig. 4.1 : Relationship between original profitability and the elements of redistribution.

Figure 4.1 shows the relationship between redistribution and original profitability, computed on the basis of the 1980 values of the industrial firms. The figure demonstrates that, if a firm was not loss-making originally, it cannot in fact expect to receive any subsidy, whereas bigger loss-making entails higher subsidies. What we see on the other side is that, with rising profitability, the rates of taxes will rise as well.

We also studied the statistical relationships between profit and profit deviation, i.e., its relative value: the indicator RR of the redistribution ratio, and the profit level. (The indicator RR is the ratio of the difference between actual and original profit to the value of assets.) The correlation coefficients of the redistribution ratio and of the original profitability indicator will be presented in Table 4.3. The higher the value of the redistribution ratio, the more preference the firm enjoys in the redistribution process. The negative correlation shows that the higher a firm's original profitability, the less preference it can expect in the course of redistribution.[9] What is more, such correlation does not only show up as a tendency, but almost as a linear function. It is quite clear that a considerable departure from

Table 4.3: Correlation coefficients between original profitability and redistribution ratio

Sample	1980	1982
Mining	−0.99	−0.99
Electric energy industry	−0.99	−0.99
Metallurgy	−0.94	−0.50
Engineering industry	−0.89	−0.25
Construction material industry	−0.98	−0.96
Chemical industry	−0.93	−0.78
Light industry	−0.97	−0.95
Other industries	−0.95	−0.96
Food processing	−0.99	−0.94
Industry	−0.99	−0.93
Building industry	−0.98	−0.79
Agriculture and forestry	−0.97	−0.78
Transport and telecommunication	−0.95	−0.28
Trade	−0.99	−0.97
Water management	−0.97	−0.48
Services	−0.96	−0.98
State-owned firms: Total	−0.99	−0.92

(–1), the correlation coefficient between the redistribution ratio and the original profitability values, appears only in exceptional cases.[10]

PROPOSITION 4. As a consequence of redistribution, profitability is evened out on a lower level.

Table 4.4 shows the proportions of the firms of different profitability levels in the major national economic branches. Firms are categorized first by original profitability, and secondly by actual profitability after redistribution. The proportions undergo considerable change. Namely, the proportion of firms with extreme values of profitability will be very low after the redistribution, whereas the overwhelming majority of firms, between 67 and 94 per cent, will come into the category of low profitability.

Similar conclusions can be drawn from Tables 2.1 and 5.2, pre-

Table 4.4: Proportion of firms at the various profitability levels in 1982

Profitability level			Proportion (%) of firms at given levels	
			before redistribution according to original profitability	after redistribution according to actual net profitability
Loss-making	(1)	(2)	13 3	2 4
	(3)	(4)	2 22	4 1
	(5)	|(6)|	19 |14|	1 |1|
Low profitability	(1)	(2)	22 3	67 94
	(3)	(4)	58 8	83 89
	(5)	|(6)|	31 |22|	82 |76|
Average profitability	(1)	(2)	45 36	23 5
	(3)	(4)	74 43	10 7
	(5)	|(6)|	27 |40|	17 |17|
High profitability	(1)	(2)	19 3	6 0
	(3)	(4)	19 27	3 3
	(5)	|(6)|	23 |24|	0 |5|

Note: The figures in parentheses refer to: (1) industry; (2) agriculture; (3) construction industry; (4) domestic trade; (5) services; (6) state-owned firms total.

sented in chapters 2 and 5 in this volume. Both tables are based on the results of the research project reported in this chapter. Other results will also be presented to demonstrate the standard dispersion of the profitability indicators. (See Table 4.5.) Narrowing dispersion of the profitability values due to redistribution is a definite[11] and unambiguous tendency. The differentiation of firms according to profitability lessens as a consequence of redistribution.

Another of our computations has led us to draw the following major conclusions:

a. Of the originally highly loss-making firms, below minus ten per cent, prior to 1980 none had been left as highly loss-making after redistribution; in 1981–82, however, some of them were not saved. Yet in 1981 still only twenty per cent of the originally highly loss-making firms were left in the group of the lowest actual profit-

Table 4.5 : Standard deviation of the profitability indicators

Indicator Sample	Original profitability	Profitability according to balance sheet	Post- redistribution profitability
1978			
Industry	32.85	7.81	8.68
Construction industry	15.15	16.00	7.58
Agriculture and forestry	6.18	3.95	2.39
Transport and telecommunication	12.22	6.49	7.90
Trade	41.86	8.22	6.08
National economy total	30.30	10.59	7.45
1979			
Industry	33.56	8.04	7.25
Construction industry	14.75	15.63	7.33
Agriculture and forestry	6.14	3.93	2.14
Transport and telecommunication	11.91	6.19	6.52
Trade	45.23	8.19	5.41
National economy total	31.31	10.39	6.48
1980			
Industry	32.20	7.51	4.77
Construction industry	24.31	14.46	6.22
Agriculture and forestry	7.45	3.91	2.11
Transport and telecommunication	15.09	7.03	6.46
Trade	37.49	9.46	4.89
National economy total	29.35	9.59	5.06

ability. In 1982 this rate fell again: only 11.2 per cent of the loss-making firms were not pulled out by the government from the lowest category. In other words, compensation for large losses is symptomatic of the entire period.

At this point, we should recall the softening of the budget constraint. (See in this volume the first part of the chapter 'The Soft Budget Constraint'.) As noted therein: '...external assistance is a random variable... The higher the subjective probability that excess expenditure will be covered by external assistance, the softer the budget constraint.' The firms in financial trouble can expect immediate and permanent assistance from the fiscal system with an 88 per cent probability. This is a high enough chance to get built into the firms' behaviour. In addition, even the case of the remaining 12 per cent is not hopeless, for the banking system may take pity on them, either voluntarily or in response to pressure from other bureaucratic branches. (See the studies [1986 a, b] by Éva Várhegyi.)

b. Firms of extremely high profitability have a low chance of keeping their position.

Table 4.6 shows the chances of keeping the highest profitability level in a period of a few years.

The figures indicate a slight improvement of the situation in this respect, yet it is still generally true that in the course of redistribution firms have little chance of not sinking from the highest profitability level down to lower levels.

The fact of levelling is, therefore, undeniable. But what is at the root of this tendency? Fiscal policy-makers have not made a conscious decision that levelling is necessary. Indeed, pronouncements to the contrary are often heard. The tendency emerges more or less

Table 4. 6: Chance of keeping the highest profitability level

Year	Sample State-owned industrial firms	State-owned firms total
1975	0.3	6.3
1978	3.6	5.3
1980	1.7	5.1
1982	8.9	13.2

Note: The values in the table show, with respect to a given sample and a given year, what percentage of highly profitable firms — i.e. more than 20 per cent — will keep their extremely high profit level after redistribution.

unintentionally, as the result of many different intentions and efforts, ideas and interests. Of this mess, four intentions will be taken in turn.

4.6.1. *Confiscation of conspicuous incomes.* The decision to take away money from those who have 'too much'.

4.6.2. *Income redistribution in the spirit of social justice — the principle of compensation for circumstances.* No higher income is due to the firm which has earned it not through good performance, but thanks to favourable circumstances (such as advantageous *initial* position or an auspicious turn in *external* conditions). In such cases, adjustments for good luck must be made: firms should be taxed on what they do not deserve. Conversely: firms which have made a loss not because of poor performance but because of adverse circumstances (such as a disadvantageous initial position, or an inauspicious turn in the external conditions), do not deserve a small income. Compensation for bad luck must be made, too: the firms must be granted all that they deserve.

4.6.3. *To guarantee the survival of all firms, and the maintenance of all jobs.*

4.6.4. *Higher centralization of the financial sources of investments.* The greatest possible part of investment resources should be allocated through central decisions, for if large development funds are accumulated by firms operating at a level of high profitability, decision-making power will fall into their hands.

One or more of the intentions specified above do prevail, if not in all the channels of redistribution, at least in a good number (some of which shift vast amounts of profit). That is why the statement can be made that, though profit is in fact derailed through redistribution, the derailing is governed by a certain tendency.

The authors are of the opinion that each one of the intentions specified above is wrong, and suggest that, parallel to the establishment of the necessary conditions, economic management should consistently eliminate those four intentions. In a previous section of this chapter it was pointed out that one of the leading ideas of the reform was, from the outset, to introduce the profit incentive. But profit incentive and profit levelling, which are as different as chalk and cheese, are impossible to reconcile, and no attempt should be made to do so. Obviously, the state budget needs revenue, but this can be raised through 'neutral' (or at least more neutral) forms of taxation which do not level profit or vitiate the profit incentive.

Let us now return to the first of the four intentions. It must be admitted that, beside other motives, two dispositions underlie it: suspicion and envy. By and large, the following train of thought (or rather sequence of emotions) leads to a drastic tapping of high incomes: 'Under any circumstances, let us tax away high income, for who knows how the owner has come by it. Perhaps some impropriety was involved.' No investigation is made to determine how the income was earned and, to play it safe, a substantial part of it is taxed away. As the saying goes: they 'have not the heart' to leave it to the firm. If income earnings are only average or even lower in some firms, why should a few earn well above the average?

This leads us to paragraph 2: the principle of compensations. Here the authors support the assertion of the principle of social justice in income distribution. This can be achieved partly, and only partly, through fiscal policy, which should accomplish its goals through proper taxation of personal income and property. (In a subsequent part of this study, we shall return to the taxation or subsidization of certain products and services for the purpose of social justice.) The 'negative income tax' is another aspect of the question: providing financial aid to those in need of it by debiting of the central or local governments' budget. And beyond the fiscal policy, redistribution for the sake of justice, the educational system, welfare policy, etc., also plays a role.

Nevertheless, while fully accepting the moral and political justification (and one might add, the social usefulness) of redistribution carried out in pursuit of social justice, we argue that this principle does not belong to the 'business' sphere of society. The market, competition, and business are not just: profits are not distributed among firms according to merit, and the state cannot, nor should it try to act either as the judge who weighs 'mitigating circumstances' before meting out punishment, or as the teacher who takes into consideration the pupil's abilities and diligence before giving him a mark. It has to be recognized that a sizeable profit may be the result of good performance and/or good luck, and a large loss may be the consequence of poor performance and/or bad luck. Firms must learn to make good use of fortuitous circumstances and to adjust to adverse conditions, but they can learn only after discarding the 'principle of compensation.'[12]

The principle of compensation is related to the *price problem*. One of the adverse external conditions for which fiscal policy may wish to compensate is a loss caused by a price kept artificially below cost through central price control. And conversely: fiscal redistribution seeks to tax away the additional profit due to a price which is raised artificially above the level of costs plus normal profit through central price control. The interrelation as well as intentions 3 and 4 will be discussed in the next section.

4.7 THE RELATION BETWEEN THE PRICE SYSTEM AND FISCAL REDISTRIBUTION

Fiscal redistribution and the price system are inseparable issues. In a way, the former is a *mirror image* of the latter. Precisely because our investigations have been based on *actual* prices and not on any 'desirable' or 'optimum' price system, the actual fiscal redistribution reflects some of the particularities of the actual price system. If the statement is made that fiscal redistribution 'derails' profit, is arbitrary, capricious, and leads to accidental and unpredictable outcomes, the same can be said of the price system.

Let us take an example for closer examination. Here, a highly simplified model will be outlined, since it is sufficient to demonstrate the relationship. It is assumed that two firms are competing in a genuinely free market. Firm A manufactures product A and firm B manufactures product B. The two products are not identical, yet are close substitutes. At the beginning of the examination, the state had not yet intervened in the market in which the situation had already been stabilized. Neither of the products was able to drive out the other totally through competition: both were manufactured and sold in a given proportion and a definite price ratio settled between them, with the selling price of either product covering costs and assuring normal profit. (For the sake of simplicity and brevity, we shall not dwell on the conditions necessary for such equilibrium.)

Now let us assume that the state wants to intervene, and on the *price* side. Based on some economic policy consideration, it fixes an administrative price for both products: the one for product A will be higher than the earlier market price, and the one for product

B will be lower. Under such circumstances, the profit of the two firms will depend on the buyers' reaction as a function of prices, and on which way production costs change as a function of quantities sold. After this point, a number of different situations might evolve, but for simplicity's sake, let us take a closer look at one of the possible changes. Following the price increase, firm A realizes excess profit, whereas firm B, because of the decrease in price, loses some of the profit. Now, if fiscal policy adopts the 'principle of compensation' described in the previous section, the state's administrative measure will be completed through fiscal means: the excess profit will be taxed away from firm A, and the loss of profit will be remunerated to firm B.

However, the process may go in the opposite direction. Fiscal policy imposes additional debts on firm A, and gives an allowance to firm B, through a partial exemption, or a subsidy. At the same time, it insists that the price should be calculated on the principle of 'cost plus normal profit'. Firm A readily takes the opportunity and raises the price, thus shifting the additional tax burden to the buyer. Naturally, firm B is reluctant to assert the prescribed principle of price calculation, which, if enforced, would lead to a decline in price.[13]

A factual examination of events can reveal the actual direction of causality regarding the price of a particular product, or the firms manufacturing the product in question. We can thus determine whether it was the state's influence on price (perhaps its administrative prescription) that led to fiscal measures, or the other way round, if fiscal measures influenced prices, or if, in the course of events further interactions developed.

And yet, regardless of the direction of causality in one or another series of events, the final outcome will be the mirror image previously mentioned.

The mirror image would not develop if the state, while keeping an active price policy, renounced the principle of compensation, for example, by raising the price of product A and letting firm A have excess profit, or by lowering the price of product B, but without caring about the financial situation of firm B. But, as we have seen, this is out of the question and, in fact, an effort is made to assert the principle of compensation, an extremely complicated task which is practically impossible to accomplish and therefore has only the consequence of making fiscal redistribution volatile in this respect, too. The mirror image thus takes shape, though in many cases only after much delay, complicated transmissions and a great many distortions.

In the official statements and classifications of fiscal redistribution, a dividing line is generally drawn in the following manner: the channels of redistribution attached to specific products or services with a view to consumer price policy should be sharply separated from all other channels. Those who support such a division wish to separate the above-mentioned redistribution channels a) from any redistribution which, though motivated by price policy, is not connected with the *consumer* price policy; b) from any redistribution which does *not* derive *from price policy*, but from other factors, for example, directly from fiscal policy; and finally, c) from any redistribution which is *not* related *to any product or service but* to a firm, its taxation or subsidization. Since we see this division as arbitrary, we argue that it cannot be consistently implemented, and will refrain from using it in our subsequent explications.[14] Our counter-arguments are as follows:

a. The price system is interdependent: in the final analysis, every price affects every other price, so that whichever one the state may derail from its market point, its influence will permeate the entire price system and affect at least the cost of consumer articles and services. And if, at that moment, the central price policy does not allow the chain-reaction to continue and exert influence on consumer prices, that in itself will constitute intervention in the consumer price system. The state's price policy in oil, steel, the dollar exchange rate, or credit interest has direct consequences on the costs and prices of consumer products.

b. Reference has already been made to it, when discussing the interaction of fiscal policy and prices. Even if intervention does not have a price policy *intention,* it does affect prices and, given the interdependence of the price system, consumer prices as well.

c. The manufacturing company could pocket the tax imposed on the product sold at an artificially high price. The fact of actual sales is proof that the buyer is prepared to pay that price, with other conditions unchanged. By taxing the product, the state deprives the firm of its potential additional income, and, conversely, subsidizing the product amounts to subsidizing the firm. If the state refrained from subsidizing, the price of the product would rise, and there is no guarantee that the firm could sell the same volume as before, or even continue to function profitably.

4.8 THE DEVIATION OF ACTUAL
AND MARKET PRICES

We shall now attempt to review the factors that cause actual prices to depart from potential market prices. Some of these factors have emerged from deliberate central schemes and their underlying policy intentions, while others assert their effect spontaneously and independently of central resolutions.

4.8.1. *Paternalistic intervention in the consumption pattern.* To start with, we wish to emphasize that the issues we are facing are related to the *selection of fundamental values.*

Therefore, to facilitate the discussion, we shall state in advance our own value premise. *We attribute high value to the sovereignty of the citizen, the consumer, and the family unit.* We do not place these above everything else, and we acknowledge that there may be higher values. Nevertheless, in matters of everyday consumption, the consumer should be as free as possible to choose from the available consumer baskets; and the cases in which the individual or the family must be protected against their own decision should be regarded as exceptional.

. And, we believe, there are exceptions. For example, the problem of externality has been sufficiently clarified in the literature.[15] If all private agents can choose, at market price and without policy restraint, between private motoring and public transport, it is to be feared that the predominance of the former will aggravate environmental pollution, make cities even noisier and the road network even more crowded. Thus it may be justifiable to raise the price of private motoring above market level and bring the price of public transport below it. This measure will 'internalize' the externality in question: the individual or the family will weigh their decision on the basis of the artificially derailed price and cost proportions. But even in this simple illustration, the question of quantity proportions arises. What should be the rate of subsidy in the public transportation tariffs? What percentage of tax should be imposed on private cars? This problem becomes worse if intervention itself does not seem to be justified. Why is it necessary to subsidize certain articles of food, thus stimulating the Hungarian population to eat more? (If undernourishment were a problem for certain strata of the population, it should be tackled by some other method.) Why is a much lower turnover tax imposed on fuel sold to the population, than on clothing articles?[16]

The contemplation of these questions leads to serious ethical and political considerations. What entitles the intervening authority to force its own preferences on the decisions made by the individual, the household, and the family? Is there any proof that the intervening authority makes more reasonable decisions than the consumer directly interested in the decision and dealing with his own money? Who controls such intervention on the part of the authority?

The public ought to be informed about the differentiations made in the field of taxes and subsidies affecting consumption. Which are the consumer items these differentiations 'persuade' one to buy, and which are those they 'dissuade' one from buying? In all likelihood, a few official preferences would be endorsed by public opinion while others be disputed. It is certain, however, that a number of differentiating interventions — expressing a set of preferences — would not survive the scrutiny of public opinion, especially if people realized that all the subsidies granted to encourage consumption of certain items are to be paid, among others, by those who do not consume those items. And the reverse relationship should also be made known: most citizens have no idea of the percentage of taxes calculated in the prices of the products they buy regularly.

We think that social decisions of high importance are involved by these matters, and that as such, they should not be prescribed by administrative orders in the form of bureaucratic improvisations. Instead, they ought to be regulated through legislation agreed upon after thorough and explicit discussion.

4.8.2. *Welfare policy considerations* constitute a problem area that partly overlaps with paragraph 1, concerning paternalistic intervention in the consumption pattern. There, intervention is meant to influence the selection of goods and services; and here, price policy and the attached taxation and subsidization policy seeks to correct inequalities in income and wealth distribution among social

classes and groups. With a slight simplification, the *intention* underlying such kinds of intervention can be summarized as follows:

The set aim is to help the disadvantaged and to guarantee equal
opportunities, in other words: increased assertion of social justice. With this in mind, the products and services consumed or used
by the poor and by those who are disadvantaged and start with
inferior opportunities, must be sold at lower than market prices.
Conversely: the products and services consumed or used by those
better off and those who enjoy a more advantageous position and
better opportunities, must be sold at higher than market prices.

Although we shall not challenge its ethical bases, it must be said
that it has been found in practice that this *intention* cannot be consistently fulfilled by means of consumer price policy (and the fiscal
policy related to the finances of the firm). Indeed, efforts often lead
to results which are exactly the opposite of the original intention,
for it is quite difficult to ensure that subsidies are received at all or
exclusively by their intended beneficiaries, just as it is nearly impossible to have only the targeted group bear the weight of increased
taxes. Convincing evidence, for example, has been supplied by several studies to the effect that state-owned housing rents kept
artificially low, and the relatively high price of privately owned
housing, do not diminish but enhance social inequality[17]. The same
can be said of many other products and services.

Redistribution made for the sake of social justice has many
different instruments at its disposal, the most important one being
an apt system of income and property taxation, including a negative
'income tax', i.e. financial aid to the needy. A part of this system
might consist of the distribution of vouchers for certain specific
consumer items, or in the undertaking of the family's expenditures
by the state. This would be a more unambiguous situation — the
market price of a given product or service would have to be paid,
even if payment were assumed by society in the form of vouchers
or direct payment — than if the undertaking takes the form of
subsidization 'without address'.

We do not categorically exclude intervention in consumer prices
from the set of instruments to be used in the accomplishment of
social policy tasks. There are a restricted number of cases in which
such intervention could be justified. It is quite certain, however,
that such cases, in which price deviations are clearly reasonable, are
much less numerous than the actual ones.

Incidentally, our conclusions in section 4.8.1 are applicable here too: the decisions involved are of such importance that intervention should take place in the glare of publicity and under public supervision, and not in compliance with a bureaucratic prescription.

4.8.3. *Protection of domestic production.* The 'infant-industry' argument for protection of domestic production from import competition is well-known. Its advocates never fail to stress that protection of the 'infant' is only temporary: the producer can expect protection only up to a clearly-set point in time. In practice, however, such protection tends to become permanent, so that the infant and the old benefit equally from the subsidization of their products or the outright prohibition of competing imports, both of which free them from the rigour of competition and allow them to produce goods of poor quality at high cost.

4.8.4. *Export incentives* should be broken down into several categories. For example, a substantial part of the taxes collected from the population is spent on maintenance of the nation-state structure, administration and defence. Clearly, the foreign buyer cannot be expected to bear this burden, and therefore exemption from this tax should not be considered a distortion of the price system nor the export incentive unjustified. Beyond this, however, many suggest that the introduction of a new domestic product in a foreign market, or the winning of a new market, should also be promoted through financial aid. This policy on the export side is symmetrical with the protection of an infant industry on the import side. The usefulness of this kind of promotion is disputed, while undoubtedly various considerations speak on its behalf. It can be stressed, however, that it is harmful if the exports in question are pushed by every means of subsidization though their design is outdated or they have made losses over a long period of time. If the domestic inputs of exports are higher than their proceeds, subsidization is, in the final analysis, a gift to the foreign buyer to the detriment of the Hungarian economy.

Of course, this statement can only really be interpreted accurately if we know which exports are 'profitable' and which 'loss-making', and to assess this, we need principally a realistic exchange rate. Unfortunately, however, the principle of a marginal exchange rate was rejected at an early stage of the 1968 reform.[18] At that time, it was officially stated, in advance, that under the exchange rate to be applied, a large part of Hungarian exports would be loss-making. To this day, like many other Hungarian economists, we have not been able to find one reasonable argument that could be marshalled to the defence of that decision. In any case, the changes that have since occurred in the world economy and in Hungarian foreign trade have further augmented the losses of Hungarian exports.

At this point, however, our analysis gets trapped in a vicious circle: all of the problems listed in sections 4.8.1 to 4.8.4 together make economic calculation impossible. We shall return to this problem later, but for the moment it is sufficient to say that we do not even really know whether some Hungarian exports are in fact loss-making. In reality, losses may well be lower or higher than their current demonstrated values.

4.8.5. *Protection of price stability.* Some subsidies are granted with the express purpose of hindering the process of rising costs leading to a rise in prices. In short, the state 'assumes' the additional costs, thus creating one of the worst distortions of the price system. In a few cases, the arguments in favour of this measure are linked to the considerations mentioned in sections 4.8.2 and 4.8.4 price increases must be avoided, since they would affect the less prosperous groups of society or would harm export chances.

4.8.6. *Principle of covering the costs.* Here it is often argued that prices are raised with reference to rising costs or because subsidies weigh too heavily on the budget. Both reasonings can take advantage of economic arguments, but the problem is that the argument mentioned in section 4.8.4 is diametrically opposed to the one that figures in section 4.8.5, with the additional complication that no unambiguous rule or criterion is declared to decide which of the two ought to be applied in any particular case. The outcome is that during an identical period, one is applied to one group of products, and the other is applied to the remainder. Examination of the price history of a particular item also shows that the two principles are alternately applied, the choice between the two principles being capricious, random, and arbitrary. In fact, arbitrariness and unpredictability of the entire price system (and, with it, of the redistribution of the firms' profit) is one of the essential elements of 'derailment'. Let us take an example. If state-owned housing or public city transport are strongly subsidized sectors, what reason is there to reduce the subsidy at a particular date and rate? Both the date and rate of cost-shifting are fixed in a totally arbitrary manner.

4.8.7. *Conservation of the proportions of fiscal redistribution.* It is assumed that, under the influence of the factors discussed in sections 4.8.1 to 4.8.5, the rules and rates of the redistribution of profit, i.e. a certain distribution of taxes and subsidies, will somehow develop. But in fact, those rates tend to get fixed: they become customary and 'normal'. And no protest is raised against a customary tax, regular subsidies are insisted upon, and both remain even after their justification has long ceased to apply. For example, a subsidy was legitimate at a certain time, but once its source of legitimation disappeared, concern for 'established rights' did not allow the necessary change to take place. (What could possibly justify today's contribution to subsidized meals at the workplace?) Or, how can we justify the fact that some extra profit, originally taxed for the benefit of the budget, continues to be taxed long after it was consumed by increased costs? If in the case of the phenomenon discussed under section 4.8.5 it is the protection of price stability that distorts fiscal redistribution, here it is the stability and rigidity of the fiscal redistribution that distort the price system.

4.8. *Spill-over effects.* These have been discussed briefly previously. At this point, however, for the sake of a complete overview, we will discuss in more detail the spill-over of cost and price effects. Any significant arbitrariness in the elements of the price system spills over to its other parts. It is well-known that prices can be seen as the variables of a vast system of simultaneous equations. Thus, if the values of the individual variables are arbitrarily determined, either the rest of the prices will change in conformity with them, or the lack of conformity will have to be counterbalanced through fiscal intervention: taxes and subsidies. Once again, we are faced with arbitrariness: in which cases do price and fiscal policy allow the spill-over, and in which cases do they apply the brakes of taxes and subsidies?

4.9 CONSEQUENCES OF THE DISTORTIONS

After this overview of the factors distorting the price system and profit redistribution, we turn to the *harmful consequences of the existing situation.*

One of these consequences is *the impossibility of a rational economic calculation.* We no longer know what is expressed by profit or by loss. As a working concept, profit has lost prestige because of the arbitrary nature of the price system; no one can be fully confident that it really reflects efficiency. It is profit-redistribution itself that makes it quite apparent that not even the economic management would be able to trust the original profit, given that it would result from the difference between proceeds and expenditures calculated in actual prices. The original distribution of profit is derailed; it is disassembled and then reassembled in unrecognizable proportions. Meanwhile, profitability is levelled; original profit is tapped where it is high, and compensated where it is low or where there is a loss. Furthermore, all these act with combined force to dampen any effort toward maximization of the original profit calculated at prevailing prices. After all, it is not worthwhile to put up a good fight for the reasonable, actual prices, since the 'profit' of the firm does not really depend on them. Under such circumstances, irrational and arbitrary prices can survive without any strong resistance. Again, one of the frequently mentioned traps becomes clear: the arbitrary price system, the arbitrary and bureaucratic profit redistribution, and the weak profit incentive mutually precondition and maintain one another.

The other harmful consequence is that *the series of partial price adjustments increases the inflationary pressure.* Partial price adjustments are almost always one-sided: as a rule, they imply not price cuts but increases. And, precisely because of the above-mentioned spill-over effects, a price increase at any one point induces compensation through wage increase; and a rise in prices and wages, in turn, entails rising costs. Thus, we get caught up in the price-wage-cost inflationary spiral.

Since the beginning of the reform almost two decades ago, a number of partial price adjustments and the related partial adjustments of taxation and subsidization have been made. Part of these adjustments was intended expressly to eliminate the arbitrary traits of the price system, as well as those of the related fiscal system.

Unfortunately, *it cannot be proved theoretically, nor has it been shown by experience that the series of partial adjustments introduced in the course of time will finally converge towards a rational price and fiscal system.* Because of the frequently mentioned interdependence, it is impossible to isolate one sufficiently arranged block of the price system from another still ruled by arbitrariness in order to gradually expand the former and reduce the latter. Especially during an inflationary process, the latter would continuously creep back into the former: if it were believed that price policy had developed more reasonable relative prices by raising the prices of products *A, B,* and *C,* while the prices of products *K, L,* and *M,...* were momentarily left unchanged, the prices of products *K, L, M,...* would be on the rise sooner or later, as would be the prices of the new products *P, Q, R,...* The substitution of the former, or arranged block, with the arbitrary one, will from the outset be made at a higher price level, and, finally, products *A, B, C,* would not be made *relatively* more expensive, or at least not as much as has been expected.[19]

Our own investigations indirectly validate the existing scepticism toward partial adjustments. The dimensions and the arbitrary and random character of redistribution have hardly diminished in the last ten years. This fact reflects the constant involvement, whether deliberate or not, of economic management in the correction and compensation of the signals and effects of actual prices.

4.10 ON THE SIMULTANEITY
OF THE NECESSARY CHANGES

The doubts formulated above concerning the series of partial adjustments, i.e., the 'policy of small steps,' suggest that the problem facing us is one to be resolved only by closely linked simultaneous measures. Below we shall summarize the measures that cannot be taken individually since each one can be lasting and effective only if combined with the rest.

4.10.1. The entire price system ought to be liberated simultaneously. That is, with a few reasonable and genuine exceptions, price formation should be left to the market. Before the 1968 reform, orthodox minds doubted that the economy could function properly if producers were not told what to produce, and users of inputs were not told what to use. As it turned out, the economy can indeed function without such instructions. Why should it be otherwise with prices? Price formation is the most obvious function of the market.

4.10.2. Reasonable interest rates should be established as an organic part of price reform, in due consideration of the demand and supply conditions of credit and capital, and of the expected rate of inflation. In addition, marginal rates of exchange must be introduced, for only then can the export transactions that are indispensable to the Hungarian economy begin to avoid wide-spread loss-making.[20]

4.10.3. At the same time as the liberation of prices, the fiscal redistribution of the firms' profit must be eliminated. Not one channel of redistribution should be spared solely for the conservation of some customary tax or subsidy. Upon the considerations specified in paragraphs 1 to 4 of the preceding section, certain taxes or subsidies may be applied in a narrow sphere. But once again, it should be stressed that there can be only a few sufficiently justified exceptions to the general rule of total elimination of profit 'derailment'.

Revenues (and even the reserve funds needed to buffer shocks) can be fully secured by introducing new tax categories, which should be 'neutral' or at least 'more neutral' with regards to production and efficiency. This can be done in parallel with the liberation of prices, for example, by gradually and continuously 'refining' taxation to include personal income.

4.10.4. The problems of the fiscal system and the necessary decisions should be discussed and made in public. The assessment and use of taxes represent one of the most ancient public concerns. Ever since its institution, parliament has discussed, first and foremost, matters of taxation and the budget, since they involve not the bureaucracy's but the taxpayers' money. Who pays the tax and in what proportion, as well as its destination, are all questions for legislative assemblies at national and local levels.

The unpredictable improvisations, continual arbitrary changes and the whole fiscal 'regulation game' must stop, as should bargaining over taxes, favouritism, and exceptions. The more stable, simple, unambiguous and hard the fiscal system is, the more the state-owned firm is compelled to consider it as a given condition as well as to seek ways of increasing profit in the market and in production.

4.10.5. Demand — that of households, firms, investments, and governmental budget — should always be firmly in hand, and even more so in the years directly following the reform. This is the key to preventing the *price level* from getting out of control, in spite of the liberation of *relative* prices. The series of partial price increases spread over years or even decades was necessarily concomitant with inflation, *which is a dynamic process*. By way of contrast, a one-shot price adjustment need not entail inflation at all.

4.10.6. The release of prices and the elimination of the greater part of profit redistribution may come as a shock to several firms. In the new market situation and at the new market prices, some firms may become entangled in serious financial difficulties. If it looks likely that they will adjust, they should be granted transitional credits, when requested, but these should be repaid according to a clearly specified and not over-long schedule. Firms *have to* adjust to the new situation, and if they cannot, they should be wound up in one form or another, turning over their physical resources to those state-owned, cooperative, or privately-owned economic units that can put them to profitable use.

Furthermore, the need for transitional credits must be anticipated in advance. Their amount should be taken into account when planning 'tight money', i.e., it should not emerge as an 'extra' over the planned demand, since it would then become an inflationary pulling force.

4.10.7. The change may cause great problems in the lives of many individuals and families, but the price and tax reform need not lead to unemployment. In the long run, employment depends on economic growth and its pattern. Naturally, some people will lose their customary employment temporarily, since specific jobs should not be guaranteed. At the same time, however, they should be adequately compensated until they locate a new job, and if necessary, should receive retraining. Conversely, no one should be permanently exempted from the obligation to adjust to the labour market that will evolve under the new circumstances.

Changes in prices affecting consumption have an incalculable impact on individual families. The general principle of the change would obviously be to leave the total volume of consumption unchanged, or to let it shrink only slightly. Nevertheless, in the course of its actual distribution among the various social strata, groups and individual families may undergo quite a considerable change. Society must make efforts to compensate at least partly the losers and to facilitate adjustment partly through aids and loans. However, aside from a few exceptions to be made upon humanitarian and welfare considerations, no one can be exempted from adjusting their consumption pattern to the new price conditions when the transition period has expired.

At this point, a warning similar to that issued in paragraph 5 must be given. An adequate reserve must be accumulated to cover aids and credits to be granted to households, which in turn should not be extended 'in addition' to the tight estimate of the total purchasing power, lest they become additional factors in the pulling force of inflation.

Erhardt's 1948 price and financial reform of West Germany may provide the best example for the operation previously outlined. In one stroke, the West German reform put an end to the regulated economy and liberalized the price system, while money and credit supply, as well as purchasing power, were firmly held in hand by the central economic policy and the banking system. It is well-known that this reform established the conditions for efficient and innovative growth in the West German economy. Obviously, economic and political conditions are different in Hungary in the 1980s from those in West Germany in 1948, but the earlier experience deserves to be studied and should be borne in mind.

One of the most important lessons of Erhardt's reform is that it is quite impossible to conjecture, within the framework of a bureaucratic apparatus, what the best actual relative prices should be. As demonstrated by the period that has passed since 1968, this is as impossible as the detailed elaboration of production and consumption volumes proved to be within the framework of similar bureaucratic apparatus prior to 1968.

Although we have suggested that many measures are to be taken *simultaneously,* together they might still constitute only a part of a 'package' of measures that are more comprehensive and extend to an even wider range of issues.[21] This book is not concerned with the total 'package', and therefore, the changes set forth above have more or less been kept within the area of the main subject treated (namely, the firms' profit and the related changes in the fiscal and price systems). We merely wished to make it clear that, in our opinion, fiscal reform is bound to fail without a thorough and comprehensive price reform, and vice versa. Both need a radical renewal in order to allow for the creation of real profit incentive.

Do the necessary political and social conditions exist for such a reform to be implemented? The single most important condition is that the decision-makers be intent on a thorough and simultaneous reform of the price and fiscal systems, as well as on taking all the necessary complementary measures; and that the population should widely support these changes, as well as the concomitant shocks and sacrifices. We doubt that these conditions exist.

In any case, our prediction is of little importance in this respect, and the strength of the intention to reform the price and fiscal system will be made apparent by the events of the coming years. Indeed, the first draft of the book that provided the basis for the present excerpt was written in the summer of 1986, but we have made little change in the printed text in the intervening time, even as preparations for a tax reform were started independently of our work. In finalizing the book's text, we did not feel it our duty to try modify its content by relying on pieces of information being leaked, or by reacting in advance to possible future changes. All we want to stress now is that in a few years' time it will be highly informative to contrast our description not with the decrees issued but with the practice pursued. It would be interesting, for example, to repeat many of our computations and compare the numerical data of the period 1975–1982 to, say, those of the early 1990s; and then to return to the question: has a simultaneous reform of the firms' positive and negative taxation and prices been put into effect? If not: what is the consequence? Have the derailment and levelling of profit, and subsidization of loss-making firms ceased? To what extent has the firms' actual profit grown from a bureaucratic category into a market category? Is a new situation being stabilized, or is the old practice of bureaucratic redistribution of profit being restored?

Finally, in explaining our reform ideas, we did not assert that they *clearly* followed from our descriptive statements. It may well be that other economists would draw different conclusions from the same factual description. We can only say that we personally have been convinced by the thorough examination of the Hungarian practice of profit redistribution and, following the train of thought described above, that the fiscal and the price system must be changed simultaneously, virtually at one stroke.

4.11 SUMMARY

In conclusion, we shall summarize the main *general conclusions* drawn from our investigations, including those not discussed in the excerpt published in this volume.

• The state-owned firm's profit, or more exactly, the financial category that is usually qualified as profit, in the final analysis, depends only slightly and indirectly on the firm's own activity and market position, and very largely on fiscal redistribution and on prices prevailing in the state-owned sector. As for the latter, we know from sources other than our own investigations that they are not substantially affected by the market and demand-supply conditions. After all, 'profit' is not so much formed by market processes as by bureaucratic influence.

• In a market economy, there is a close connection between the firms' profit and its development. Such a connection does not exist in Hungary, where a more profitable firm has no greater chance of investment, and investment does not create conditions conducive to increased productivity.

• The profit incentive is totally illusory for the firm's employees.

• The most characteristic tendencies of the fiscal redistribution of profit are the composition of losses and the taxing of high profits, both of which undermine the power of the profit incentive. The tendency of 'spiriting away' losses by fiscal means, however, has weakened since 1980.

• The fiscal redistribution of profit is an inextricable mesh in which the various measures diminish one another's influence.

• Because the state-owned firms' budget constraint is rather soft, it prevents the assertion of natural market selection. More specifically, a loss-making company can count on compensation for its losses, and may be certain its profitability will be raised to the level of the 'general average' by means of fiscal redistribution. As a result, profitability does not exert any considerable influence either on survival chances or on access to investment resources (especially external ones).

• Based on the above, the assertion can be made that *the declared intention in the elaboration of the 1968 reform — assigning a major role to profit as a basic force of the market mechanism — has yet to become a reality.*

4.12 APPENDIX

The excerpt published in the present volume sets forth propositions 1–4 of the research. Proposition 5, which deals with the role of the various redistributive measures, cannot be included in the present excerpt, since it refers to many notions elaborated in the original book but not discussed in the present abbreviated version.

6. No true linkage exists between the profitability and bankruptcy of firms.

7. No positive linkage exists between the firm's profitability in an earlier period, and investment activities later.

8. Profitability in a later period is not actually dependent on investment activities in an earlier period.

9. Profitability criteria are typically not applied in investment allocation. There is no strong relationship between self-financed investment and the firm's original profitability. Lower profitability increases the chances of acquiring external investment resources.

10. Profit-sharing does not promote development of collective interest for two reasons: the share in the total earnings is very low and its value deviates strongly from the firm's profitability.

11. No positive linkage exists between the firms' profitability and the earnings of the employees.

12. The value of original profitability is largely determined by the original profitability of the earlier period. In actual profitability, however, similar definite auto-correlation is no longer asserted.

13. The different impacts of redistribution display considerable fluctuations over time. The value of the subsidies fluctuates, primarily in the mining and construction sectors, in the services industry, and in the smallest firms.

14. In the early 1980s the extent of redistribution diminished somewhat in comparison with earlier values, but not generally. At the same time, the levelling that follows in the wake of redistribution has grown in a somewhat lop-sided fashion: large profits are still heavily taxed, but the concealment of firms' losses is now less frequent.

15. The diminishing rate of redistribution found in 1980–82 did not result in strengthening the linkages between original and actual profitability. The importance of redistribution in shaping actual profitability has not decreased, either.

16. Although a negative linkage exists between the size and the

profitability of the state-owned firms, it is not demonstrable for each profitability indicator or in each national economic sector or industry. Even if the negative linkage does exist, its effect is rather weak.

17. The role played by the firm's size in redistribution is neither negligible nor of fundamental importance. No generally valid relationship can be demonstrated to exist between the firm's size and preferential treatment which would prevail equally in all sectors of the national economy. Yet in state-owned industry, the tendency clearly prevails for preferential treatment to be an increasing function of the firm's size.

18. The rate of distribution among large state-owned firms is in general no different from that of the sector's majority. Large firms do not enjoy preferential treatment in every respect, but they do have an obviously advantageous position with regard to exemptions, investment allocation, and tax rates.

19. The sectoral location of the firms is one criterion in the bias manifested in the redistribution. As for its final joint impact, however, redistribution does not display essential differences in the different sectors.

20. Exports do not clearly imply an advantageous position in redistribution. The redistribution largely levels the profitability differences between exporting and non-exporting firms.

NOTES

1. 'Redistribution' is a widely comprehensive category and plays a central role in several schools of social science. Here, K. Polányi's (1944) work must be mentioned, and with respect to the socialist economy, I. Szelényi's (1978) article, and Gy. Konrád's and I. Szelényi's book (1979). In this study, we discuss only a narrow partial process of total redistribution without looking at other areas.
2. Monetary reallocation through the credit system is closely connected with fiscal redistribution. Although our research work covered this area, the book from which this excerpt is taken does not discuss it.
3. '... the stock market values the performance of management and exerts pressure for efficiency and innovation. When a firm's management does not appear to be exploiting the opportunities available to it, the company's stock will be priced at a level that encourages a takeover bid by another firm.' This quotation is taken from the book of T. Mayer–J. S. Duesenberry–R. Z. Aliber (1984) (p. 110).
4. In a number of cases, however, even a momentary grave loss may cause

serious difficulties. The stock exchange may overreact to bad business news, the stockholders, in panic, may want to get rid of shares, etc. The intensity with which short- or long-range interests are asserted in the sector of the shareholding companies is an open issue.

5. This description differs from the opinions expressed in *Anti-equilibrium* (1971) by J. Kornai. Then it was stressed that the assumption of profit maximization unduly simplifies the complex motives of the firms' decision-making. Although that criticism was not groundless, in retrospect, the author finds it somewhat exaggerated. What he has read and seen since then has convinced him that, simplification and abstraction notwithstanding, profit maximization does represent the most important feature of the capitalist firms' attitude.

6. The original Hungarian quotation applies the term 'income', without qualification. It is clear, however, from the context, that R. Nyers refers to net income. (Translator's note.)

7. The problem arose a long time ago. As a matter of fact, it came under discussion as soon as profit incentive appeared in its initial forms in Hungary. Profit sharing was first introduced in 1958. J. Kornai wrote an article in 1958: 'Kell-e korrigálni a nyereségrészesedést?' (Should the Profit Sharing System be Corrected?). The following quotation comes from that article: 'One criticism, often heard especially among company managers, runs as follows: "Anyway, profit share does not depend on our work, but on how much the ministry wants to give us."

The problem became prominent again at the time of the 1968 reform. For example, in her article published in 1968, A. Deák called attention to the proliferation of taxes and subsidies.

8. A few *propositions* will be emphatically formulated. This term is applied only when substantial evidence supports the statement, and no such evidence from any other author has been found to prove the opposite convincingly. All propositions are presented with due reservation; in fact, these are qualitative statements which cannot be 'proved' in the strict epistemological sense of the word. At most it can be said that the evidence we have supplied is reproducible: relying on the same data, and using the same computation methods, anyone else would arrive at the same results.

Altogether twenty propositions are set forth in the book. In this excerpt, numbers 1, 2, 3, and 4 are given, together with some of the factual statistical evidence. A considerable part of the statistical evidence has been left out for the sake of brevity.

Fifteen other propositions set out in the Appendix provide more complete information but, given the lack of space, without supporting evidence. Readers interested in statistical data should turn to the book.

9. The strong correlation that exists between the indicator RR and the original profitability is significant. We were not able to find a theoretical relationship between the variables which would explain a deterministic function underlying the correlation close to -1. (In any case, the existence of such a deterministic relationship is contradicted by the fact that in a few exceptional cases the correlation coefficient is rather low.)

10. A similar conclusion is reached by G. Kertesi and E. Cukor (1987). Relying

on a different set of data, their study presents statistical results concerning the strong negative relation between the total effect of redistribution, and profit stripped of taxes.

11. In order to compare the variances of original profitability and post-redistribution profitability, F-tests were made in a few cases. The difference between the variances appeared significant without exception.

12. One of the biggest American pharmaceutical companies, Johnson and Johnson, used to manufacture an analgesic called Tylenol. Some years ago a criminal case took place when cyanide was mixed with the drug. The product was prohibited, control of the manufacture and packing had to be reorganized, and finally the product could be introduced again. The confidence of customers was restored. Then a second catastrophe came: cyanide was again added to a few packets. The product was instantly withdrawn, the company incurred vast losses, and the value of its shares immediately began to fall. This was a perfectly 'unjust' outcome since the owners and managers of the company were in no way culpable; but the stock market does not mete out justice. Instead, it keenly reacts to expected profit, while the owners and managers of the company have nowhere to turn for compensation. There is only one thing they can do: strive to improve the firm's operations so that it can compensate itself for the serious loss. In the last instance, 'unjust' loss moves the firm to improve performance.

13. In reality, the following series of events takes place: as a consequence of rising costs, firm B is granted a subsidy to cover additional costs, on the condition that it should keep the price unchanged and not shift the increased costs to the buyers. As for the relationship under examination, this is analogous to what has been said of firm B: it is the fiscal action that affects the price, and not the other way round.

14. It is an entirely different matter that, with the aid of our figures and system of indicators, we too can make this kind of 'official' separation, relying on official definitions, if necessary. And, as demonstrated in the book (in a section not included in this excerpt), we did make the separation for the purpose of eventual comparisons, but in keeping with our theoretical stance concerning the arbitrariness of the separation.

15. See, for example, the book by R. A. Musgrave and P. B. Musgrave: *Public Finance in Theory and Practice* (1980), especially Chapters 3–6 on public goods and the ethical principles asserted in distribution.

16. See B. Csikós–Nagy (1985).

17. For example, see Zs. Dániel (1982, 1984).

18. In Hungarian debate about the reform two principles of determining the exchange rate are distinguished. Both principles are based on the consideration of the domestic costs of goods produced for export. Let us take the example of the Hungarian Forint/US Dollar rate. The *average* exchange rate reflects the average costs (measured in Hungarian Forint) of goods exported for U. S. Dollars. In contrast, the *marginal* exchange reflects the marginal costs of the goods exported for US Dollars. The latter is regarded as a first approximation of a genuine market rate, which of course cannot be determined without the convertibility of the Hungarian currency.

19. It can be discovered, whether or not such price increases such as the

raising of public housing rents, or of public transport fares, brought about any considerable change in *relative* prices, i. e. vis-à-vis prices of substitutes, such as privately-owned housing and private motoring.
20. See Footnote 18.
21. Comprehensive reform programs are outlined in the works of L. Antal (1982), L. Antal et al. (1987), T. Bauer (1984), M. Tardos (1982). The ideas presented in our book on the subject of changing the price and fiscal systems are in close intellectual kinship with the studies mentioned above.

REFERENCES

Antal, L. (1979) 'Development with Some Digression. The Hungarian Economic Mechanism in the Seventies', *Acta Oeconomica, 23, (3-4)* pp. 257-73.
Antal, L. et al. (1987) 'Change and Reform', *Acta Oeconomica, 32,* pp. 187-213.
Antal, L. (1982) 'Gondolatok a gazdasági mechanizmus reformjáról' (Thoughts on the Reform of the Economic Mechanism), *Medvetánc, 2,* pp. 63-95.
Bauer, T. (1984) 'The Second Economic Reform and Ownership Relations: Some Considerations for the Further Development of the New Economic Mechanism', *Eastern European Economics, 22,* pp. 33-87.
Csikós-Nagy, B. (1985) *Árpolitikánk időszerű kérdései* (Timely Issues in Our Price Policy), Budapest: Közgazdasági és Jogi Könyvkiadó.
Dániel, Zs. (1982) 'Bérlakás, jövedelem, állami rediszttribúció' (Rented Housing, Income, State Redistribution), *Gazdaság, 16,* pp. 43-54.
Dániel, Zs. (1984) 'Még egyszer az igazságos lakáselosztásról az adatok tükrében' (Once again on a Just Distribution of Dwellings as Confronted with Facts), *Gazdaság, 18,* pp. 22-45.
Deák, A. (1968) 'A reformot előkészítő pénzügyi számítások tapasztalatai' (Financial Calculations Made to Prepare the Reform), *Közgazdasági Szemle, 15,* pp. 854-868.
Kertesi, G.-Cukor, E. (1987) 'Mitől függ a vállalatok kereseti pozíciója?' (What does the Income of Enterprises Depend On?). Manuscript, Institute of Economics of the Hungarian Academy of Sciences.
Konrád, Gy.-Szelényi, I. (1979) *The Intellectuals on the Road to Class Power,* New York: Harcourt Brace Janovich.
Kornai, J. (1971) *Anti-Equilibrium,* Budapest: Közgazdasági és Jogi Könyvkiadó.
Mayer, T.-Duesenberry, J. S.-Aliber, R. Z. (1984) *Money, Banking and Economy,* New York: Norton.
Musgrave, R. A.-Musgrave, P. B. (1980) *Public Finance in Theory and Practice,* New York: McGraw Hill, (1973).
Nyers, R. (1969) *25 kérdés és válasz gazdaságpolitikai kérdésekről. Interjú Nyers Rezső elvtárssal,* (25 Questions and Answers on Issues in Economic Policy), Interviewers: Bagota, B. and Garam, J., Budapest: Kossuth Könyvkiadó.
Polányi, K. (1944) *The Great Transformation,* New York: Ferrar and Renehart.

Szelényi, I. (1978) 'Social Inequalities in State Socialist Redistributive Economies', *International Journal of Comparative Sociology*, *19*, pp. 62–87.

Tardos, M. (1982) 'Development Program for Economic Control and Organization in Hungary', *Acta Oeconomica*, *28*, pp. 295–315.

Várhegyi, É. (1986a) 'A hitelrendszer hatása a vállalati költségvetési korlátra', (Impact of the Credit System on the Firm's Budget Constraint), Manuscript, Economix-Econoware.

Várhegyi, É. (1986b) 'A bankhitel működése restrikciós időszakban' (The Functioning of Banking Credit in the Period of Restriction), *Gazdaság*, *20*, pp. 47–62.

5 The Hungarian Reform Process: Visions, Hopes, and Reality*

5.1 INTRODUCTION

The Hungarian economy has undergone major systemic changes in the last 30 years. The impact of the reform is felt by every Hungarian citizen. The influence of the Hungarian experience, however, does not stop at the borders of this small Eastern European country. At least the temptation to follow a similar road appears in other socialist countries. The leaders of the Chinese economy are studying the Hungarian situation carefully in an effort to learn from its successes and failures. In the Soviet Union and in a few smaller Eastern European countries, where a genuine reform has not yet begun, the advocates of more far-reaching changes frequently refer to Hungary. It is probably not an exaggeration to say that the Hungarian reform has some global relevance.

*First of all, I am greatly indebted to Moses Abramovitz, for his encouragement and constructive help. I am grateful to many colleagues, especially to Tamás Bauer, Abram Bergson, Zsuzsa Dániel, Katalin Farkas, Károly Fazekas, János Gács, Gregory Grossman, Edward A. Hewett, Pál Juhász, János Köllő, Mária Lackó, Mihály Laki, Paul Marer, Ágnes Matits, Tamás Nagy, Richard Portes, András Simonovits, Aladár Sipos, Márton Tardos, and Laura D'Andrea Tyson for helpful suggestions and criticism of the first outline and the drafts. I should like to express my thanks for the support of the Institute for Advanced Study (Princeton), the Institute of Economics of the Hungarian Academy of Sciences, and the Department of Economics at Harvard University. The devoted assistance of Mária Kovács is gratefully acknowledged. Naturally, responsibility for the views expressed and any remaining errors is exclusively mine.

According to a widely held view, the Hungarian economy has become or is close to a system of 'market socialism'. Referring to Oscar Lange's (1936–37) famous model of socialism, Paul R. Gregory and Robert C. Stuart (1981) write: 'In a general way, NEM [the New Economic Mechanism of Hungary] bears a close resemblance to the Lange model' (p. 299). I am convinced that this interpretation of the Hungarian reform is erroneous and the purpose of this chapter is to support my rejection of this view. At the end different 'visions' of market socialism will be reviewed and confronted with Hungarian reality. But before this confrontation of 'vision' with reality, a positive description is needed. I will try to answer the following question: if it is not 'market socialism', what is the true nature of the present Hungarian system? For an answer, we have to go into some detail in reviewing the Hungarian situation, so as to avoid oversimplification.

This chapter addresses the general readership of this journal, not only the specialists in comparative systems and socialist economies; therefore it cannot avoid including information known to the experts. The approach is largely 'institutional'; data are used for illustration. There is no attempt to support rigorously formulated hypotheses with econometric analysis. Many important questions remain unanswered; the paper stops at the present frontier of research in Hungary and elsewhere.

There are dozens of books and hundreds of journal articles about the Hungarian reform[1,2]. The chapter is not an utterly mechanical compilation of every treatment. It recognizes and presents the principal alternatives, but, in the end, it describes and appraises the Hungarian reform in the light of my own views. It is best to say at once: This is a *subjective* description and appraisal of the Hungarian reform, its intellectual background, and its real development. Another personal remark is in order. Although my writings are not without some intellectual influence in my country, I do not claim to be regarded as one of the 'architects' of the reform. I was not and am not a government official or a member of any decision-making body, or a formally appointed adviser. In other words, I am accountable neither for the great results of the reform, nor for its shortcomings. At the same time, I was and still am a firm supporter and a critical observer of the reform process. It is hoped that this special position gives me a certain closeness to the events, but also the necessary distance for a frank and fair appraisal.

Subjectivity is not identical with originality. The chapter contains some ideas originating in my own writings but also the ideas of other economists whose contributions will be acknowledged. In some cases the originator cannot be traced, because the thought or formulation has been generated anonymously and now belongs to the folklore of the Hungarian economics profession. In some respects this chapter reflects a rather wide consensus shared by a larger group of Hungarians. That does not imply that something like a universally accepted 'Hungarian view' exists. Economists in Hungary are no less divided in their opinions than their colleagues in any other country.

The review is not impartial; my own set of desiderata will become clear to the reader as he or she goes through the chapter. Yet the article will remain in the domain of positive analysis and discuss a few intellectual currents; there is no attempt to present my own updated blueprint of an 'ideal' socialist system.

Because this chapter deals with institutional changes, it inevitably touches on problems in the fields of sociology, social psychology, political science, and political history. Nevertheless, this is the work of an economist concentrating on economic issues without aiming at a thorough analysis of their political aspects.

The Hungarian reform was not a sudden action, but a slow process. Its intellectual history started with papers of György Péter (1954a H, b H) presenting a penetrating criticism of the old system and a draft of the reform.[3] The history of practical reform measures began in 1956–57 with the abolition of compulsory deliveries in agriculture, although the dominant feature of the period 1957–64 was the conservation of the old bureaucratic economic mechanism. An important milestone was reached in 1968, when a whole package of substantial changes was introduced. Further steps came later. But the reform process did not follow a one-way road even after 1968: phases of progress were followed by reversals. After the great reform wave of the late sixties the years 1972–79 again represented a period in which anti-reform forces could break through. A new wave of reform measures started in 1979 and has been going on since. Apart from consecutive ups and downs, proreform and counterreform tendencies have been manifest side by side continuously.

Unfortunately, limitations of space do not allow a discussion of the historical evolution of the reform. This chapter focuses on phe-

nomena that prevailed throughout the 1968–85 period and character-
ize the present state of affairs, with only occasional backward
glances.

The Western reader will recognize many issues familiar to him or
her from his or her experience in his or her own economy or, at least,
in the public sector and administration of his or her own country. It
would certainly be instructive to discuss similarities and differences
between different socio-economic systems. There is also an extended
theoretical and empirical literature on certain issues, which are the
Western counterparts of problems discussed in this chapter for the
Hungarian case. For example, there are many valuable studies on
taxation, price and wage control, regulation, privatization, and the
relationship between government- and state-owned firms in non-
socialist economies. Except for a few occasional hints, such comparative study and a survey of the Western literature on the analogous issues go beyond the limitations of the present chapter.

5.2 CONCEPTUAL CLARIFICATION

There are a few general concepts that represent key building blocks
in our thought, concepts that are not unambiguous. We do not
pretend to arrive at generally applicable exact definitions. The purpose of section 5.2 is more modest: to clarify in a rather pragmatical
manner the meaning of certain concepts in the context of the present paper.

5.2.1 Economic systems
We use the term *economic system* to mean not only 'grand' systems,
like 'capitalism' or 'socialism', which could rather be regarded as
system 'families', but also the particular members of such a family.
Contemporary Czechoslovakia, Hungary, and Yugoslavia, for instance, have different systems, although all three are socialist countries.

Instead of an abstract definition, I give a summary list of the
main components of an economic system:

1. The organizations functioning in the economy: for example,
   administrative organs, non-profit institutions, firms, households,
   associations;

2. The distribution of the various forms of ownership and property rights;
3. The distribution of decision-making power;
4. The information structure: types of information flowing between organizations;
5. Incentives motivating the decision-makers;
6. The role of political organs and the government in economic affairs;
7. Laws and governmental resolutions, that is, the formal legal regulation of the economy's operation;
8. Informal 'rules of the game': routine behavioural patterns enforcing, hindering, or complementing the formal legal regulation.

The list is not exhaustive.[4] The components are interdependent; they cannot be chosen arbitrarily.

In the Hungarian literature the terms *economic mechanism* or simply *institutional circumstances* are used more or less as synonyms for *economic system*.

We contrast the concept of *policy* with the concept of *system*. The former is the determination of certain variables by policy makers within the framework of a given system. In this respect we follow the usage of Hungarian discussions, which consistently apply the distinction between issues of economic policy and issues of the economic mechanism.

5.2.2 Bureaucratic and market coordination

A system coordinates the activities and interactions of its members, i.e. individuals and organizations. For the sake of our study we distinguish two pure types of coordination.[5]

1.: Bureaucratic Coordination.[6] There is a *vertical* relationship between the coordinating individual or organization and the coordinated individuals or organizations. Control is exerted by a multi-level hierarchy. Administrative coercion and legal sanctions compel individuals and organizations to accept orders and prohibitions from above. The vertical relationship is lasting and institutionalized; it is mutually acknowledged both 'above' and 'below'. The transactions are not necessarily monetized, but if they are, the subordinated individual or organization is financially dependent on the superior. The bureaucracy is active in the allocation of resources and in the redistribution of income.

2.: Market Coordination. There is a *horizontal* relationship between the buyer and the seller individual or organization; the two participants are equal from the legal point of view. The individuals or organizations are motivated by financial gain. In its pure form market coordination takes place at prices based on agreement between buyer and seller. The transactions are monetized.[7]

Some writers prefer a wider definition; the present paper, however, will apply consistently the narrow definition outlined above. We refer to market coordination only if money, prices, and profit are at work.

The debate over the reform of socialist systems can be translated into the language of the above classification: the participants suggest alternative combinations of the basic forms. Systemic changes in the real world can be described as new combinations of the two basic forms with shifts of relative weights and new linkages between them.

5.2.3 Reform

Reform is a notion widely used by many parties and political movements all over the world. The present chapter will apply a narrow definition designed especially for our discussion. We reserve the term *reform* for the change in a socialist economic system, provided that it diminishes the role of bureaucratic coordination and increases the role of the market.

The modernization of a highly bureaucratic regulation of the economy with the aid of computers is not 'reform'. Nor do we give this name to efforts aimed at tighter labour discipline. Useful as these policy measures might be, they do not imply change of the system; they do not lead to a reduction in the role of bureaucracy and to an increase in the role of the market.

In this sense there are only three countries where a genuine reform process is in progress: in the order of inception these are Yugoslavia, Hungary, and China. There are signs that perhaps Poland will follow suit.

5.3 THE STATE SECTOR

We divide the economy into two main *social sectors:* organizations working with capital owned by the state and the rest of the economy, that is, the non-state sector. (The adjective *social* will be used throughout to refer to the sectors distinguished by ownership.) Systemic changes associated with the state sector are discussed in section 5.3 and with the non-state sector in section 5.4.

The state sector, it must be emphasized, was and still is the dominant sector of the Hungarian economy. As shown in Table 5.1, about two-thirds of officially recorded total national income is produced by state-owned firms.[8]

5.3.1 The abolition of mandatory plans

We begin with a brief description of the *command economy* by which the state sector was administered in the pre-reform period.[9] Usual synonyms are the traditional centrally planned economy or classical socialist economy, economy of the Soviet type, or simply, the 'old' economic mechanism contrasted with the reformed 'new' one.

The national plan is elaborated by the Central Planning Board and approved by the highest political bodies. After that, the plan is strictly mandatory. The economy is governed by a bureaucracy, organized in a multi-level hierarchy.[10] The plan indicators at the top are successively disaggregated from higher to lower levels. At the bottom, the state-owned firm gets hundreds or thousands of mandatory plan indicators each year, containing four sets. Firstly the set of output targets, whenever possible, in physical terms or in aggregate real terms expressed in base-year fixed prices. A multiproduct firm may get as many output targets as it has products or groups of products. Secondly, input quotas, again in physical or real value terms. This set contains the rations of centrally allocated materials and semifinished products, indicating not only quantity and quality, but also the supplier obliged to deliver. There are also labour quotas and wage funds. Thirdly, mandatory financial indicators concerning production costs, profits, credit ceilings. Fourthly, a list of certain actions to be taken by the firm: introduction of new technologies or products, investment projects, and so on. Although all plan indicators are compulsory, certain 'priority indicators' are enforced more strictly. Typically this is the case with at least one indicator of aggregate output, with some ceilings on wage expenditures, and also sometimes with a few specific export targets.

The flow of information is not unidirectional. The firms submit proposals in the course of plan elaboration and they report results

Table 5.1: Share of social sectors in employment and national income (percentage distribution)

	Distribution of active income earners				Contribution to national income		
	1966	1975	1980	1984	1975	1980	1984
1. State sector	65.0	70.9	71.1	69.9	73.3	69.8	65.2
2. Non-state sector							
a Cooperatives	30.7	24.9	25.5	25.9	17.8	19.8	20.6
b Household farming	–	–	–	–	4.0	3.2	2.8
c Auxiliary production of employees	–	–	–	–	3.0	3.7	5.9
d Formal private sector	4.3	4.2	3.4	4.2	1.9	3.5	5.5

Source: Column 1: CSO H, 1967, pp. 52–53.
Column 2: CSO H, 1976, pp. 92–93.
Column 3–4, CSO H, 1985a, p. 23.
Column 5: CSO H, 1976, p. 58.
CSO H, 1982, p. 87.
CSO H, 1983b, p. 93.
Column 6–7: CSO H, 1985a, pp. 55, 60.
CSO H, 1982, p. 85.
CSO H, 1983b, p. 98.
CSO H, 1985c, p. 77.
H. Data broken down according to our classification are not available for the contribution to national income in 1966.
Note: The non-state sectors are discussed in section 5.4. 'National income' is a net output concept within the framework of the 'Material Product System' (MPS), the accounting system used in socialist countries. Except for sectors 2b and 2c, the table does not cover the informal private sector.

during and after the plan period. The more important flow, however, is the flow downward: commands given by the higher level to the lower level of the hierarchy.

One of the most tormenting properties of the command system is rigidity. Commands once given are hard to change. Any change must go through a multi-stage process of approval in different sections and different levels of the hierarchy. The system of detailed plan indicators is, of course, interdependent; it is a kind of a 'general equilibrium' image of future economic processes. It is required that the spill-over effects of any significant change should be followed in all other segments affected and appropriate adjustment should be made. Planners understandably are not fond of such extra work. As a consequence, response to unexpected shifts in supply, demand, or technology is slow and incomplete.

Top planners seek to assure 'taut planning' (Holland Hunter 1961). The plan must have a 'mobilizing' effect, extracting maximum output from given resources. This is one more reason for rigidities: there are no easily accessible reserves left to be used for quick adjustment. Furthermore the plan leads to defensive tactics on the part of subordinates. It is in the interest of the firm's manager to hide the genuine capabilities of the firm and to fix a more lax target that can be fulfilled comfortably even if supplies do not arrive on schedule. Of course the staff of the higher authorities knows this. 'Plan bargaining' evolves: the superior planner wants more output out of less input, the subordinate wants the opposite. In the course of realizing the plan, the manager's motivation is to achieve target, perhaps even to exceed target slightly, but this must not be overdone. Otherwise the exceeded target of this year will be incorporated into the mandatory target of the next year. As a consequence, a restrictive practice is common.[11]

Input-output combinations are distorted. The direction of distortion depends on the exact nature of the 'priority' indicators. If, for example, gross output in aggregate value terms is enforced rigorously, the manager's interest is to produce goods containing large quantities of expensive material. If the output target is given in tons or, as in textile industry, in metres, the manager is motivated to produce heavy goods or thin textile. Output plans must be fulfilled at any price, neglecting all other 'non-priority' objectives or those the authorities are less able to check, like the improvement of quality, the introduction of new products, reduction of costs, and proper maintenance of machinery and buildings.

The abstract model of the command economy operating in the state-owned sector is a strictly vertical bureaucratic control, executed by a disciplined bureaucracy in a consistent way. Real command economies are not as 'pure' as the model; some horizontal coordination exists too. This proceeds partly on a non-pecuniary basis: informal agreements of reciprocal help are made between cooperating producer and user firms, complemented by some incentives in money terms to the suppliers for the sake of more reliable deliveries (i.e. a half-tolerated, half-forbidden 'market' relationship). In any case, the system in the Hungarian state sector in the early fifties was rather close to the model of a pure command system.

There were minor changes introduced in the late fifties and early sixties, for example, some limited forms of profit sharing for employees. When the dispute over reform revived in the mid-sixties, there were discussions about how far the country should go in the abolition of commands. Finally, the leadership opted for a radical solution. After careful preparation, the whole short-term command system was completely abolished in one stroke, beginning with the first of January, 1968. The state-owned firms were formally declared to be autonomous regarding short-term output and input plans.

Orthodox economists in Eastern Europe had been afraid that the socialist system would collapse without mandatory planning. It turned out that they were wrong. This chapter will make many critical comments about the Hungarian reform, but this must not overshadow one of the most impressive and undeniable conclusions concerning the Hungarian systemic changes: the radical abolition of short-term mandatory planning is viable even without a fully developed market mechanism.

5.3.2 Dual dependence

What replaced the command system? A state-owned firm of the reformed Hungarian economy operates in a condition of *dual dependence*. It depends vertically on the bureaucracy and horizontally on its suppliers and customers. A brief look at the life of a state-owned firm will illustrate how the system of dual dependence works.

Entry. The creation of a state-owned firm is the result of a lengthy bureaucratic process. It may be initiated by an individual or a group, but the very active support of bureaucratic organs is needed for success.

Recently the legal conditions for establishing small state-owned enterprises have been eased. Existing firms can 'branch out' and create subsidiary enterprises half subordinate to and half independent of the founder. There is also some possibility of entry by non-state producers as potential competitors of the state-owned firm, but this is subject to severe restrictions.

Exit. There are state-owned firms that go out of business, but their number is rather small and the exit (both final liquidation and absorption by another state-owned firm) is decided by bureaucratic producers. 'Death' is not the outcome of a natural selection process on the market. No substantial positive correlation can be found between exit and persistent loss-making or insolvency.[12]

Selection and appointment of top managers. This remained the most important vertical linkage. Until some changes in the mid-eighties the leading executives of a firm were appointed by a superior authority. A successful manager will be promoted either by moving upward within the same firm or by transfer to another firm or to some state agency. Similarly, a successful official in a ministry may be appointed to the directorship of a large firm. There is no genuine 'job market' for managers; their career depends to a large extent on the opinion of the top bureaucracy. Therefore, it is understandable that one of the main objectives of managers is to please their superiors.

In 1985 new regulations were introduced. The top managers in the majority of state-owned firms are no longer appointed by the higher authority, but elected, directly or indirectly, by the employees of the firm. The administrative and political organizations have formal or informal veto powers over both the preselection of the candidates and the outcome of the election. It is too early to appraise the results of these arrangements.

Determination of output. The firm's autonomy has increased a great deal in this respect. Short-term annual plans are determined by the firm. The superior authority does not set aggregate output targets and that is an important change. It still puts forward, however, informal 'requests' telling the firm what is 'expected' from the managers. Typically, certain deliveries are urged for export or for a customer who is a protégé of the intervening official or for the elimination of certain pressing shortages. In any case, the management of the firm will usually be willing to comply.

Determination of inputs. The all-encompassing system of formal material rationing and allocation has been dissolved, though a few goods are still centrally allocated. There are, however, informal quotas, licenses, or other restrictions (János Gács, 1982).

Horizontal linkages between state-owned firms in their capacities as sellers and buyers certainly have become stronger than they were before the reform. The linkages are mixtures of genuine market contracts following business negotiations about prices, quality standards, and delivery dates, and of 'gentlemen's agreements' based on reciprocal favours. But the horizontal linkages are still not insulated from the decisive influence of vertical regulation. In case of disagreement or contract violation, complaints are addressed to the bureaucracy, which is asked for judgment and intervention.

Choice of technology. Administrative intervention occurs, but it is not wide-spread. The firm's autonomy has increased substantially in this respect.

Determination of prices. Prior to the reform, the price of almost all goods produced by state-owned firms was set arbitrarily by administrative organs. The relative prices were grossly distorted. The rules have changed several times in the course of the reform process. Some prices are still determined administratively, although usually under some influence and in quite a few cases under strong pressure on the part of the firms. The majority of prices ceased to be administrative, at least nominally, after 1968. Most of such prices have still not become genuinely free market prices, either. Bureaucratic price control has different ways and means to exert strong, in some cases, decisive influence on price formation.

Firstly, for many goods strict rules prescribe how to calculate the price. Regulations determine the cases in which a 'cost-plus' principle must be implemented. For such calculations there are strict instructions as to how costs should be calculated and what are the permitted profit margins. In some other cases the application of the so-called competitive pricing principles is mandatory. Profit margins for goods sold on the domestic market must not exceed the profit margins achieved on export markets. Similar correspondence is prescribed between price increase for domestically sold and exported goods (critical comments can be found in Róbert Hoch, 1980 H, Lajos Zelkó, 1981 H). There are many exceptions to the declared calculation principles, again determined by a long sequence of bureaucratic rules.

Secondly, many of the changes nominally decided within the firm must be reported in advance by the producer to the price authority, which may or may not intervene, formally or informally.

Thirdly, there are laws against 'unfair profit' and 'unfair price'. These are, of course, vague concepts; much depends on interpretation and arbitrary judgment. Because firms are audited frequently, there is always the concern that their pricing practice may be condemned.

Unfortunately, there is no study available that would give a clear appraisal of how the present Hungarian relative price system compares with a rational one, reflecting relative scarcities more or less correctly. Some authors argue that prices have come much closer to rational proportions than they did before the reform, mainly because the main raw materials, energy, and many tradable goods are closer to relative prices on the world market (Béla Csikós-Nagy 1985 H). Others, the author among them, accept these results but maintain that a large degree of arbitrariness still prevails, because of the wide-spread and bureaucratic interventions mentioned above. In an interdependent price system each arbitrary aspect spills over and leads to further distortions. As we shall see later, an arbitrarily differentiated system of positive and negative taxation exists, which inevitably leads to price distortions. An indirect piece of evidence supporting the views of the critics is provided by a study of László Halpern and György Molnár (1985), who calculate a 'cost-plus' shadow price system based on uniform profit rates with the aid of an input-output table. The calculation (p. 824) shows a strikingly wide dispersion of the shadow-price/actual-price ratios.

The impact of prices on firms' decisions has become somewhat stronger in the wake of the reform, but it is still not decisive; we will discuss that later. But even if firms eagerly watch prices, they may still give the wrong signals.

Determination of wages and employment. An important change: absolute ceilings on the total wage bill that had been one of the most powerful target figures in the prereform era were completely abolished. There are still several bureaucratic instruments of interference in wage formation. The instruments have changed several times since the beginning of the reform process. To mention just a few: progressive taxation of the firm linked to average wages or to wage costs or to the increase of wages; wage policy guidelines associated with strong pressures to follow them.

As a result of the reform, mandatory employment quotas were abolished, but formal and informal restrictions on hiring labour reappeared in the seventies, as a reaction to growing labour shortages (Károly Fazekas and János Köllő, 1985b H).

Credit. Hungary has a highly centralized monetary system. There is permanent excess demand for credit. The banking sector, except for new institutions to be discussed later, acts as a credit-rationing administrative authority and not as a genuine bank following commercial principles (György Tallós, 1976 H). It is strongly connected with the planners' and the other authorities' supervision of the state-owned firms. Granting or denying credit is almost uncorrelated with the past or present profitability and credit worthiness of the firm. To some extent, the opposite relationship is true. The credit system is used frequently to bail out firms failing on the market. Perhaps a more market-oriented practice will evolve soon following recent changes in the financial sector. We return to this issue in section 5.5.3.

Taxes and subsidies. Before the reform firms had to pay all gross profits, except for a minor profit retention, to the central budget. The introduction of taxation, which leaves the post-tax profit with the firm, is an important change. The tax system is, however, extremely complicated. The total number of taxes and subsidies of different sorts to be paid by or to state-owned firms is between 290 and 300 (Vilmos Falubíró 1983 H). Few of them are based on rules that affect all firms uniformly. Many tax or subsidy regulations appear to be general, but a closer look shows that they are calibrated to affect only a small targeted group, in many instances only a few dozen out of 1,600–1,700 firms. These are 'tailor-made' rules. In addition, *ad hoc* tax exemptions are granted or payments due are postponed to help firms in financial trouble. Firms suffer from the unpredictability of taxation. Any time that the central authorities feel that firms have 'too much money', tax rates may be arbitrarily increased or new taxes introduced or firms might be forced to save (for example, by prescribing mandatory deposits or reserves).

The total of all subsidies for the entire state-owned sector is about equal to the total gross profit before taxation; the total taxes are even larger than total gross profit because the state sector is a net tax payer. This means that a huge reshuffling of gross profits goes on taxing away and distributing money through hundreds of channels.

Investment. Investment decisions and financing were highly centralized before the reform. As a result of the reform, the firm's discretion has increased; a substantial fraction of profit can be retained for investment purposes. Nevertheless, central power is still very strong. For major projects the firm needs additional capital either from the bank or from the governmental budget. Only a small part of state sector investments, about one-fifth of the total, is really decided at the firm's level and financed exclusively from the firm's own savings. As for the rest, the firm must come to an agreement with those who give external assistance; consequently the bureaucracy can have a decisive influence on the allocation of investments (Várhegyi 1986 H.) Another form of intervention is to freeze the firm's savings originally reserved for investment purposes.

The central allocation of investment resources is not based on profitability criteria. Almost the opposite is true. Redistribution assists the losers with money taxed away from firms making large profits. A closer look at the financial data of firms in the study of Kornai and Matits (1983 H, 1984), Matits (1985 H), and Várhegyi (1986 H) shows that there is no substantial correlation between pre- or post-tax profitability in a certain year and investment activities in later years (no effect of past and present profitability). And there is no substantial correlation in the opposite direction, either, namely, between investment activity in a certain year and pre- or post-tax profitability in later years. Thus, expected future profitability has no effect, assuming that there is substantial correlation between expected and actual profitability.

The situation is eased to some extent by recent developments. New financial intermediaries have been created, and new ways of raising capital are permitted. We shall come back to that in section 5.5.3.

5.3.3 Soft budget constraint and weak price responsiveness
In official declarations, profitability is the main criterion in appraising the performance of a firm. The bonus of the managers is profit-linked and there is also profit sharing for employees.[13] It was hoped that these measures would transform the firms into genuine profit maximizers. This has not happened. The situation is illustrated in Table 5.2.

Table 5.2: Transition probabilities due to fiscal redistribution in the state sector of manufacturing in 1982

From original profitability	To final profitability			
	Loss-maker	Low profitability	Medium profitability	High profitability
Loss-maker	.233	.500	.122	.145
Low profitability	.038	.853	.103	.006
Medium profitability	.000	.734	.206	.060
High profitability	.008	.394	.515	.083

Source and detail: Matits (1984a H, p. 48).
Note: The research background of this table is indicated in note 12. *Transition* means the proportion of firms in any given original profitability class that became members of a given final profitability class as a result of fiscal redistribution. The transition from 'original' to 'final' profitability means the transition from the pre-tax and pre-subsidy position to the post-tax and post-subsidy position.

First let us look at the losers. Loss, even if long term, can be compensated for by different means: *ad hoc* or permanent subsidies, *ad hoc* or permanently favourable tax conditions or bail-out credits. Price authorities can be permissive, allowing increase of the administrative price or deviation from certain interventionist price rules. The author (1979, 1980, 1986) coined the term *soft budget constraint* to describe this phenomenon. The financial position of the state-owned firm is not without influence. Although there *is* a budget constraint that forces some financial discipline on the firm, it is not strictly binding, but can be 'stretched' at the will of the higher authorities. In principle, the firm should cover expenditures from revenues made on the market. In practice, earnings from the market can be arbitrarily supplemented by external assistance.

The crucial issue is the fate of the chronic loss-makers. Their fate will clearly show whether profit is something 'dead serious' or only an illusion. The state bureaucracy exhibits a paternalistic attitude toward state-owned firms. This is understandable, for they are creations of the state, and the creator cannot let them down. There are strong social and political pressures to keep ailing firms alive for many reasons, for example, for the sake of job security (Granick 1984) or of import substitution. But many observers ask the following question. If the firm is in deep financial trouble and for socio-political reasons it cannot be closed down, why at least are the managers not fired? Such harsh treatment would— so these observers say — increase the influence of the profit motive. In fact the managers may either stay or are transferred to another job without significant loss in income and prestige. The reason is simple. Because of the thousands of bureaucratic interventions, the manager does not have full responsibility for performance. In case of failure he can argue, perhaps with good reason, that he made all crucial decisions only after consulting superiors. Furthermore, many of the problems are consequences of central interventions, arbitrarily set prices, and so on. Under such circumstances, the bureaucracy feels obliged to shelter the loss-makers.

At the other end of the spectrum are firms making large profits. Table 5.2 shows that there is a peculiar egalitarian tendency operating to reduce larger profits. The budget constraint is not only soft, but also perverse. Because of the ceaseless and unpredictable changes of financial rules, taxes, and subsidies, firms feel insecure and exposed to the arbitrary improvisations of the bureaucracy (K. A. Soós 1984).

There are differences in terminology, but in substance a large group of Hungarian economists agree: financial discipline is lax, and there is no strong market coercion to enforce the search for profits. This 'soft budget constraint' syndrome has many negative consequences. Only one will be mentioned at this point, namely, weak responsiveness to prices, especially on the input side. If a wrong adjustment to relative prices does not entail an automatic penalty through a well-functioning selective market process, the firm does not have a strong stimulus for quick and complete adjustment. There are some studies, unfortunately not many, that show the firms' weak response to relative prices. Judit Szabó and Imre Tarafás (1985), with the aid of multiple regression analysis, demonstrate that changes of the foreign exchange rate have only a weak impact on producers' choice of the output and still less of inputs.

We are facing a vicious circle between the arbitrariness and irrationalities of the relative price system on the one hand and the soft budget constraint syndrome on the other, as argued by Halpern and Molnár (1985), Antal (1985a H), and Kornai and Matits (1984). Because prices are arbitrary and distorted, firms have legitimate reasons to ask for compensation. And when external assistance is granted, it leads to the preservation of the wrong price.

5.3.4 Size distribution, monopolies

The size distribution of firms in Hungarian production is much more skewed in favour of large units than in developed capitalist economies (Iván Schweitzer 1982 H, Gábor Révész 1979, Éva Ehrlich 1985a,b H) as illustrated in Table 5.3. In 1975 in Hungarian industry the three largest producers supplied more than two-thirds of production in 508 out of 637 product aggregates (Zoltán Román 1985).[14] The extremely high concentration weakens or eliminates potential rivalry and creates monopolies or oligopolies in many segments of production.

There are quite a few organizations that have the legal status of a 'state-owned firm', but are practically playing the role of a state authority. Their number now is smaller than before the reform, but still not negligible. They have the power to determine the rationing of the goods or services they supply to customers. For example, this is the situation with the monopoly company delivering automobiles. There is a monopoly bank with the exclusive right to grant consumer credit and mortgage loans.

Table 5.3: Size distribution of firms in manufacturing

	Hungary	Sample of capitalist economies
Average number of employees per firm	186	80
Percentage distribution of employees by size categories		
10–100	14	35
101–500	26	33
501–1,000	19	13
more than 1,000	41	19

Source and detail: Ehrlich (1985b H, p. 92).
Note: The figures refer to averages of various years in the seventies. The right column covers the following sample of countries: Austria, Belgium, France, Italy, Japan, and Sweden.

In the last few years, there have been serious efforts to break up monopoly positions and to partition large entities into several smaller ones. The size distribution has become somewhat less extreme, shifting a little toward smaller units. But the process is slow and meets with strong resistance.

There is a peculiar disparity in the treatment of large and small state-owned firms. On the one hand, large firms are much more successful in lobbying for favours, particularly for investment resources. Some of them are in great financial trouble; nevertheless large credits or subsidies are granted to them (Mária Csanádi 1979 H, 1980 H, 1983 H, Erzsébet Szalai 1982, Matits 1984c. H). On the other hand, smaller units count for less in the eyes of the supervisors. They suffer less from frequent inspections, and it is easier for them to evade certain rigid regulations than it is for large firms (Tamás Bauer 1976, 1985b).

5.3.5 Summary: from direct to indirect bureaucratic control
The reform has improved the performance of the Hungarian state sector. Firms now have more room for manoeuvre; they have become less rigid and more adaptive. They respond in a more flexible way to changes in demand and pay more attention to quality improvement and technical progress. These achievements become even more visible if one compares Hungary with the unreformed socialist economies.

This appreciation notwithstanding, the reform went only half-way. Hungarian state-owned firms do not operate within the framework of market socialism. The reformed system is a specific combination of bureaucratic and market coordination. The same can be said, of course, about every contemporary economy. There is no capitalist economy where the market functions in the complete absence of bureaucratic intervention. The real issue is the relative strength of the components in the mixture. Although we have no exact measures and, therefore, our formulation is vague, we venture the following proposition. The frequency and intensity of bureaucratic intervention into market processes have certain critical values. Once these critical values are exceeded, the market becomes emasculated and dominated by bureaucratic regulation. That is exactly the case in the Hungarian state-owned sector.[15] The market is not dead. It does some coordinating work, but its influence is weak. The firm's manager watches the customer and the supplier with one eye and his superiors in the bureaucracy with the other eye. Practice teaches him that it is more important to keep the second eye wide open: managerial career, the firm's life and death, taxes, subsidies and credit, prices and wages, all financial 'regulators' affecting the firm's prosperity, depend more on the higher authorities than on market performance.

In the course of the reform the bureaucracy itself has changed: it has become less tightly centralized. It is a peculiar complex of partial multi-level bureaucracies that often act in an inconsistent manner; it is more polycentric than before the reform. The head of each branch has his own priorities and performs his own interventions, granting favours to some firms and putting extra burdens on others. The more such lines of separate control evolve, the more they dampen each other's effects.

The 'rules of the game' are not generated in a natural, organic way by economic and social processes; rather they are elaborated artificially by the officers and committees of the administrative authorities. They are, of course, never perfect: they do not produce exactly the results expected and are therefore revised time and time again. Hence they are unable to provide stable guidance for the behaviour of the firm. Once the reactions of the firms become manifest, the rules are revised again.

The role of the state is not restricted to determining or influencing a few important macro-aggregates or economy-wide parameters like the exchange rate or interest rate. As we have seen, there are millions of micro-interventions in all facets of economic life; bureaucratic *micro-regulation* has continued to prevail.

The firms are not helpless. Every new tactic of the higher organs evokes new countertactics. First of all, bargaining goes on about all issues all the time. This is a bargaining society, and the main direction is vertical, namely bargaining between the levels of the hierarchy, or between bureaucracy and firm, not horizontal, between seller and buyer. All issues mentioned in section 5.3.2 — entry, exit, appointment, output, input, price, wage, tax, subsidy, credit, and investment — are subject to meticulous negotiations, fights, lobbying, the influence of open or hidden supporters and opponents. The Hungarian literature calls this phenomenon 'regulator bargaining'; it has taken the place of 'plan bargaining' which had prevailed in the command economy. Firms had quite a bit of bargaining power even in the classical command system and their bargaining position improved substantially in the new system, especially in the case of large firms.

If bargaining does not succeed, there is one more instrument in the hands of the firm: to evade the regulations preferably not in an explicitly illegal way, but by using some tricks, seemingly following the letter of the law, but violating its intentions. And then, when the law-maker recognizes that there are loopholes, he tries to create a new, more perfect decree — and the game starts again.

Let us sum up. For future reference we need a short name for the system that has developed in the Hungarian state-owned sector. We propose calling it *indirect bureaucratic control,* juxtaposing it with the old command system of *direct bureaucratic control.* The name reflects the fact that the dominant form of coordination has remained bureaucratic control but that there are significant changes in the set of control instruments.

5.4. THE NON-STATE SECTOR

5.4.1 Digression: the reform in agriculture

Sections 5.3 and 5.4 proceed generally by reviewing the various social sectors based on different types of ownership. Here in this section we digress to take a closer look at all ownership types in one particular branch, agriculture. This is perhaps the most successful area of the reform. It is therefore instructive to discuss agriculture as a whole (Ferenc Donáth 1980, Swain 1981, Csaba Csáki 1983, Michael Marrese 1983, Aladár Sipos 1983).

Contradictory tendencies have developed in the last 25–30 years. The share of state-owned farms remained rather stable. There were two big waves of 'collectivization', that is, the forced formation of agricultural cooperatives: the first in the early fifties and the second in 1959–61. The latter brought more than two-thirds of arable land from private ownership into the hands of the cooperatives. Members of the cooperatives were allowed to hold only a small private plot and a few animals. The present shares of the various types of ownership are shown in Table 5.4. Still, in spite of dramatic changes in the direction of collective ownership, Hungarian agriculture is different from the prototype 'collectivized' organization of agricultural production.

Cooperatives. This has remained the largest social sector in agriculture. Many important changes have occurred in their functioning. In the prereform system the position of a cooperative was not far from that of a state-owned farm. It was tightly fitted in the framework of a command economy; it received detailed mandatory plan targets like state-owned firms. As a result of the reform process, the system of mandatory plans was abolished in 1966, just as in the state sector two years later. Frequent informal interventions, however, remained.

Even in the old system leaders of the cooperatives were elected and not appointed; that was the essential legal difference between a state-owned and a cooperative enterprise. In practice, however, elections were manipulated and there was only a formal approval of the preselected managers by the membership. This practice has not been rooted out, although the participation of the members in the selection and appointment of managers has become more active; the word of the membership carries more weight than it did.

Table 5.4: Contribution of social sectors to total agricultural gross output (percentage distribution)

	1966	1975	1980	1984
State-owned farms	16.4	18.0	16.8	15.3
Cooperatives	48.4	50.5	50.4	51.1
Household farming	23.7	19.0	18.5	18.4
Auxiliary production and private farms	11.5	12.5	14.3	15.2

Source: Column 1, 2, and 3: CSO H, 1983b, pp. 28, 37 and 116.
    Column 4: CSO H, 1985c, p. 73.

In the cooperatives of the early fifties material incentives were weak. Compulsory delivery quotas at very low administrative prices absorbed the largest part of production. In other words, the peasantry carried a heavy tax burden. In years of poor harvest even seeds for the next year and foodstuff for the farmers' own consumption were barely left in the village. In the expression coined during those times, the attics of the farmers' houses were swept clean by compulsory deliveries. The sale of surplus on the market was legally permitted, but little or no surplus was left to sell.

There have been substantial changes in this respect. Some (though not all) price distortions, both on the output and on the input side, have been eliminated. Material incentives are strong. As has been mentioned, the compulsory delivery system was abandoned as early as 1956–57. The cooperatives can sell to state trade organizations on a contractual basis, but they are allowed to do their own marketing if they prefer. The cooperative as a whole is motivated to earn more income and more profit. The cooperatives have more autonomy in deciding how to use their own profit. In many areas a special kind of decentralization is applied within the cooperatives: working teams or individuals are in charge of a certain line of production and get their own share of their production line's net income.

Before the reform, agricultural cooperatives were prohibited from engaging in any but agricultural activities. In the reform process non-agricultural activities have developed. The cooperatives have engaged in food processing, in the production of parts for state-owned industry, in light industry, in construction, in trade, and in the restaurant business. The share of non-agricultural production in the total output of agricultural cooperatives was 34 per cent in 1984. In this way profits have increased and seasonal troughs of employment can be bridged more easily (Kálmán Rupp 1983).

Private household farms of cooperative members. Here one finds the most dramatic changes. Whereas the legal limitations on the size of the household plot have remained unchanged,[16] much more family work is devoted to this special kind of private agriculture. Restrictions on keeping animals and on owning machinery have been lifted. Household farms produce a large percentage of meat, dairy and other animal products, fruits and vegetables. With few exceptions, there is no legal restriction on selling output, and prices are determined by supply and demand on the free market for foodstuffs; hence the peasants have a strong incentive to work hard and produce more. The attitudes of both the cooperative and of the agricultural administrative apparatus towards the household farm are now very different from what they were. In the old system the cooperative was hostile; private household farming was regarded as a 'bourgeois remnant' that should be replaced soon by collective forms of production. Now private household farming is declared a permanent component of agriculture under socialism. Cooperatives render assistance in different ways: they provide seeds, help with transport, lend machinery, give expert advice, and assist in marketing. A remarkable division of tasks has evolved in which the cooperatives concentrate more on grain and fodder, which can be produced most efficiently by large-scale operations, while private household farms focus on labour-intensive products where small-scale operations succeed better.

We do not want to paint an idealized picture: in fact, there are many problems in this area. There have been periodic capricious bureaucratic interventions into the household farming sector, confusing the farmers and weakening their confidence. There are gross distortions in prices offered to the private producers by the state trade organizations, who are the main buyers of many agricultural products. In spite of these problems, the household farms are relatively successful.

Auxiliary agricultural production. Hungary is a country with a strong agricultural tradition. People working in non-agricultural professions like to have a garden or a small plot, where they can grow fruit and vegetables, or raise poultry or pigs. The liberalization measures in agriculture gave new impetus to these activities. Auxiliary agricultural production turns out to be a non-negligible proportion of total output, covering not only a substantial portion of the participating households' own consumption, thereby decreasing demand for marketed products, but also contributing to the marketed supply. Some of these producing units developed into specialized, capital-intensive private farms producing commodities almost exclusively for the market.

State-owned farms. The share of state-owned farms in total agricultural output has not changed much, but their situation is now different. All the systemic changes discussed in section 5.3 also apply to the state-owned area of agriculture. Here we also find dual dependence, but the relative strength of the market is stronger and that of bureaucratic coordination is weaker than in other branches of the state-owned sector. Prices are more reasonable, managers are more 'entrepreneurial', and the profit motive is more intense. The difference is explained mainly by the fact that in agriculture a small number of state-owned enterprises are surrounded by a very large number of more competitive, more market- and profit-oriented cooperatives and private household farms. The minority's behaviour adjusts to some extent to the behaviour of the dominant parts of the branch.

To sum up: Hungarian agriculture shows a particular blend of spectacular successes and unresolved problems. The main achievements are the significant improvement of domestic food supply, some good results in exports and the stronger motivation for work in all subsectors. But all these results were obtained at high cost: with the aid of a very large investment of capital and of the peasants' hard 'self-exploitation'.

The present size distribution is unsatisfactory; medium size units, smaller than the large-scale state-owned and cooperative units and larger than the 'mini'-scale units in household farming are almost non-existent. In other countries with highly developed agriculture the dominant form is a farm operating with a small number of people, but with high capital intensity. Such an efficient and highly productive form has not yet developed in Hungary either in the cooperative or in the private sector. Development in that direction has been hindered by the privileges of the existing large-scale units and by conservative bureaucratic restrictions.

5.4.2 Non-agricultural cooperatives
We now return to our main train of thought, discussing the various social sectors one by one. Our next topic is the cooperative sector and because we have discussed agricultural cooperatives in section 5.4.1, we focus here on the non-agricultural cooperatives. Their significance has increased in the reform process in manufacturing, construction, commerce, and services. They are similar to the agricultural cooperatives in many respects; we will not repeat what has been said already.[17] One important distinction: there is less favourable treatment of non-agricultural than of agricultural cooperatives as far as credit, tax, subsidy, and import are concerned.

What are the main similarities and differences between state-owned firms and cooperative enterprises? Everything described in sections 5.3.1 and 5.3.2, the abolition of mandatory plans and the dual dependence of the enterprise, applies to the cooperatives as well. There is, however, a difference in relative weights; in all issues (exit, entry, selection of managers, price, wage, tax, credit) there is somewhat less bureaucratic intervention and somewhat stronger influence of market forces than in the state sector. The budget constraint is somewhat harder; non-agricultural cooperatives (especially the smaller ones) cannot expect unconditional survival[18] and almost automatic bail-out by the bureaucracy. The cooperative is much more responsive to prices; its profit motivation is stronger.[19] The cooperatives receive less favourable treatment than state-owned firms in the allocation of investment credits and subsidies.

The average size of the cooperatives is much smaller than that of the state-owned firms, and this has been so especially in recent years, because more possibilities have opened up for establishing so-called small cooperatives that work under easier and more flexible legal and financial conditions than do the rest of the cooperatives.

The situation of cooperatives is important from the viewpoint of socialist ideology. The idea that cooperatives will be one of the basic forms of ownership in socialism, or even *the* basic form, has a long-standing intellectual tradition in the Hungarian Left. The advocates of the traditional cooperative idea have always stressed the principle of voluntary participation. Nowadays this principle is more or less consistently applied in the non-agricultural sector. (The same cannot be said about the formation of cooperatives in the past.) There is general shortage of labour in Hungary. The vast majority of present members therefore, have a genuine choice between entering and remaining in a cooperative or getting a job in other sectors. Those who stay seem to prefer this form because it combines the efficiency of a medium size firm with a certain degree of participation in managerial decisions. The linkage between individual and collective performance and individual earning is more direct than in the state-owned firm. Of course, a conclusive test can come only if the economic environment of the cooperative sector becomes more competitive and market oriented, and the cooperatives have to demonstrate efficiency and profitability against more vigorous competition.

5.4.3 The formal private sector

The most spectacular trend of the Hungarian reform process is the growth of the private sector. From the point of view of ideology, this is the boldest break with orthodoxy.

The term *private sector* has both narrower and wider definitions. In the present section we discuss only a well-defined part of it, the *formal* private sector; other parts and also some definitional problems will be the topics of the next section. What distinguishes the formal private sector from the other private ventures is that it is officially licensed by the bureaucracy.

Tables 5.5: The size of the formal private sector (in thousand of persons)

	1953	1955	1966	1975	1980	1984
1. Private craftsmen	51.5	97.6	71.3	57.4	63.7	76.1
2. Employees and apprentices of private craftsmen	4.0	16.0	26.7	19.7	20.1	26.9
3. Private merchants	3.0	9.0	8.5	10.8	12.0	22.4
4. Employees of private merchants	–	1.0	1.5	3.4	8.2	28.5
5. People working full time in business work partnerships	–	–	–	–	–	11.0
6. Total number of people working full time in the formal private sector	58.5	123.6	108.0	91.3	104.0	164.9

Sources: Row 1 and 2 in Column 1, 2 and 3: CSO H, 1972, pp. 12–13.
   Row 3 and 4 in Column 1 and 2: CSO H, 1957, p. 61.
   Row 1 and 2 in Column 4, 5 and 6: CSO H, 1985a, p. 324.
   Row 3 and 4 in Column 3: CSO H, 1967, p. 56, 199.
   Row 3 and 4 in Column 4 and 5: CSO H, 1981, pp. 132–133, 325 and CSO H, 1976, p. 93.
   Row 3 anv 4 in Column 6: CSO H, 1985a, pp. 52–53, 210.
Note: Since 1968 individuals who have a regular full-time job in the state-owned or cooperative sector can get a license for a second part-time job in the formal private sector. Data for 1984: 47.2 thousand individuals work as part-time licensed private craftsmen, and 31.5 thousand individuals as part-time members of business work partnerships.

Table 5.5 shows the size of the formal private sector. The majority of personnel are craftsmen, construction contractors, shopkeepers, and restaurant owners. They work alone or are assisted by family members or a few hired employees. The size of this sector has increased rapidly in the last few years when the authorities began to grant licenses more liberally. Also the regulations concerning employment became less restrictive: at present the maximum number of employees, apart from family members, is seven. This is, of course, a very small number for those accustomed to private market economies, but large in comparison with other socialist countries. It means the legalization of 'small capitalism'. We must add that medium- or large-scale capitalist business is prohibited in Hungary.

A new form has appeared recently: the so-called business work partnership, a small-scale enterprise based on the private ownership by the participants. It is a blend of a small cooperative and a small owner-operated capitalistic firm. This form also belongs to the formal private sector.

The formal private sector is still a minor segment of the economy (see Table 5.5). Nevertheless, its rate of growth is remarkable: mere permission to exist and perhaps also some encouragement in official speeches were enough to induce a sudden boom. Apparently thousands of people had a latent desire to enter private business; at the first opportunity, they ran to join the formal private sector. And this happened in the face of many difficulties. Private business is at a disadvantage in getting inputs from the state sector. It rarely gets credit from the state-owned banking sector and therefore must rely on raising money through private and frequently illegal channels. Private credit does not have satisfactory legal backing.

It is widely believed that tax evasion is quite common; in any case, enforcement of the tax law is rather lax. Tougher enforcement could easily scare away many people from private business. This leads to a wider issue, namely the problem of confidence.

At present the majority of people working in the formal private sector are probably satisfied with their current income. Perhaps they are not all aware that their relative position in the income distribution is much better than that of small business people in a private market economy. There, craftsmen or small shopkeepers usually have very modest incomes. In Hungary, many of them are in the highest income group. Yet they cannot be sure how long that will last. These individuals or their parents lived through the era of confiscations in the forties. In spite of repeated official declarations that their activity is regarded as a permanent feature of Hungarian socialism, deep in their hearts they have doubts. That is why many of them are myopic profit maximizers, not much interested in building up lasting goodwill by offering good service, and quick and reliable delivery or by investing in long-lived fixed assets. Encouragement and discouragement alternate; quiet periods are interrupted by orchestrated media campaigns crying out against 'speculation' and 'profiteering'. A confidence-strengthening experience of many years is still needed to extend the restricted horizon.

5.4.4 The informal private sector, the second economy

We must start with conceptual clarification. Hungarian experts dealing with private activities and income earned outside the state-owned and cooperative sector do not agree on terminology and definitions.[20] The present chapter applies the following notions.

To the *informal* private sector belong (a) all private activities pursued outside the formal private sector as defined in the earlier section and (b) all income that does not originate as payment for labour service rendered in government agencies, officially registered non-profit institutions, state-owned firms, cooperatives, and formal private business. The activity and income components (a) and (b) of the definition are not completely overlapping.

The *first economy* is composed of the governmental agencies, officially registered non-profit institutions, state-owned firms, and cooperatives. The *second economy* is the total of the formal and informal private sector.[21] A caveat: the decisive mark distinguishing 'first' and 'second' economy in this usage is not legality versus illegality, or payment of taxes versus tax evasion. (That is the common criterion in the Western literature on the 'shadow economy'.) Many activities in our second economy are legal; a part of second-economy income is taxed. We apply a system-specific classification. The first economy is the sphere that was regarded by the prereform orthodox interpretation as the genuine 'socialist' sector, the second economy was classified as 'non-socialist'. We discuss this manifold sphere from various angles.

Working time. Hungary, with some delay, follows the tendency of industrialized economies by reducing hours of work in the first economy. Simultaneously, activities in the second economy consume more time than ever before. Some people work in the second economy as their main activity. Some members of a family are active full time in the private household farm, while other members of the family are employed in the state-owned farm or in the cooperative. Many pensioners have a full- or half-time (illegal or 'half-legal') activity. But the majority work in the second economy as an activity supplementary to a first job in one of the formal sectors. They 'moonlight' in the evenings, weekends, during paid vacations. It happens, illegally, that people work while on sick leave, paid by the national health service, or during regular paid working hours at their first job.

Aggregate data are shown in Table 5.6. The incredibly high (one to two) ratio between total working time spent in the second and

Table 5. 6: The relative size of the second economy

	First economy (State-owned firms and cooperatives) (per cent)	Second economy (Formal and informal private sector) (per cent)
1. Distribution of total active time (excluding time spent on household work and transport) in 1984	67	33
2. Contribution of social sectors to residential construction (measured by the number of new dwellings) in 1984	44.5	55.5
3. Contribution of social sectors to repair and maintenance services in 1983	13	87

Sources: Row 1: Timár (1985b H, p. 306); Row 2: CSO H, 1985a, p. 139; Row 3: Drexler and Belyó (1985 H, p. 60). Both studies rely on micro-surveys (interviews and questionnaires).

Notes: The table covers both the officially recorded and unrecorded part of total activities. The figures concerning the latter are based on estimates elaborated by the researchers who compiled the data base of the table. Figures in row 1 are aggregates of all branches of production, including residential construction. The latter is also surveyed separately in row 2. The 'first economy' figures include the activities of so-called enterprise business work partnerships, which will be discussed in section 5.4.5. The 'second economy' figures include household farming and 'auxiliary production of employees'. The 'second economy' figures in row 3 are the sum of three parts: formal private sector 14 per cent, informal private sector excluding 'do-it-yourself' activities 19 per cent, and 'do-it-yourself' activities within the household 54 per cent.

first economies demonstrates the high preference of a large part of the Hungarian population for more income and higher consumption over leisure. This is just one of the secrets of the 'Hungarian miracle': people are willing to work more if allowed; they will exert themselves for the sake of higher consumption. In a large percentage of families, members are working to the point of psychological and physical exhaustion.[22]

Of the 33 per cent of active time spent on second-economy activities, a smaller part is spent in the formal private sector, thus contributing to the officially recorded GDP. The larger part of the 33 per cent is spent in the informal private sector. Depending on how productivity is measured in the informal private sector, this subsector may add perhaps 20 per cent or more to the officially recorded GDP.

Production for own consumption: the role of the household. Before the reform there was a strong tendency to reduce the role of the family and the household as a producing and property-owning institution and to shift more and more activity and property into the domain of large and preferably state-owned organizations. The reform reversed this trend to some extent.

The reversal is not consistent and is accompanied by many frictions. A kind of vacuum is present in some areas: the old forms of socialized services are no longer fully responsible for meeting demands on them while the household and the family are not yet in a position to take over these responsibilities satisfactorily (Bauer 1985b).

We have already discussed an important form of production for own consumption: the extension of private household farming and auxiliary agricultural production. These activities serve partly the household's own needs. The other extremely important area is housing. The trend in the prereform system was towards public housing. All apartment houses were nationalized; tenancy was rationed by the bureaucracy. This trend has been reversed. In 1980 71.4 per cent of the total housing stock was in private ownership and the rest was owned by the state. The trend continues: 85.7 per cent of the dwellings built in 1984 were private.[23] The new shift is associated with severe social and economic tensions (Iván Szelényi 1983, Zsuzsa Dániel 1985).

A further example is transport. Khrushchev advocated the complete abolition of private cars in favour of public transport as a desirable trend in socialism. Present-day Hungary is overcrowded with private cars. The number of privately owned cars increased 13.7 times from 1966 to 1984. But repair service and the building and maintenance of the road network cannot keep up with the increasing number of private cars.

There are many more examples of the reversal from 'socialization' toward self-sufficiency within the family and household: child care, sick care, cooking and other household work, and do-it-yourself repair and maintenance. How far the latter trend has gone is demonstrated in Table 5.6.

Contribution to consumer supply. Another approach to indicate the importance of the second economy is to look at the contribution to consumer supply. Table 5.6 presents a few characteristic data demonstrating the extremely large share of the second economy in this respect. And, of course, there are many more areas not shown in the table.

Yields of private property. The preceding paragraphs of section 5.4.4 discussed activities where the participant in the second economy combined his own labour with his own equipment, say the toolkit of a repairman. It may happen, however, that he uses, illegally, the equipment of his first-economy employer. There is also another category of person: income earners whose source of second economy income is a return from some private property. The most common example is the subletting of privately owned housing or the renting out of second homes in recreation areas, either to long-term lessees or to short-term visitors and tourists.[24]

Legality. There is a wide continuum running from perfectly legal, 'white' and perfectly illegal, 'black' activities, the latter being only the cases where law is strictly enforced. An informal private sector or a second economy exists in all socialist countries. Quantitative comparison is not possible, but experts are convinced that the share of this sector in Hungary is much larger than in most other socialist economies. This is a direct consequence of the state's attitude. There is a deliberate effort to legalize formerly illegal activities, or to be tolerant of ambiguous cases, provided that these activities are regarded as socially useful or at least not harmful. This tolerance awakened tremendous energy in a large part of the population. It is certainly not a very satisfactory organization of human activity; it is full of conflicts and unfair actions, but still, without the tolerance, this energy would remain dormant. It must be added, however, that the spirit of tolerance and the trend toward legalization do not work consistently. What has been said about alternations of encouragement and discouragement of the formal private sector applies even more to the informal sector. As a consequence, the situation here is rather unstable.

5.4.5 Combined forms

A characteristic feature of the Hungarian reform is the experimentation with different mixed forms, combining state ownership with private activity or private ownership. We discuss briefly three forms.

Firms in mixed ownership. A few dozen firms are owned jointly by the Hungarian state and foreign private business. A sharing of business by the Hungarian ownership state and Hungarian private business does not exist.

Leasing. This form is widely applied in trade and in the restaurant sector. Fixed capital remains in state ownership, but the business is run by a private individual who pays a rent fixed by a contract and also taxes. He keeps the profit or covers the deficit at his own risk. The lessee is selected by auction; the person offering the highest rent gets the contract. In 1984 about 11 per cent of the shops and 37 per cent of the restaurants were leased this way (CSO H, 1985a, p. 210).

Enterprise business work partnership. In contrast to 'business work partnership', which is a form clearly belonging to the formal private sector as shown in section 5.4.3, here we look at a group of people who are employed by a state-owned firm. They do some extra work under special contract for extra payment, but in some sense within the framework of the employer state-owned firm. In many cases the team is commissioned by its own firm. Or it gets the task from outside, but with the consent of the employer. In many instances the members are allowed to use the equipment of the firm. The 'enterprise business work partnership' can be established only with the permission of the managers of the firm; each member needs a permit from his superiors to join the team. More detailed description and analysis can be found in Teréz Laky (1985) and David Stark (1985).

The purpose of creating this new form is clear. It gives a legal framework for certain kinds of activities, formerly not legal, mentioned in section 5.4.4, and at the same time allows the employing firm to keep some control over these activities. Many managers support this arrangement because they can get around central wage regulation in this way: the partnership undertakes work for extra payment that it would otherwise do (perhaps in regular overtime) within the framework of its regular job. The number of such units is increasing rapidly. It was 2,775 in 1982 and grew to 17,337 by the end of 1984 (CSO H 1985a, p. 326). Many observers are highly critical and question whether it is really efficient to have a first and a second job within the same organization. On the other hand, the arrangement may perhaps lead to some healthy intrafirm decentralization later on.

5.4.6 Summary: strong market orientation and bureaucratic constraints

As we have seen, the reform process has created or strengthened a large variety of non-state ownership forms and activities. It is a great merit of the reformers that they allowed or initiated such experimentation with courage and an open mind.

In the midst of the variety of forms, there are a few common features. The economic units in the non-state sector (perhaps with the exception of large cooperatives) have a hard budget constraint; they cannot rely on the paternalistic assistance of the state as far as survival and growth are concerned. They enter business in the hope of profits and they go out of business if they fail financially. All activities are more market oriented and price responsive than those carried out by the state-owned firms.

The non-state sector acts as a built-in stabilizer of the economy, which is less sensitive to the 'stop-go' fluctuations so strongly felt in the state sector. It is able to grow even when there are troubles with the balance of payments or restrictions on import and investment.

The non-state sector is, however, not free from bureaucratic control. There are permanent restrictions and regulations, and also unpredictable, improvised interventions and frequent changes of the rules. The same phenomenon we have just praised, namely, bold experimentation, can also be rather confusing. The lack of stability and the many bureaucratic restrictions do not give full scope to the initiative of the individuals engaged in the non-state sector.

Nevertheless, with all its shortcomings, the appearance of a vital non-state sector represents something brand new and important in the history of socialist countries.

5.5 OVERALL RESOURCE ALLOCATION AND DISTRIBUTION

In sections 5.3 and 5.4 we surveyed various social sectors. In this section we shall be studying issues that cut across the economy, regardless of the breakdown by ownership forms. We shall also make a few remarks concerning the relationship between the social sectors.

5.5.1 Planning

In the usage of socialist countries 'planning' has a double meaning. First, it refers to an *ex ante* exploration of possibilities and comparison of alternative solutions. A plan sets targets and assigns instruments to fulfil the targets. The 'product' of the planners' work is the plan itself — a document accepted by the political and legislative bodies, which serves as a working program for the government. Second, the term *planning* is also used to denote what this chapter calls direct bureaucratic control. The official ideology of the command economy deliberately wanted to convince people that these two concepts are inseparable.

We suggest a strict separation of the two concepts and reserve the term *planning* only for the first. The official documents of the Hungarian reform adopt this interpretation when they repeat that, although mandatory targets and quotas are abolished, planning must be maintained.

Nominally, these resolutions have been implemented. The planning apparatus is at work, and plans are elaborated in due course. Nevertheless, a closer examination shows that planning has not found its appropriate new role. One would expect that after being freed from the nuisances of 'dispatcher work' (that is, setting quotas, checking performance, urging deliveries, etc.), the planner's time and intellectual energy could finally be spared for his genuine tasks of exploration, calculation, comparison, and *ex ante* coordination. These possibilities have not been fully exploited. There are efforts to elaborate long-term plans, but the linkage between these plans and the actual regulation of economic affairs is rather weak. Planners have achieved impressive results in coordinating short-term macro-policy and the micro-regulation described in section 5.3.2 in a state of emergency (for example, when tensions developed in Hungary's international credit position). Yet the problem has not been solved. The old methodology suitable for imperative planning is no longer applicable and a consistent new methodology compatible with the systemic changes is not yet available.

5.5.2 Fiscal system

The fiscal system has remained extremely large (Mihály Kupa, 1980 H, László Muraközy 1985 H). Total central government expenditure was 52.8 per cent of GDP in 1970, grew to 62.7 per cent by 1980, and decreased slightly to 61.3 per cent by 1983.

In capitalist economies this ratio is strongly correlated with the level of development (GDP/capita). For the sake of comparison we look at European capitalist countries that have reached about the same level of development as Hungary: in 1980 the government expenditure/GDP ratio was 37.7 per cent in Finland, 36.5 per cent in Greece, and 29.4 per cent in Spain.[25]

There are several reasons for the high degree of centralization of financial flows through the government budget. Most of them are associated with issues already discussed, the huge burden of subsidies, the deep fiscal involvement in financing investment, and the expenditures of the large bureaucratic apparatus. These properties of the fiscal system provide remarkable evidence that genuine decentralization of economic processes through market coordination has not gone very far.

The next section will discuss the role of banks and the capital market. One remark can be made in advance. The fact that a very large proportion of the economy's net income flows through the central government budget allows less scope for the activity of banks, other financial intermediary institutions, enterprises and households in the reallocation of funds. This is eminently clear in the case of investment allocation. The larger the proportion of investment financed by the central budget, the less disposable capital is left to the discretion of other actors and the less possibility arises for the creation of a well-functioning capital market.

In that respect there is a trend toward decentralization. The share of investment financed by the central government budget was 40 per cent in 1968–70 and diminished to 21 per cent in 1981–1984; the share of investment financed by bank credit and by the producers' own savings increased accordingly (János Dudás 1985 H).

5.5.3 Monetary system, capital market
In a fully monetized market economy money is a means of integrating the whole national economy. That is assured by the possibility that money is a universal medium of exchange, which can be used by each money holder for any purpose he chooses. The classical pre-reform system fragmented the economy in this respect. Certain types of money flows between different segments of the system were permitted while others were strictly prohibited. The state sector paid money wages to the households, but, except for minimal tightly restricted consumer credits granted by the monopoly savings bank, it could not give credit to customers. The household paid the price for goods and services marketed by the state sector, but could not invest its savings in real capital formation by the state sector. Even within the state sector money was 'earmarked'. The firm had at least three kinds of money: 'wage money', 'money covering current costs other than wages', and 'investment money'. These categories of money could be used only for the assigned purpose (Brus [1961] 1972, Grossman 1966, Kornai 1980, Tardos 1980).

The reform has brought some relaxation in this respect; the economy has come closer to a system integrated by money. It is, however, still far from one with free flows on funds.

Banks. Until recently, Hungary has had a 'monobank system'. In that respect it has remained similar to the classical socialist economy. The Hungarian National Bank has combined two functions: it plays the usual role of a central bank and also acts as a commercial bank, practically as the monopoly commercial bank for most financial operations of the state-owned and cooperative sectors. There have also been a few specialized banks, for example, the foreign-trade bank and the bank for household savings, but these have enjoyed only a seeming autonomy.

There are now resolutions to establish a two-level banking sector in the near future. There will be a central bank at the top with the usual functions and a set of state-owned, but competing commercial banks on the lower level, regulated by the central bank. Even before this plan is realized, a few small financial intermediaries that can lend for specific purposes (certain kinds of investment, innovation, export promotion) have been established. In any case, we do not know yet how much genuine autonomy the units of the decentralized banking sector will enjoy and to what extent they will subject to the pressure of the central and local bureaucracy.

Firms. Before the reform, the state-owned firm had almost no choice concerning financial decisions.[26] The portion of working capital that had to be deposited in the Central Bank was strictly regulated; there was a very small part of gross investment financed from retained profit and depreciation funds. Trade credit was prohibited. The bank had a strictly protected monopoly in granting credit to the firm.

Now the situation is different. Let us start with the asset side. A firm can deposit money in the bank and in the near future it will also be able to choose between banks. It can grant trade credit to other firms buying its output.[27] It can invest in its own plant or it can establish a small subsidiary, holding only a part of equity in the newly created firm. It can contribute to the capital of a newly founded company jointly with other firms or institutions. It can buy bonds issued by other firms or local authorities and traded on the bond market. Table 5.7 provides information about the size of the bond market.

Table 5.7: The availability of bonds, May 1986

	Total nominal value (billion forints)[a]	Yield (per cent)	Relative size (per cent)
Available to private citizens	4.5	7–13	2.0[b]
Available to firms and institutions	2.0	7–15	9.7[c]

Sources: Data on nominal values, information given by the State Development Bank. Data on yield, *Heti Világgazdaság* (1986 H, p. 55).
[a] Covers all bonds issued prior to May 1986.
[b] Total nominal value / stock of household deposits in savings banks.
[c] Total nominal value / stock of outstanding bank investment credit.

On the liability side the situation is symmetrical; only a few additional remarks are needed. Interest rates have been raised several times since 1976. The average interest rate for medium- and long-term credits granted to state-owned firms was 13 per cent in 1985, that is, a real interest rate of about 5 per cent. There is no conclusive evidence concerning how firms responded to the increase in interest rates (Miklós Breitner, 1985 H, Tivadar Grósz, 1986 H). There is permanent excess demand for credit, though the ratio of rejected to accepted credit applications has declined a little. Most observers agree that the sudden decrease of investment activity was achieved mostly through direct bureaucratic intervention into the approval and execution of large projects, and by cutting credit supply — not by the influence of interest policy.

Formerly the only source of credit for the firm was the central bank. Now if the firm wants to raise capital, it can apply to one of the newly created intermediaries just mentioned. As for bonds, they can be bought by households, which opens a new source of fund raising.

The long list of options gives a more favourable impression than does a closer look at the real situation. There are still many formal and informal restrictions both on the asset and the liability side: blocked or temporarily frozen deposits, constraints on self-financed investment. Many of the options are promises for the near future and not yet facts. For example, it is remarkable that firms are not very enthusiastic about buying bonds; the total number of bonds is very small. Most firms prefer to use their savings for reinvestment in their own production even if the expected yield is lower than the return of bonds issued by other firms or local authorities.[28]

Households. The set of options open to households has also become wider. Before the reform households could deposit money in the savings bank.[29] They could also buy, under strong legal restrictions, precious metal or real estate. The reform extended the potential portfolio recently by permitting the purchase of bonds. The first steps were taken to establish a kind of institutionalized bond market. This is an important new possibility, but its true significance is hard to judge at this early stage.

As mentioned earlier, individuals can lend to other individuals or invest money in a 'silent partnership' of a private business. Without sufficient legal protection, however, this may involve high risks.

To sum up: the first vague contours of a credit and capital market are emerging, but the Hungarian economy is still far from overall 'monetization' and from the solidified institutions of a full-grown, well-operating, flexible credit and capital market.

5.5.4 Labour market

While steps toward an extended capital market are modest, movement towards a free labour market is substantial. At the peak of direct bureaucratic centralization, labour was rigorously tied to the workplace. There were various restrictions: administrative prohibition on changing jobs except on the explicit instructions of the authorities, prohibition against taking employment in cities without a special permit, and distribution of many goods and services through employers, the state-owned firms, of such items as housing, child care, recreation, food, and other consumption goods in kind. In the course of reform the first two of these restrictions on individual choice have been abolished. Remnants of the third still exist in housing, recreation, health care, and child care. These are, however, less binding ties than before.

Not only has overall full employment been achieved, but hidden rural unemployment was also absorbed in the early seventies. This is an important success. The general chronic excess demand for labour, however, is accompanied by labour hoarding and does not exclude minor frictional unemployment in certain professions or regions (Péter Galasi and György Sziráczky, 1985, Károly Fazekas and János Köllő, 1985a). Excess demand, together with the elimination of administrative ties, results in high quit rates: 15.7 per cent in 1982, as compared, for example, to 7 per cent in Czechoslovakia in the same year. Labour is sensitive to benefits and also to differentials between the wage offers of different firms and moves quickly in the direction of better terms (Fazekas and Köllő, 1985b H). This is true of the labour movement within the state-owned sector. It applies even more to the relationship between the state-owned and the private sectors. Income offered by the formal and informal private sector attracts labour away from state-owned firms, which pay much less. The formal private sector can offer full-time employment. Or employees of the first economy can engage in informal private activities, such as 'moonlighting' or even working illegally during regular working time. In any case, the extra activities exhaust the individual and use up much of his energy; hence he will work with less attention and diligence at his first job. Here lies a hidden cost of bureaucratic regulation. State-owned firms are restricted in raising wages, but the formal and even more so the informal private sector can get round the restrictions. This is a painful dilemma; simple deregulation of wages would not help if all other circumstances such as excess demand for labour, weak profit motive, soft budget constraint remain unchanged. It would only lead to more forceful wage-push inflationary pressures (István R. Gábor and György Kővári, 1985 H, Katalin Falus–Szikra, 1985 H).

5.5.5 Summary: coexistence and conflict of the social sectors

This completes our description of the systemic changes. Our observation can be summarized as follows.

Hungary has a multi-sectoral economy; different forms of ownership coexist and compete with each other. But competition is on unequal terms. With some simplification we may speak about a preference ordering of the bureaucracy: 1. large state-owned firms, 2. small state-owned firms, 3. agricultural cooperatives, 4. nonagricultural cooperatives, 5. formal private sector, 6. informal private sector.[30] This ordering is followed in bail-outs (for 1, 2, and 3; with more certainty for 1), and in handing out credits (1, 2, 3, 4). The formal private sector only occasionally receives these favours; the informal private sector gets nothing. It does not mean, however, that the actual relative position of the various sectors follows the same ranking. Again with some simplification one may say, that the same ordering prevails regarding the following troubles and burdens: frequency and intensity of micro-interventions, inspections and auditing, especially interference with price and wage determination, and enforcement of tax laws. In these respects the informal private sector has the advantage of being farther away from the eyes of the bureaucracy. This is an important, although not the only reason why many people prefer, in spite of fewer formal favours, to work in sectors placed lower on the state's preference scale.

Bureaucratic and market coordination are thoroughly intertwined in all sectors. The lower we go on the state's preference scale, the more freedom for market coordination. That is not necessarily because the bureaucracy would deliberately grant this freedom, but at least partly because it is less able to apply the same methods to several thousands of business units or millions of individuals that it can to a few hundred large firms. But even the formal and informal private sectors do not work in a 'free' market; the bureaucracy regulates the scope of legality and has many other instruments of restriction and intervention.

There is a feeling of complementarity, but also a feeling of rivalry between the various sectors; and there are collisions between them. The sectors lower on the state's preference scale suffer because in many allocative processes regulated by the bureaucracy, they are 'crowded out' by sectors higher on the scale. At the same time, the same lower-preference sectors may be successful in 'crowding out' the favourites of the state in the competition on the market. The most important example, namely bidding for labour in short supply, has just been mentioned.

In short: the Hungarian economy is a symbiosis of a state sector under indirect bureaucratic control and a non-state sector, market oriented but operating under strong bureaucratic restrictions. Co-existence and conflict exist between the social sectors in many ways and all the time.

5.6 TENSIONS AND IMBALANCES

The idea of market socialism is associated with the expectation that the 'marketization' of the socialist economy creates equilibrium of supply and demand. It is a crucial litmus test of reform to see whether such equilibrium has been established in Hungary or whether tensions and imbalances characteristic of the former bureaucratic command economy have remained or others appeared.

5.6.1 The classical shortage economy
The prereform classical system in Hungary suffered from chronic shortages, and shortages are characteristic of other socialist economies. The first studies were Kornai [1957] (1959), Franklyn D. Holzman (1960), Herbert S. Levine (1966). The shortage phenomenon and its causal explanation are analysed in more detail in the author's book *Economics of Shortage* (1980). There is wide-spread excess demand on many markets, associated with queuing, forced substitution of less desired but available goods for the goods desired, forced postponement of purchases, and forced saving. Shortage phenomena torment both the consumer and the producer, the latter in his capacity as buyer of inputs. There is also excess demand for investment resources, for foreign exchange, and, in the more industrialized socialist economies, shortage of labour as well. There are spill-over effects: short supply of inputs creates bottlenecks retarding production and generating shortage elsewhere. The unreliability of deliveries induces hoarding of inputs. Shortage breeds shortage.[31]

Chronic shortages do not exclude the appearance of underutilized resources, excess capacities, and excess inventories. On the contrary, shortages even contribute to the creation of unnecessary surpluses, because of hoarding and because of frequent bottlenecks that leave complementary factors of production underutilized.

Chronic shortages damage consumer welfare; the buyer feels frustrated because of unsatisfied demand and/or forced adjustment to available supply. It means the dominance of the seller over the buyer: the latter is treated rudely and is frequently humiliated. In production, the disturbances of supply and improvised forced substitutions in input-output combinations cause losses of efficiency. The seller has a safe market and the buyer is willing to accept unconditionally what he gets. This leads to the most detrimental consequence of shortage: the lack of stimulus for quality improvement and product innovation.

Chronic shortage is the joint result of several interactive causal factors.

In spite of restrictive efforts on the side of macro-policy, there are systemic tendencies for demand to run to excess. The strongest force is the so-called *investment hunger,* the insatiable demand for investment resources. The hunger appears at all levels of hierarchical control, starting with the top policy makers and planners who seek high growth rates and ending with firms' and shops' managers, who also have a drive to expand. This is closely linked to the 'soft budget constraint' syndrome discussed in section 5.3.3. Because potential investment failure does not threaten severe consequences, there is little voluntary restraint on the claimant's demand for investment resources, that is, for project permits, subsidies, or credits. If the budget of the decision-maker is not strictly constrained, his desire to expand remains unconstrained as well.

The rush to investment is more intensive in periods when central economic policy is pushing more aggressively for accelerated, forced, growth. Central policy pulsates in this respect; stop and go periods, decelerations, and accelerations alternate causing cyclical fluctuations (Bauer 1978, 1981 H, Soós 1975–76, Mária Lackó 1980, 1984).

Demand for intermediate goods is amplified by the tendency to hoard mentioned before. The buyer does not insist on getting just what he needs right now, but is willing to purchase everything that may be of some use at a later time.

Demand of producers for imported intermediate goods is very strong. As a counterbalance, central policy wants to push exports. Importers' demand in foreign economies is, of course, constrained.[32] Yet the foreign trade companies in the socialist country are willing to sell at lower prices just to increase the total amount of foreign exchange earned by export. If dumping leads to losses domestically, the loss will be covered by the manifold instruments of the soft budget constraint. In other words, the demand of the state-owned foreign trade sector vis-à-vis producers of exportable goods is almost unlimited, adding a further component to runaway total demand.

Households have a hard budget constraint; in the classical system their income is under tight central control. Therefore excess household demand may or may not appear, depending on macro-demand management exercised, in the first place, through wage and consumer price policy. In some countries in certain periods, however, excess household demand is one of the main sources of runaway total demand (for example in Poland in the last 5-10 years.)

Relative prices are distorted. Many goods and services have absurdly low prices or are distributed free of charge, generating almost insatiable demand.

The adaptive properties of the system are poor for many reasons. That applies to short-term adjustment: quick modification of input-output combinations requires mobile reserves of all complementary factors at all points of production. If there are shortages of one or two factors, bottlenecks do not allow flexible adjustment. Long-term adaptation is also slow. Uncommitted slack capital should be available for entrepreneurs who want to make use of unforeseen opportunities. But the irresistible investment hunger ties up *ab ovo* all investment resources. The great concentration of net income in the central governmental budget, the bureaucratic procedures of project approval, and the lack of a capital market hinder a fast decentralized adjustment of investible resources.

Adaptation is also dependent on motivation. The producer-seller is in a contradictory position. On the one hand, he cannot be indifferent to the urging of the dissatisfied customer, who is supported by his own higher authorities in many cases. On the other hand, he is interested in preserving shortage, which makes his life easier on the output side, because he need not pay much attention to quality, delivery time, and costs.

The relative weight of the different shortage-causing factors is controversial (Soós, 1984, Szabó, 1985 H, Stanislaw Gomulka, 1985, Kornai, 1985a, b). There is, however, general agreement in that all these factors play an important role in explaining chronic shortage.

The issues described in sections 5.3.1, 5.3.2 and 5.3.3 – direct bureaucratic control, soft budget constraint, weak price responsiveness – and the problems discussed above concerning the causes and consequences of chronic shortage are closely interrelated, or more precisely, they are interacting properties of the same system. Chronic shortage is the necessary consequence of a system that is dominated by bureaucratic coordination and that almost totally excludes market coordination. At the same time, shortage is indispensable for the command economy as a legitimation ('rationing, intervention, taut planning are needed because of shortage'), as a stimulant ('produce more because your output is urgently demanded by the buyer'), and as a lubricant of the creaking mechanism of adaptation (in spite of poor quality, unreliable delivery, and poor adjustment to demand, all output is accepted).

5.6.2 Preservation and elimination of shortages

Hungary has moved away from the classical shortage economy. In important spheres the change is apparent. All observers agree that the supply of food and of many industrial consumer goods is much better in Hungary than it is in other Eastern European economies. In the winter of 1985–86, when the present chapter was written, Hungarian households are provided with electric energy and heating, while in Rumania and Bulgaria drastic measures were introduced to force people to cut energy consumption.

Highly visible signs of improvement notwithstanding, careful examination is needed, because the situation is complex and diverse. We focus on areas where shortages persist and start with a review of *consumer goods and services*.

Service supplied exclusively by non-business state organizations free of charge or at nominal prices.[33] The most important example is medical care. Almost insatiable excess demand prevails: long average waiting time for hospital admission (except for emergency), overcrowded hospitals and clinics, hurried examinations, and so on. There is legal private practice, but only for office visits to the physician. Shortage is accompanied by large gratuities to doctors and other medical staff.

Service supplied exclusively by state monopolies at effective prices. The most important example is the telephone service. Shortage is very severe in this field. The number of telephone lines increased at an annual rate of 4.5 per cent and the number of applications for a line at an annual rate of 7.6 per cent in the last 25 years. The average waiting time is getting longer and longer; at present it is about fifteen years *ceteris paribus.* The network is overutilized: customers have to wait a long time for a dial tone, lines are almost always busy, and wrong connections are frequent.

Goods and services supplied by a dual system. The most important example is housing. Most urban apartment houses are publicly owned and rented out at very low rates covering only a small fraction of construction and maintenance costs. Although the right to join the queue (different entitlements based on income, family size, etc.) has been subjected to more severe restrictions, the waiting time in the capital is still several years. The other subsector is composed of condominiums in private ownership, owner-occupied family houses, and sublets. In the private sector, prices and rents are very high. The market operates but with many frictions; real estate intermediaries are few (Dániel 1985).

Another example of duality is the allocation of cars. The supply of new cars is monopolized by a state-owned company. The average waiting time is two to three years. Supply responses tending to preserve shortage can be observed. If the growth of demand is retarded by price increase, authorities and the car sellers monopoly retard supply as well (Zsuzsa Kapitány, Kornai, and Szabó 1984, Ágnes Tibor 1984 H). About one-tenth of all new cars is sold to privileged customers jumping the queue. The other subsector is the private market for second-hand cars. Here, prices are determined by supply and demand.

Imported consumer goods. The bulk is both imported and distributed by state-owned firms. Supply is capricious. Equilibrium or excess supply occurs in some cases. Sometimes demand is created by introducing a new good imported from the West and then supply is cut, causing shortages. A small supplement is the private import of Hungarian tourists: imported (in many instances smuggled) goods are sold on the informal market.

Goods and services produced and sold simultaneously by various social sectors, including the formal and informal private sectors. A variety of situations exist. The most typical is equilibrium in the aggregate of a larger commodity group. For example, a sufficient quantity of 'shoes' or 'meat products' in the shops does not necessarily mean that demand is satisfied: frequently the consumer does not find the kind of shoe or meat product he is looking for, and must therefore resort to forced substitution. Excessive inventories and empty shelves may exist side by side. Concerning the attitude of the seller, in some markets one finds a healthy competition, where attention is paid to the demands of the customer. In some other markets, where shortage persists, the private seller exhibits all the well-known traits prevailing on a sellers' market: he can be rude, may try to cheat, and so on.[34]

As for *intermediate goods*, shortages are rather frequent. Firms do not suffer from brutal cuts of energy supply as in some other Eastern European countries or as in Hungary in the early fifties. It is rather the unreliability of deliveries that causes many losses. That is particularly true for imported intermediate goods, where short supply can cause great troubles in production (Gács, 1982). There is an enlightening index, the composition of inventories. In a shortage economy firms hoard on the input side and output is easily sold: therefore, the ratio of input inventories to output inventories is relatively high. In an economy where selling difficulties are predominant, the reverse tends to be true (Ervin Fábri, 1982, Attila Chikán, 1981, 1984 H). Table 5.8 shows that the Hungarian

Table 5.8: International comparison: composition of inventories in manufacturing industry

Country (Years of observation)	Ratio of input inventories to output inventories	
	Lowest	Highest
1. Austria (1975–76)	1.04	1.07
2. Canada (1960–75) .	1.06	1.40
3. United Kingdom (1972–77)	1.20	1.56
4. Hungary (1974–77)	5.72	6.38
5. Hungary (1978–84)	4.90	5.25

Sources: Rows 1–4: Chikán (1981, p. 84). Row 5: CSO H, 1979, p. 190; CSO H, 1980, p. 194. CSO H, 1981, p. 198; CSO H, 1982, p. 134; CSO H, 1983, p. 127; CSO H, 1984a, p. 130; CSO H, 1985a, p. 128.
Note: 'Input inventory' covers stocks of purchased materials and semifinished goods; 'output inventory' covers goods ready for sale. For more detailed definitions see the sources.

state-owned production sector is still closer to the characteristic situation of a sellers' than to that of a buyers' market.

As mentioned earlier, there is excess demand for credit in general, and for long-term investment credit in particular. Pressure for credit became stronger, because credit supply was cut in the late seventies. These cuts were parts of the general macroadjustment programme to improve Hungary's position on the international financial market. Following tough central intervention, investment activity and demand for investment goods fell off.

To sum up: Hungary today is less of a shortage economy than it was before the reform, and some segments have been able to rid themselves of tormenting shortages to some degree. The change has been due more to changes in the proportionate weight of the various social sectors and less to the changes within the dominant state sector. The formal and informal private sectors play a substantial role in filling the gap left by the state sector. But even then, shortages have not been eliminated, because many of their causes have not disappeared.[35] A vicious circle exists: recentralization contributes to the generation of shortages and shortages contribute to the trend of recentralization.

5.6.3 Inflation

Table 5.9. shows that inflation has accelerated in the past decade.[36] According to a wide-spread view, the acceleration in Hungary was caused by the reform. This is an oversimplification, although it is not without some truth. Before the reform started, prices and wages had been tightly controlled and fixed for longer periods.

Firms were not particularly interested in profits; hence they had

Table 5.9: International comparison of inflation

Rate of increase of average annual consumer price index (per cent)

	1960–67	1967–73	1973–78	1978–84
Austria	4.8	4.9	6.8	5.2
Finland	4.8	6.6	13.8	9.2
Portugal	3.4	9.3	22.1	22.9
Spain	4.1	6.8	18.8	13.9
Hungary	1.0	1.6	3.9	7.5

Sources: United Nations (1970, pp. 524–29), (1979, pp. 690–96), (1983b, pp. 200–206), and (1985b, pp. 220–24).

no strong reason to raise prices. Some creeping inflation, however, had been going on already long before the first reform measures (not sufficiently reflected in the official price indices). True, the reform relaxes price and wage control in many spheres and strengthened somewhat the firms' interest in higher profits. Yet these changes are not enough to constitute a full explanation of the acceleration; there are other explanatory factors at work as well.

First of all, in the last few years, central macro-policy has been deliberately using inflationary measures as instruments of an austerity program. Hungary has serious problems with foreign indebtedness and with the deterioration of the terms of Hungarian trade; policy-makers decided to shift the balance of trade from deficit to surplus by every means possible. As a precondition of such a shift, the growth of domestic consumption had to be stopped or cut back. Prices of many basic consumer goods and services were, therefore, raised again and again by government decrees accompanied by decisions to raise nominal wages as a partial compensation. The deliberate central price and wage increases have put in motion the whole price level, including prices and incomes in the formal and informal private sectors.[37] Using the terminology introduced in section 5.2.2, we can see that the change in *policy* and not the change in the system is the main causal factor. A similar policy was also applied in certain periods before the reform, for example, in the early fifties when the standard of living was deliberately kept down using the instrument of sudden price increases.

Central policy is ambivalent in this respect. While centrally decided price increases lead the inflationary process, there are official statements attacking managers of firms and the formal and informal private sectors for forcing prices up and for profiteering. Quite a few academic adherents of the reform show a similar ambivalence. They think that inflation, provided it is not too fast, may help the reform, because it makes the correction of distorted relative prices and wages easier. Actually, the same argument comes up also in the official statements justifying some of the price increases. Other economists, the author among them, feel that, with the protracted sequence of partial price increases, Hungary is walking a dangerous path. Each partial price rise has spill-over effects in costs of production and/or in the cost of living. The interminable series of partial upward corrections puts in motion the well-known *dynamic process* of the price-cost-wage-price spiral (Klára Csoór and Piroska

Mohácsi 1985 H). That can do much harm to the core of decentralization: to financial discipline and rational calculation based on prices and profits. Inefficiencies can be comfortably covered up by passing over cost increases to the buyer.

One last remark on the interaction between shortage, inflation, and reform. Shortage, acceleration of inflation, deficits in the trade balance, the growing burden of indebtedness, liquidity troubles, or any other type of tension and unhealthy disequilibrium are good excuses for recentralization. They provide legitimation for suppressing market forces and reviving tight control, formal and informal interventions, and rationing of intermediate goods. This is a trap, because recentralization solidifies the deeper systemic causes that created most of the troubles. In some cases recentralization is accompanied by solemn promises that the measures are only provisional and will be applied only as long as the troubles prevail. The trouble is that the provisional bureaucratic measures tend to become permanent, because they restore the systemic roots of the difficulties.

5.6.4 External imbalances

Disequilibrium in the balance of trade and current accounts is not a system-specific phenomenon; many non-socialist economies are suffering from the same problem. What deserves special attention in this paper are some characteristic linkages in Hungary between external imbalances on the one hand and systemic changes and macro-policies on the other.

There is an ongoing dispute in and outside Hungary about the cause of the external imbalances. Did they occur mainly because of the deterioration of external conditions (worsening terms of foreign trade, intensified protectionism of Western importers, less access to foreign credit, increase of interest rates), or because of the delayed and inefficient response to the changing conditions? Nobody denies that both classes of factors played a certain role; the controversy is about their relative importance. The author joins those who put the emphasis on the latter group of explanatory factors, that is, on the deficiencies of Hungarian adjustment to the changes in the external world.

The dividing point in the time series shown in Tables 5.10 and 5.11 is 1973–74, the first world-wide oil shock. Before this event Hungarian growth rates were rather similar to the rates achieved by European private market economies. (As in an earlier table, the small sample contains countries that are close to the level of development of Hungary.) There is, however, a striking difference in the response to the oil shock. While the capitalist economies sank into stagnation and recession following the oil shock, Hungary was progressing on the path of forced growth. The expansion drive continued without interruption; foreign credit was easily available. The accumulation of foreign debt was a consequence of two closely intertwined factors: macro-policy aiming at uninterrupted growth at any cost and the lack of genuine decentralization, that is, the inconsistencies in reforming the economy. It is difficult to separate 'policy' and 'system' in this respect. The incomplete change of the system produces (or at least intensifies) the expansionary policy at all levels of the hierarchy. Firms were sheltered from the losses due to the contraction of Western markets and the deterioration of the terms of foreign trade by softening the budget constraint and delaying appropriate changes of domestic relative prices.[38] This is striking evidence that the reform of the state-owned sector remained superficial: the national troubles were not 'decentralized' down to the firms, which consequently were not forced to adjust to the new world market situation. Instead of restraint in undertaking new investment and in carefully selecting projects well adapted to the new composition

Table 5.10: Indicators of growth in Hungary, 1957–84

	Average annual growth rates (per cent)			
	1957–67	1967–73	1973–78	1978–84
	(in real terms)			
1. National income	5.7	6.1	5.2	1.3
2. Investment	12.9	7.0	7.8	−3.0
3. Real wage per wage earner	2.6	3.1	3.2	−1.4
4. Consumption per capita	4.2	4.6	3.6	1.4
	1971–73	1973–78	1978–84	
5. Gross convertible currency debt				
In forints	13.8	20.0	9.1	
In USD	23.8	26.8	2.6	

Sources: Row 1: CSO H 1985a, p. 3; Row 2: CSO H 1985a, p. 4; Row 3–4: CSO 1985a, p. 17; Row 5: National Bank of Hungary

Table 5.11: International comparison of growth rates in construction
activity

	Annual growth rates (per cent)		
	1968–73	1973–78	1978–81
Austria	5.5	1.0	0.0ᵃ
Finland	3.9	1.1	1.8
Portugal	8.9	0.9	–
Spain	5.9	–2.1	–1.9
Hungary	6.6	5.7	–0.6

Sources: United Nations (1979, pp. 365–68; 1983a, pp. 827–30; 1985a, pp.
828–29.
Note: We use construction activity as a proxy for investment activity.
ᵃ Last period for Austria: 1979–80.

of external demand, an undiscriminating investment hunger continued and was even encouraged by the macro-policy of forced
growth.

Finally, after a long delay, macro-policy responded to the dangers
emerging in the external position of the country. Suddenly brakes
were applied: radical investment cuts followed by austerity measures
and a decline of real wages as mentioned earlier. Again, this has
been and has remained mostly a centralized policy. It is not the
market response of decentralized agents to price and quantity signals
(external prices and quantity signals converted into decentralized
domestic signals). Or more accurately, such decentralized signaling
plays only a relatively minor role. It is more a result of recentralization, a revival of administrative interventions in favour of important
substitution and of a costly forced export drive that helped in solving
the most burning troubles of trade imbalances and international
liquidity. Hungary's balance of trade improved: its credit worthiness
is rather exemplary compared to many other socialist and developing countries. But the deeper roots of external imbalances are alive.
Bureaucratic control, both direct and indirect, is incapable of
'fine tuning'. A system cannot have two faces: rigidities, delays in
deliveries, slow innovation and technical progress for domestic use
and the opposite for the foreign customer. Efficient foreign trade
can be assured only by a breakthrough in the reform process (Marer
1981, Balassa and Laura Tyson 1983, András Köves and Gábor
Obláth 1983).

5.6.5 Individual choice and distribution

We have now arrived at the end of the descriptive parts of the paper. There is one more problem to be raised before turning to the discussion of 'visions'. How do the systemic changes and the remaining or newly emerging tensions and imbalances affect the individual citizen? As shown in Table 5.10, real consumption was increasing impressively for a while, but was then followed by a slowdown. We pointed out in the previous section that the deceleration cannot be charged to the account of the reform. It is explained by an unfortunate coincidence of deteriorated external conditions, policy mistakes, and poor adjustment to the external changes due to the inconsistency of systemic change. Something more should be said, however, not about real consumption recorded in official statistics, but about a different aspect of the quality of life: the individual's rights of choice.

We limit the discussion to economic aspects; choice in political, cultural, and moral dimensions is not the topic of the present chapter. One more qualification: freedom of economic choice is not a simple question of 'yes' or 'no', but a matter of degree. We shall glance at the change in the degree of freedom in the different aspects of economic choice.

In the classical command economy the household could choose between marketed goods and services within its budget constraint. But the situation was very far from consumer sovereignty for many reasons.[39] A large part of total consumption was distributed through non-market channels by bureaucratic procedures as fringe benefits. As for the marketed part, chronic shortages created a situation in which the buyer bought not what he wanted but what he could get. Recurrent forced substitution is a violation of economic freedom. Prices did not reflect relative scarcities, and supply did not respond to prices. The consumer's choice had only a weak influence on the composition of supply. On the contrary, arbitrary relative consumer prices shaped demand.

A part of saving was forced by shortage; even after forced substitution some money remained practically unspendable. There was no choice between alternative schemes of sick care or retirement; these were fully institutionalized by bureaucratic arrangements. Savings could not be used for productive investment.

The individual's choice of work was limited. He was free from the great suffering of unemployment, but his choice of profession was, if not dictated, at least 'channelled' in the prescribed directions. The working place was assigned in many instances and movement to another job was greatly restricted by administrative prohibitions.

The great achievement of the Hungarian reform is the significant extension of choices. And the great shortcoming of the reform is that it did not go far enough in this extension.

Consumers' choice has become wider. Shortages are less intensive and less frequent, but they still exist. The domain of bureaucratically rationed goods and services has become narrower but has not been eliminated. There are goods and services where prices convey the consumers' signals to the producer, who responds to them with changes in supply. But this linkage is restricted to certain spheres, mainly where the consumer is served by the non-state sector and even there the functioning of the market is distorted. In the rest of the economy the composition of supply is controlled by a peculiar combination of influences: in part by legitimate protection furthered by well-considered plans that promote society's general long-term interests against myopic and individualistic decisions, but also by arbitrary paternalistic bureaucratic interference with the consumer's free choice,[40] and by the influence of the consumer's decision and, finally, also by merely random effects.

The choice set concerning saving and investment has become wider as well. The most important change is that individuals can invest in their own private housing instead of passively waiting for bureaucratic allotment. True, the purchase or building of a private house or condominium requires tremendous sacrifices caused by bureaucratic obstacles, shortages, and scarcity of credit. There are new options in holding financial assets, although the number of alternatives is still small. There is still little choice between alternative schemes of medical insurance or retirement.

The individual now has much more choice in deciding on a profession and job. Administrative restrictions of labour movements have been eliminated. The most important new opportunity is the impetus given to the formal and informal private sector. Those who feel they have entrepreneurial abilities have some (rather modest) possibilities of using them. Those who are willing to work more for the sake of higher consumption can enter the second economy. The study by Róbert Tardos (1983 H) showed that in response to the stagnation or decline of real wages, 47% of the families opted for working more in the first and second economy, because they wanted to maintain their standard of living. Again, the choice set is still rather restricted by frictions and administrative limits.

The problem of individual choice is strongly linked to income distribution. The prereform system associated the narrow limitations of individual choice with a certain type of egalitarian tendency. Income differentials of employees of the state-owned and cooperative sectors were moderate, although there was never a perfectly egalitarian distribution. Privileges existed for people higher up in the bureaucracy, not so much in the form of higher money wages as in perquisites: a service car, allotment of better housing, special shops with better supply, special hospitals and places of recreation and so on.

Table 5.12: Income distribution

| | Shares in total recorded money income (per cent) | | | |
	1967	1972	1977	1982
1st decile	4.1	4.0	4.5	4.9
2nd decile	6.0	5.9	6.3	6.4
3rd decile	7.1	7.0	7.3	7.3
4th decile	8.0	7.9	8.1	8.1
5th decile	8.9	8.8	8.9	8.8
6th decile	9.9	9.8	9.8	9.6
7th decile	10.9	10.8	10.8	10.7
8th decile	12.2	12.1	12.0	11.9
9th decile	14.0	14.0	13.7	13.7
10th decile	18.9	19.7	18.6	18.6
Measure of inequality	1.92	1.96	1.84	1.82

Sources: Column 1: CSO H, 1975a, p. 65.
Column 2, and 4: CSO H, 1985d, p. 13.
Note: The interpretation of the first 10 rows is as follows. The population is ranked in increasing order according to recorded per capita money income and divided into 10 classes. The first figure in the first column means: the poorest. 10% of the population received 4.1% of the total recorded money income of the population in 1967.

The term *recorded money income* excludes recorded but non-money income (for example benefits in kind), and also unrecorded income, mostly earned in the second economy.

The last row shows a synthetic measure of inequality calculated by the Central Statistical Office in Hungary. Income earners are divided into [two classes. Group 1: income earners above average; group 2: income earners below average. 'Measure of inequality': ratio of average income of group 1 to average income of group 2.

As mentioned earlier, the Hungarian economy achieved full employment and job security. The latter is a controversial issue; several economists point out negative side effects on working morale and on the artificial preservation of inefficient production lines. Income differentials in the first economy exhibit a mild decreasing trend as demonstrated in Table 5.12. There are suggestions that the rapid growth of the second economy counterbalanced this change or perhaps led to some increase of inequality, but there is no reliable evidence supporting these conjectures. Careful studies (Kolosi, 1980 H, Szelényi, 1983) show that Hungary now exhibits neither the characteristic inequalities prevailing in the prereform classical socialist system, nor the typical inequalities of a capitalist economy, but a peculiar combination of these. We still see differentials based on one's position in the hierarchy, but these appear less in the form of fringe benefits handed out in kind; they are more often reflected in money income differentials. (Although the shift is not complete, privileges in kind still exist.) At the same time, new inequalities have been created by the market, and in particular, by the appearance of the formal and informal private sector. While incomes at the upper end of distribution increased, social policy at the lower end did not develop sufficiently. For a long time, reformers had a one-sided technocratic orientation, concerned only with growth, efficient adaptivity, trade balance, and financial regulators and did not pay sufficient attention to the great moral objectives of social justice (Zsuzsa Ferge 1984 H).

In this respect as well, Hungary is a mixture of the distributional consequences of both bureaucracy and market.

5.7 CONFRONTATION OF VISIONS WITH REALITY

Having described the reformed Hungarian economy we turn to alternative visions of market socialism,[41] discuss past ideas (sections 5.7.1; 5.7.2) as well as contemporary Hungarian thinking (sections 5.7.3; 5.7.4). Some visions took the form of pure theory as in the Lange model; others are blends of normative theory and practical proposals.

5.7.1 Oscar Lange's market socialism
The literature of the celebrated debate about socialism in the thirties, including the original writings and the later appraisals, fill

up a library.[42] This chapter does not survey the literature but concentrates on Lange's classical paper (1936-37) which is the central piece in the debate.

The first question is a positive one: is the reformed Hungarian system a 'Lange economy' or anything that comes close to a Lange economy? Based on information provided by sections 5.3 and 5.4 the reader has the answer already: a definite 'no'.

Caution is needed in formulating a fuller reply. Lange presents in a brief paper a *model*. Model building inevitably abstracts from complications of reality irrelevant to the main line of argument. It is a cheap and unfair criticism of a theoretical model to point out that reality is richer than the model. With certain simplification we focus on the most substantial assumptions and properties of the theory, both in a comparison with Hungarian reality and in considering the criticism of the theory that follows later.

Because a description of the Hungarian system has been presented already, very brief references will suffice. Lange thought of the possibility that socialism would be a dual economy consisting of a public and a private sector, but he formulated his disputed suggestions for the sector in public ownership. Therefore, it is legitimate to compare the Lange model with the Hungarian state-owned sector.

The Lange economy has a Walrasian information structure. Sufficient information is provided by the price system and by the observation of excess demand. A trial and error method generates Walrasian equilibrium prices or at least prices that converge toward them. Agents respond to prices. In contrast to that, the prices of the output produced by Hungarian firms even since the reform are not Walrasian prices and do not converge to such prices. Official declarations do not reveal even an intention to generate market-clearing prices everywhere in the economy (Csikós-Nagy 1985 H). The prices of products or services originating in the state-owned sector do not reflect relative scarcities. The prices of products and services originating in the non-state sector may come closer to Walrasian prices but only with severe distortions. The non-market-clearing prices of the state sector spill over to the rest of the price system. Apart from the question whether prices give the right signal, the main problem is that price responsiveness of the state-owned firms is weak. They give as much or, in many cases, more attention to other signals.

In the Lange economy the firm is essentially a profit maximizer. In contrast, the Hungarian firm has multiple objectives; the search for more profit is only one of its set of objectives and not necessarily the strongest one. The profit incentive is weakened by the soft budget constraint syndrome. The firm's vertical dependence on the superior bureaucracy dominates its horizontal dependence on the market.

In the Lange economy the central authorities restrict their activities to price determination. In the Hungarian economy the bureaucracy is busy intervening in all dimensions of economic life. Intervention into price formation is only a small part of its hyperactivity.

The question is still open: is the establishment of a Lange economy viable and desirable? The first is the primary question, because in case of infeasibility, the second question loses relevance. Of course the experience of a single country cannot give a convincing answer, but can help in the reconsideration of speculative argumentation.

Lange's model is based on erroneous assumptions concerning the nature of the 'planners'.[43] The people at his Central Planning Board are reincarnations of Plato's philosophers, embodiments of unity, unselfishness, and wisdom. They are satisfied with doing nothing else but strictly enforcing the 'Rule', adjusting prices to excess demand. Such an unworldly bureaucracy never existed in the past and will never exist in the future. Political bureaucracies have inner conflicts reflecting the divisions of society and the diverse pressures of various social groups. They pursue their own individual and group interests, including the interests of the particular specialized agency to which they belong. Power creates an irresistible temptation to make use of it. A bureaucrat must be interventionist because that is his role in society; it is dictated by his situation. What is now happening in Hungary with respect to detailed micro-regulation is not an accident. It is rather the predictable, self-evident results of the mere existence of a huge and powerful bureaucracy. An inherent tendency to recentralization prevails (Teréz Laky 1980).

Lange's model is based on an equally erroneous assumption concerning the behaviour of the firm. He expects the firm to follow the Rule designed by the system engineer. But society is not a parlour game where the inventor of the game can arbitrarily invent rules. Organizations and leaders who identify themselves with their organizations have deeply ingrained drives: survival, growth, expansion of the organization, internal peace within the organization, power and prestige, the creation of circumstances that make the achievement of all these goals easier. An artificial incentive scheme, supported by rewards and penalties, can be superimposed. A scheme may support some of the unavowed motives just mentioned. But if it gets into conflict with them, vacillation and ambiguity may follow. The organization's leaders will try to influence those who imposed the incentive scheme or will try to evade the rules.

These remarks are well-known in the modern sociology, economics, and social psychology of bureaucracy, hierarchy and organizations. The Lange of the thirties, although a convinced socialist, lived in the sterile world of Walrasian pure theory and did not consider the socio-political underpinning of his basic assumptions.

Lange hoped that a market could be *simulated* by a bureaucratic procedure. This hope appears time and again in contemporary writings, for example in Hungary (Csikós-Nagy 1985 H). There is an inner contradiction in the logic of the idea. An army of bureaucrats is needed to adjust and readjust millions of prices almost continuously. The contemporary successor of Lange might say: determine with the aid of computers only price indices of large aggregates and give Rules to the actors prescribing calculation principles for breaking down the aggregates. This is happening, more or less, in Hungary. But as was said above, the firm can get around the calculation principles if these conflict with its interest. As a countermeasure, the authorities will add more detailed instructions, restrictions, and prohibitions. What emerges from this procedure is not a successfully simulated market, but the usual conflict between the regulator and the firms regulated by the bureaucracy.

The next objection concerns competition. Lavoie (1985) rightly points out that in the neoclassical debate about socialism, the emphasis shifted one-sidedly to the issue of computing the correct price signals. What got lost was the crucial Mises-Hayek-Schumpeter idea regarding 'rivalry'. In a genuine market process actors participate who want to make use, and can make use, of their specific knowledge and opportunities. They are rivals. In that sense the market is always in a state of dynamic disequilibrium. The total potential of all rivals normally exceeds actual demand. Some win and some lose. Victory brings rewards: survival, growth, more profit, more income. Defeat brings penalties: losses, less income, and in the ultimate case, exit. Using the vocabulary of this chapter, the Mises-Hayek-Schumpeter market implies a hard budget constraint and a buyers' market. As long as the system and the policy do not assure the prevalence of these two conditions, there is no genuine market. The great shortcoming of the Lange model is that it does not even contemplate these conditions and many of Lange's followers committed the same error.

This argument is related to our last remark. Lange had in mind a market using a Walrasian feedback mechanism that equilibrates supply and demand. There are, however, built-in tendencies in a centrally controlled system based on state ownership generating chronic excess demand in various spheres of the economy as described in section 5.6.

5.7.2 The naive reformers
This is a name given by the author to a group of economists who were the pioneers of the reform process. In Hungary, György Péter (1954a H, b H, 1956 H, 1967) must be mentioned first. Others are Sándor Balázsy (1954 H), Péter Erdős (1956 H), Tamás Nagy (1956 H), and István Varga (1957 H). The author, when writing his first book, *Overcentralization,* in 1955–56 (published in English in 1959), can be put in the same category.[44] Brus [1961] (1972) in Poland, Evsey G. Liberman [1962] (1972) in the Soviet Union, and Ota Sik (1967) in Czechoslovakia belong to the same group. This is an arbitrary and all too short list, just to illustrate the concept of naïve reformer. We refer here to early works of authors who, with the exception of Péter and Varga, are still alive; most have deviated more or less from their early theoretical position.

The group is heterogeneous; the members did not share identical opinions. We shall point out a few common characteristics. These seem to be all the more significant because it was exactly this set of common ideas that was so clearly reflected in the official resolutions and documents of the Hungarian reform in 1968.[45] What is more, rather similar ideas appear in Chinese official writings today. Most Hungarian economists have lost their naïveté through long and sometimes bitter experience. But many of their colleagues in other socialist countries, impatiently advocating the start of a reform, having no first-hand experience as yet, show the same naïveté today and are irritated by the critical attitude of Hungarians.

Before turning to critical remarks, first a word of acknowledgement. The fact that the author's early work is included in the list above must not restrain us, out of false modesty, from recognizing the intellectual and political courage of the pioneering works. The descriptive part of these studies contains a deep and still valid critical analysis of the prereform system. The prescriptive part points in the direction of the later practical reforms in Hungary and China and to the reform attempts in Czechoslovakia and Poland: firms' autonomy, right price signals, profit incentive, use of market forces, shift toward a buyers' market, and so on. But the pioneers did not foresee many complications which, as it turned out, are the barriers to consistent applications of their proposals.

The naïve reformer does not recognize the conflicts between indirect bureaucratic control and the market. He thinks that abandoning the command system and turning from direct to indirect control is a sufficient condition for the vigorous operation of a market. His line of thought can be characterized as follows. Let us have a profit-maximizing, almost autonomous firm. It will respond with appropriate changes of supply and demand to the signals of relative prices, interest rates, taxes, credit rations. If so, there is no contradiction between central regulation and market. On the contrary, the market is an 'instrument' in the hands of the central policy-maker. The officers in the central authorities pull all the strings of indirect control and the profit-maximizing agents respond like obedient puppets. As Hungarian experience demonstrates, this fundamental assumption is wrong.

The underlying philosophy is an optimistic belief that perfect harmony can be achieved or at least approached. A market is a rather good, but not perfect automation. Market imperfections should be corrected by central interventions, because the centre knows social interests *ex officio* better than do blind market forces. The naïve reformers admit that central planners are not infallible. But then, planners' imperfections can be eliminated with the aid of the market, which makes some corrections automatically. The faith placed in the harmonious, mutually correcting duality of 'plan' and 'market' (or, in the language of the present chapter, bureaucracy and market) is the centrepiece of the pioneers' naïveté.

The coexistence of bureaucratic and market coordination does not guarantee that we get 'the best of both worlds'. It does not lead inevitably to the opposite case either, — 'the worst of both worlds'. These are extreme simplifications. Certain mutual corrections are possible. If market forces lead to income distribution that is judged to be unfair by society, or to undesirable externalities damaging to the environment and so on, the bureaucracy can and should apply corrective measures. (Even these corrections, however, are not made sufficiently in Hungary.) If state interventions have undesirable side effects, market disequilibria can give a signal and the planner can make adjustments provided that he listens to the signal. But such favourable complementarity cannot be relied on too much. As section 5.3.5 pointed out, the greater the bureaucratic intervention, the more one intervention weakens the effect of the other. Each string puller thinks that he can control the firm; the firm, confused by a hundred strings, starts to twitch. It does not respond clearly to bureaucratic regulation, but does not respond to market signals either. This is what László Antal (1979) aptly termed the 'illusion of regulation'.

The naïve reformers searched for a reasonable line of separation between the role of the bureaucracy and the role of the market. Many of them thought that such a separation line could be drawn like this: 'simple reproduction' (in Marxian terms) regulated by the market and 'extended reproduction' by the planners. In other words, current production controlled by the market and investment by the planner. It turned out that this separation is not viable. On the one hand, the bureaucracy is not ready to restrict its activity to the regulation of investment. On the other hand, the autonomy and profit motive of the firm become illusory, if growth and technical development are separated from the profitability and the financial position of the firm and are made dependent only on the will of higher authorities.

The pioneer reformers wanted to reassure all members of the bureaucracy that there would be ample scope for their activity. Their intention is understandable. The reform is a movement from 'above', a voluntary change of behaviour on the side of the controllers and not an uprising from 'below' on the side of those who are controlled. There is, therefore, a stubborn inner contradiction in the whole reform process: how to get the active participation of the very people who will lose a part of their power if the process is successful. The reassurance worked too well in the Hungarian case; the bureaucracy was not shattered. The number of people employed by the apparatus of economic administration changed hardly at all (Kornai 1984). Small wonder that, instead of the harmonious coexistence of 'plan' and 'market' or the establishment of a 'regulated market', we got the phenomenon of dual dependence, described in section 5.3.2 which actually gives dominant influence to the bureaucracy. And as was explained earlier, once bureaucratic intervention exceeds a certain critical threshold, the market is more or less deprived of energy.

The naïve reformers were concerned with the problems of the state-owned sector and did not spend much hard thought on a reconsideration of the non-state sectors' role. It turned out, however, that up to the present time, it has been just the non-state sectors that have brought the most tangible changes into the life of the economy.

5.7.3 Galbraithian socialism

The present Hungarian economic community cannot be easily classified. In a certain sense, every economist and government official is an adherent of reform: reform is the officially declared policy of the political leadership and the government. What really matters is not general notions but the concrete appraisal of the present system and the practical proposals for the future. In these respects the views are heterogeneous; debates go on about dozens of issues. We economists who agree about one issue may disagree about a second. Each individual has his own personal collection of criticisms and proposals. Nevertheless, for the orientation of the foreign reader this section and the next will delineate two 'schools'. A warning is in order: there is some arbitrariness in my characterizations. Those who undeniably belong to one or other school may still maintain some individual reservations or dissents. What we present are rather stylized 'prototypes' of two somewhat amorphous currents of thought.

We call the first school *Galbraithian socialism*. This is a name coined by the author; it may easily be that neither the members of the school nor Galbraith would be pleased. Anyway, Galbraith's work is a very characteristic reference in the writing of the school (László Horváth 1976 H, Ferenc Kozma 1983a H, b H, Tamás Sugár 1984 H, Andrea Szegő 1983a H, b H). A dispute, marked sometimes by rather sharp polemics, goes on between them and the school of *radical reformers* whose thoughts will be reviewed in the next section. The ideas of the first school can be understood best in the framework of the dispute.

The Galbraithians contend that the radicals advocate an anachronistic system. The radicals, they say, want to introduce a mechanism into a socialist economy that would recall early 19th-century Manchester capitalism: a market free from any governmental intervention and the predominance of small economic units. They are socialistic Friedmanites — so the rebuke goes — although the true nature of contemporary capitalism is quite different. And here comes the emphatic reference to John Kenneth Galbraith (1967a, b) and to other authors describing modern private market economies. Contemporary capitalism is a dual economy. The first sector is a small group of huge and very powerful corporations, many of them in monopolistic or oligopolistic positions, intertwined with and sheltered by the government. It operates in an environment created by a large and powerful bureaucracy that intervenes in the economy continuously through Keynesian demand management, price and wage regulation, protectionist measures, and so on. The second sector is composed of small producers, small merchants, and the households, whose activities are coordinated by the market. Although both sectors do exist, the first is the really powerful and dominant one and the second is ancillary and subservient. If that is true in case of modern capitalism — so the argument of the Galbraithian school goes — there is no reason to require more decentralization in socialism. On the contrary: a socialist system has the possibility and the obligation to apply central planning and coordination more consistently and establish more thorough links between the central planners and the large enterprises. The crucial role of central planning must not be disguised bashfully, but should be openly and proudly declared and, of course, much better organized than before. The large monopolies, oligopolies, and the state associated with them must become 'entrepreneurial'; 'entrepreneurship' should not be a privilege of the small units.

The Galbraithian school is accused in some writings of desiring the restoration of the prereform command economy. As far as their published writings are concerned, these do not suggest a return to an all-embracing command economy. What they do suggest is the legitimation of the *status quo*. They justify the dualities of the present system: the coexistence of public and private sectors, bureaucracy and market, large and small firms, provided that the first component in all these pairs has the undisputed upper hand. Some of their writings suggest that they do not have much confidence either in the market or in the private sector and would rather see their roles diminished. They would legitimate the actual state of affairs, suggesting minor changes for improvement, but reject any further radical change that would go much beyond the present situation. For that purpose the school proposes to utilize all theoretical results and practical experience of contemporary capitalism: Kaleckian and Keynesian macro-economics, the textbooks of Western business schools, the lessons drawn from study tours to ministries, large banks and corporations in industrialized countries. Every bit of experience that points in the directions outlined above is welcome.

It is, of course, a paradoxical 'ideological' support for present Hungarian practice to say: 'Look, the system is in many respects not so very different from the practice of modern capitalism.' The trouble is that the similarity is exaggerated. True, modern capitalism is a system very different from a perfectly competitive atomistic Walrasian world. Admitting that, there are decisive differences between today's Hungarian economic mechanism and the system of highly developed capitalist economies (the 'West' for short in what follows). Without seeking completeness we underline only a few attributes relevant in the present context.

There is a state- and a non-state sector in the agriculture, industry, and commerce of both systems, but the proportions are radically different. The state sector is dominant in Hungary, while it is an important but minor sector in the West.

There are powerful large firms in both systems, but the size distribution is very different. The concentration in Hungary is much higher than in the West, as shown in Table 5.3.

The 'soft budget constraint' syndrome appears in both systems. In Hungary it is the normal way of life; in the West similar phenomena are more nearly an exception. Related to this is the issue of price responsiveness, which is rather weak in the Hungarian state-owned sector and strong in Western business life, including large corporations.

There are bureaucratic interventions in both systems. In Hungary it is all-encompassing; millions of micro-interventions make the astate-owned firm highly dependent on the authorities. In the West the influence of the governmental bureaucracy is not negligible, but the frequency and intensity of intervention are much smaller. By and large it does not exceed the critical threshold where the vigour of the market would be diminished.

Shortage and surplus coexist in both systems. In Hungary shortages are wide-spread; strong competition of the sellers for the favour of the buyer is rather exceptional. In the West, the reverse is true. Shortages appear sporadically, but the typical situation is rivalry between competitors for the buyers' attention. That applies not only to small business but to the large corporations as well. They too feel the threat of actual or potential competition, of new-comers, large or small, of new products brought to the market by firms in the same sector or in other sectors, and also the competition of foreign sellers.

In the dialectics of the debate, however, the proponents of the 'Galbraithian' school deserve full attention, because they put their fingers on some weak points in the argumentation of the other school, the radical reformers.

5.7.4 The radical reformers

This is not a group with a commonly accepted consistent reform programme. We are talking about economists working in different research institutes or in the apparatus of some higher authorities who share more or less similar opinions about the reform. The most characteristic writings are those of Nyers and Tardos (1978, 1979, 1984), Tardos (1986), Bauer (1984, 1985a), Antal (1985a H, 1985b), but there is a much larger set of articles written in a similar spirit.[46]

Radical reformers elaborate profound critical analyses of the present situation; this chapter has made extensive use of these studies. We focus here on their normative proposals. Out of the fragments a blueprint of market socialism takes shape. These are more circumspect suggestions than those of the naïve reformers of 20–30 years ago. The main ideas may be summarized as follows.

A system of market-clearing prices is needed; this and only this price determination principle is acceptable. Price determination must be left to the market. Deviation from these principles can be allowed only exceptionally. Profit incentives should be strengthened to make them sufficiently responsive to prices. Beyond that, new incentive schemes must be introduced; firms should be stimulated to try to increase their net worth as their primary goal.[47]

The distortion of the size distribution should be corrected. It would be good to encourage the appearance of medium- and small-size economic units by a variety of policies to support the free entry of new units and the breakup of monopolies or overconcentrated, excessively large units. Large firms are needed only when they generate economies of scale and are able to operate successfully in world-wide competition.

Barriers to competition must be eliminated. Various forms of competition should be promoted: rivalry between units belonging to different social sectors between large, medium, and small units between domestic production and import.

A reform of the system dedicated consistently to these objectives, together with appropriate macro-policy, should greatly extend the scope of the buyers' market.

Barriers to a free labour market must be eliminated. The state sector must not be at a disadvantage relative to the rest of the economy in acquiring labour. More flexibility of wage determination is needed.

Tough financial discipline, the hardening of the budget constraint, must be assured. This effort must be combined with more decentralization in the allocation of funds and with the creation of a flexible capital market. The possibility of bankruptcy must be an ultimate threat. At the same time, prosperous firms must have the opportunity to expand quickly by self-financing, by loans or by raising capital on the capital market. As a precondition for such changes the share of the government budget in the total flow of income must be diminished.

A commercial banking system must be fully developed and must operate according to business principles.

More competition must be allowed in export and import activities. Realistic exchange rates must become more influential. Conditions of import liberalization and full convertibility must be created.

Laws are needed that protect private business and clarify unambiguously the legal possibilities and limitations of private activities.

Political conditions of systemic economic changes must be created; the various social and economic groups must get appropriate political representation. At the same time, the state must continue to play an active role in the economy. Its main obligations are the macro-management of demand, the regulation of monopolies, the development of the infrastructure, the protection of society against harmful externalities, the redistribution of personal income for the sake of social justice.

The changes listed above and perhaps a few more important measures must be introduced in a consistent manner, as a 'package'.

Any one of these changes, implemented separately without the appropriate conditions created by the other necessary changes can be risky or harmful.

The author is convinced that the implementation of these proposals is highly desirable. Yet quite a few substantial questions are left open. The problem of ownership and property rights is not clearly elaborated in the writings of the radical reformers. This large issue can be divided into two subproblems.

First, what should be the future of non-state ownership and, in particular, private ownership in the blueprint of a reformed socialist system? Can its share be enlarged? Is a small unit with seven employees the upper limit of a private enterprise acceptable in a socialist country?

Second, is the traditional form of state ownership compatible with the proposed changes listed above, including strong profit motivation, free entry, hard budget constraint, flexible wage determination, workable capital market?[48] Different authors offer various solutions for separating the firms' management from the governmental bureaucracy. Some economists suggest labour-management, because that might assure independence from the bureaucracy (Bauer 1984, István Csillag 1983 H).[49] There are counterarguments: the history of Yugoslav labour-management and also the first experiences with the participation of employees in the selection and appointment of managers are not sufficiently reassuring. Others, for example Tardos (1982), suggest the separation of management from a special institution that would be the declared representative of 'ownership interests'. The latter, like a board of directors in a capitalist joint stock corporation would appoint and supervise the managers. Critics are sceptical: can ownership interest be simulated by an artificially created body, which is commissioned (by whom? by the bureaucracy?) to represent society as the 'owner'?

Many arguments put forward in earlier sections of this chapter come to mind. Is genuine autonomy of the public firm under the conditions of the Hungarian political structure feasible? Will the bureaucracy observe a voluntary restraint of its own activity without exceeding the limits assigned by the proposals surveyed above?

Such questions lead to the ultimate problem: can a reform process in a socialist country go much beyond what has been accomplished in Hungary? Or does contemporary Hungary exhibit more or less the ultimate limits of reform?[50] Other minor systemic changes, whatever their desirability, are irrelevant when considering the essence of this question.

The author must frankly confess his own ambivalence. As a Hungarian citizen he sincerely hopes that the answers to the series of questions raised above will be positive. As an occasional adviser he may try to help the process go in the direction outlined. As a researcher he reserves the right to doubt.

One lesson that can be safely drawn from study of the socialist economies is the large degree of unpredictability as far as deep system-wide changes are concerned. The questions raised above cannot be answered by speculation, only by historical experience. Up to now, Hungary does not provide a conclusive answer. We must wait and see what may be revealed by Hungarian or Yugoslav or Chinese experience or by the history of any other socialist country that may take the route of reform.

NOTES

1. This chapter refers to works in English or in Hungarian. The latter references are distinguished by the letter 'H' in the text.

   The tables of the chapter frequently refer to reports of the Central Statistical Office, published in Hungarian. To save space, the tables indicate the source only in the following general form: CSO H. The supplementary bibliography provides detailed information about the CSO sources for each table.

2. A brief sample of summary reviews and appraisals of the Hungarian reform: Rezső Nyers and Márton Tardos (1979), József Bognár (1984), László Antal (1985a H), in the Hungarian literature; Richard Portes (1977), Béla Balassa (1978, 1983), Edward A. Hewett (1981), Paul Hare, Hugo Radice, and Nigel Swain (1981), Paul Marer (1986a, b) in the foreign literature. My intellectual debt to these works is gratefully acknowledged.

3. The history of the reform, including its intellectual history is surveyed in Iván T. Berend (1983 H) and Iván Pető and Sándor Szakács (1985 H). The studies of László Szamuely (1982, 1984) and János Mátyás Kovács (1984 H) discuss mainly intellectual history.

4. The literature of comparative economics offers various, mostly overlapping interpretations of the notion *economic system*. See for example Egon Neuberger and William Duffy (1976) and John M. Montias (1976).

5. For further elaboration see Kornai (1984). The influence of Max Weber [1922] (1947), Karl Polányi (1944), Charles Lindblom (1977), Oliver Williamson (1975), and György Konrád and Iván Szelényi (1979) is acknowledged.

6. The term *bureaucratic* is frequently used pejoratively in the Eastern European literature. The present chapter does not follow this usage: according to

the Weberian tradition, the term is a value-free denomination of a particular form of coordination.

7. Other basic 'pure' forms exist also. As important as these might be, for our topics the consideration of forms No. 1 and No. 2 will be sufficient.
8. The size of the officially unrecorded output will be discussed later.
9. More detailed description in English can be found in David Granick (1954), Joseph Berliner (1957), Balassa (1959). Wlodzimierz Brus [1961] (1972), Alec Nove (1983, a , b). Morris Bornstein (1981), Gregory and Stuart (1981).
10. Here and throughout the paper we do not discuss the role of the Party separately. The Party is not simply a political movement as in a non-socialist country, but also an apparatus in charge of running all affairs. Although from a legalistic point of view the Party and the government are separate entities, in practice they are intertwined and they work jointly in all relevant control processes. The Party has the leading role in the joint operation. Hence the term *bureaucracy* or *bureaucratic control* in this paper refers to the role played by the Party apparatus.
11. The problem has been discussed in Eastern Europe since the fifties. There the phenomenon is called 'base-year approach'. The Western literature introduced the apt name 'ratchet principle' (Berliner 1957, Michael Keren 1972, Keren, Jeffrey Miller, and James R. Thornton 1983).
12. This observation and a few more to which we refer in the chapter are based on a large-scale project examining the balance sheets of all Hungarian state-owned firms during 1975–82. This project is directed by the author and Ágnes Matits; results are discussed in Kornai and Matits (1983 H, 1984), Matits (1984a H, b H, c H), and Éva Várhegyi (1986 H). See also Mihály Laki (1982, 1984), Galina Lamberger, György Matolcsy, Erzsébet Szalai, and Éva Voszka (1986 H), Gábor Papanek, Péter Sárkány, and Erzsébet Viszt (1986 H).
13. Two remarks. First, a manager's bonus is linked to post-tax profitability, giving the manager an extra stimulus to fight for less tax and more subsidy. Second, profit sharing is levelled off; in contrast to the high variance of profitability, the ratio of profit sharing and wage per worker has a very small variance (Kornai and Matits 1983 H, 1984).
14. The 637 product aggregates cover about 75 per cent of total manufacturing.
15. Portes (1972, p. 657) made the same general point much earlier, writing that 'there is a threshold beyond which decentralization must go to take firm roots', He was, however, rather confident that Hungarian 'strategy and tactics has brought the reform across this border'. These views were shared by many outside observers. The opinion expressed in the present chapter is different: the Hungarian reform did not cross the critical threshold that separates a genuine market economy (associated with a certain degree of bureaucratic intervention) from an economy basically controlled by the bureaucracy (with certain elements of market coordination).
16. The cooperative members are entitled to a household plot not larger than 0.57 hectares.
17. See Gábor Agonács et al. (1984 H) and Gyula Tellér (1984 H) for important studies about the indirect bureaucratic control of cooperatives.
18. Agricultural cooperatives are much more sheltered. Small wonder that this

segment of the economy stubbornly opposes the introduction of bankruptcy laws and other measures of hardening the budget constraint.

19. All these differences are smaller and the similarities greater between *large*
cooperatives and state-owned enterprises.

20. The most important Hungarian writings are by István R. Gábor (1979,
1985), Gábor and Péter Galasi (1981 H), Tamás Kolosi (1979 H), Pál Belyó
and Béla Drexler (1985 H), János Timár (1985a H, b H), and Katalin
Falus-Szikra (1986). In the foreign literature pioneering work was done by
Gregory Grossman (1977) concerning the Soviet second economy; a detailed
bibliography is presented in Grossman (1985).

21. Here we follow more or less the definition of the second economy used by
Gábor, the leading Hungarian expert in the field.

22. As mentioned in the note to Table 5.5, many individuals have a first job in
the state or cooperative sector and a second job in the formal private sector.
Although we count this activity as part of the formal private sector, the
comments above concerning the extension of working time apply also to
this group.

23. Source: CSO H (1984, p. 470), (1985b, p. 10).

24. Tenants in a public apartment have in practice a 'quasi ownership' under
the conditions of chronic shortage. Tenancy can be inherited, sold for
money illegally to a new tenant or legally to the state. Therefore it is not
out of place to put the arrangement of subletting in a public apartment
in the same category as using the equipment of a first-economy employer.

25. The Hungarian ratio in 1980 was somewhat higher even than the ratio of
Sweden, Denmark, and the Netherlands, although all three countries are at
much higher level of development and spend relatively much more on welfare purposes. The ratio of governmental expenditure on production
(mainly investment and subsidies) in industry, agriculture, transport, commerce, and service as a percentage of GDP was 25 in Hungary and less
than 9 in the average of a sample of 14 industrialized capitalist countries.
The figures are calculated on the basis of definitions assuring comparability.
They refer to the same set of expenditures (including central and local governmental expenditures). GDP is calculated according to Western definitions for Hungary.
Source of all data is Muraközy (1985 H, pp. 746–47) and an unpublished
paper of Muraközy.

26. Because space is limited, we cannot discuss the same issue as far as other
social sectors are concerned.

27. This is only partly a sign of healthy 'commercialization' of trade relationships. A large fraction of trade credit is involuntary; the buyer simply does
not pay the bill in the agreed time, in this way forcing the seller to grant
credit. Actually this arrangement is becoming a common method of
'softening the budget constraint'. Involuntary trade credit was, of course,
known before the reform.

28. This phenomenon indirectly supports the observation that state-owned
firms are not highly profit motivated. They are more interested in the
expansion of their own capacity.

29. The interest rate paid for a one-year deposit to households by the savings

bank is 5 per cent, while the inflation rate in the last few years has been about 6–9 per cent according to the official statistics.

30. In some instances large agricultural cooperatives get more favourable treatment than small state-owned firms.

31. There is an important school of thought (frequently called, rightly or wrongly, the 'disequilibrium school') dealing with centrally planned economies which denies that shortage is chronic in the classical prereform socialist system or at least on the consumer market of this economy. The intellectual leader of this school is Richard Portes (Portes and David Winter 1977, 1978, 1980; Portes, Richard Quandt, Winter and S. Yeo 1983; Portes 1986). Many remarkable and valuable studies have been produced using the theoretical ideas and econometric methods of this school. An extended bibliography can be found in Portes 1986.

The author has an ongoing debate with the disequilibrium school (Kornai 1980, 1982). The controversy concerns questions of aggregation, measurement and interpretation of the notion of aggregate excess demand, the insulation of the consumer market from the rest of the economy, independence versus co-determination of demand and supply, the existence of forced saving, the relationship between shortage and labour supply, etc. This is not the place to go into these controversial issues. We shall come back to some empirical results of the disequilibrium school in the next section.

32. Except for the import hunger of other shortage economies for certain goods.

33. Each price has a critical value. Under this value the own-price elasticity of demand is zero; that is, the price is nominal. Above the critical value the own-price elasticity of demand is non-zero; that is, the price is effective. Many goods and services have nominal prices in socialist economies.

34. The attitude of the seller vis-à-vis the buyer is determined by the seller's membership in a certain social sector (state-owned firm versus private business) and by the state of disequilibrium in the market (sellers' versus buyers' market). Hungarian experience shows that the second factor is the more important.

35. The most important Hungarian representative of the disequilibrium school mentioned in footnote 31 is Katalin Hulyák (1983 H, 1985 H). Based, at least partly, on a different theoretical foundation and the estimation methods applied by Portes and his associates, her empirical results are in conformity with the observations presented above. She demonstrates chronic excess demand for housing, automobiles, and investment resources. As for aggregate consumption, she shows fluctuations in the intensity of general shortage. The chronology and the signs of the fluctuations are closely correlated with fluctuations revealed by other studies, for example Kornai (1982).

36. We compare Hungary with a small sample of capitalist countries that are close to the Hungarian level of development (measured by GDP/capita). We do not make comparisons with other socialist countries concerning inflation rates, because adequate information about the statistical methodology of constructing price indices in these countries is not available.

Many analysts agree that some hidden inflation exists in all socialist countries all the time. Certain kinds of price increases are not sufficiently reflected in the official price indices because of systematic bias in measurement methods (Kornai 1980, section 15.4, and Domenico M. Nuti 1985).

37. Unfortunately, the observation of prices and incomes in the formal and informal private sectors is not organized in a satisfactory manner. Petschnig (1985a H, 1985b H) provides many examples of the fact that price increases in these sectors are much faster than in the rest of the economy.

38. The effect of the oil shock was also dampened by the fact that Hungary could obtain Soviet energy at prices below world market level.

39. The problem is discussed in a wider context by Ferenc Fehér, Ágnes Heller, György Márkus (1983).

40. The arbitrariness of intervention in consumer choice is demonstrated by the high dispersion of turnover tax rates on consumer goods. No reasonable social preference imposed on individual preferences can explain a turnover tax of +11 per cent on household chemicals, +5 per cent on shoes, of −11 per cent on sugar and of −26 per cent on fish (Csikós-Nagy 1985 H, p. 58).

41. The alternative visions of *market* socialism are only a small subset of the much larger variety of visions concerning alternative forms of socialism.

42. The most outstanding works in the Great Debate were Enrico Barone [1908] (1935), Ludwig von Mises [1920] (1935), Fred M. Taylor (1929), Friedrich Hayek (1935), and, of course, Lange's paper. The classical summary is Abram Bergson's (1948) review. Important new points have been added by Bergson (1967), Alec Nove (1983), and Don Lavoie (1985).

43. What Lange had in mind concerning the role of the Central Planning Board and the market when he wrote his paper is controversial. In a private letter addressed to Hayek he stressed the importance of market forces directly determining prices in sectors where genuine competition prevails (Tadeusz Kowalik 1984). This chapter does not discuss Lange's thinking in the thirties, but the so-called Lange model as perceived by the profession (in textbooks and papers referring to Lange) from the time of publication up to now.

44. References to surveys are listed in footnote 2.

45. The most significant documents can be found in the collection by Henrik Vass (1968 H). See also the book of Nyers et al. (1969). Nyers was the secretary of the party in charge of economic affairs at the time of the 1968 measures and can be regarded as the chief architect of the 1968 blueprint.

46. A pioneer of radical reform was Tibor Liska (1963 H, 1969 H). Later he elaborated a blueprint of socialism based on leasing state-owned capital to individuals. His ideas are clearly distinguishable from the proposals of other radical reformers listed above. Space does not permit me to take up his suggestions and their criticism. Liska's program is discussed in Jenő Bársony (1982), Norman Macrae (1983), and István Siklaky (1985 H).

47. This is a reasonable desideratum. Unfortunately the doubts raised in earlier sections against the viability of artificial 'rules', 'incentive schemes' imposed on living organizations with inherent endogenous motivations, apply to this proposal too.

48. This is an objection raised repeatedly by the opponents of these proposed changes. Szegő (1983b H).
49. A comprehensive survey is presented in Tamás Sárközy (1982).
50. Those few sentences require additional explanation. The socialist system referred to in this study and in the other writings in this book has certain specific distinguishing marks: 1. the communist party exercises undivided political power. 2. Marxism-Leninism serves as the official ideology, and 3. state ownership is predominant. These attributes are assumed in the lines above when the limits to the reform process are discussed. If any essential change should occur in any of these three fundamental attributes, that counts not as a reform of the prevailing system any longer but as a *revolutionary* transformation, i. e. a transition from one system into another, even if it takes place gradually and without any violence.

In this sense the events that were taking place in Hungary and Poland in 1988 and 1989 went beyond the limits, of what this book refers to as a 'reform process'. (An additional note appended by the author in August 1989 while the English edition was being prepared.)

REFERENCES

This list does not include works in Hungarian. These are distinguished in the text by letter 'H' (See Note 1.)

Antal, László (1979) 'Development with Some Digression. The Hungarian Economic Mechanism in the Seventies', *Acta Oeconomica, 23*, pp. 257–273.

Antal, László (1985b) 'About the Property Incentive', *Acta Oeconomica, 34*, pp. 275–86.

Balassa, Béla (1959) *The Hungarian Experience in Economic Planning*. New Haven: Yale U. Press.

Balassa, Béla (1978) 'The Economic Reform in Hungary. Ten Years After', *European Economic Review*, Oct. *11*, pp. 245–268.

Balassa Béla (1983) 'Reforming the New Economic Mechanism in Hungary', *J. Comparative Economics*, September 7, pp. 253–276.

Balassa Béla and Tyson, Laura (1983) *Adjustment to External Shocks in Socialist and Private Market Economics*, Mimeo. Washington, DC: World Bank Development Research Department.

Barone, Enrico (1935) 'The Ministry of Production in the Collectivist State', in *Collectivist Economic Planning*, Ed.: Friedrich A. Hayek. London: Routledge & Kegan Paul (1908), pp. 245–290.

Bársony, Jenő (1982) 'Tibor Liska's Concept of Socialist Entrepreneurship', *Acta Oeconomica, 28*, pp. 422–455.

Bauer, Tamás (1976) 'The Contradictory Position of the Enterprise Under the New Hungarian Economic Mechanism', *Eastern European Economics*, Fall, *15*, pp. 3–23.

Bauer, Tamás (1978) 'Investment Cycles in Planned Economics', *Acta Oeconomica, 21*, pp. 243–260.

Bauer, Tamás (1984) 'The Second Economic Reform and Ownership Relations: Some Considerations for the Further Development of the New Economic Mechanism', *Eastern European Economics*, Spring/Summer 22, pp. 33–87.

Bauer, Tamás (1985a) 'Reform Policy in the Complexity of Economic Policy', *Acta Oeconomica, 34,* pp. 263–274.

Bauer, Tamás (1985b) 'The Unclearing Market', Mimeo. Institute of Economics.

Bergson, Abram (1948) 'Socialist Economics', in *A Survey of Contemporary Economics.* Ed.: Howard S. Ellis, Homewood, IL: Irvin, pp. 1412–1448.

Bergson, Adam (1967) 'Market Socialism Revisited', *Journal of Political Economy* October, 75, pp. 655–673.

Berliner, Joseph S. (1957) *Factory and Manager in the USSR.* Cambridge, MA: Harvard U. Press.

Bognár, József (1984) 'Further Development in Economic Reforms', *The New Hungarian Quarterly*, Autumn, 25 (95), pp. 45–54.

Bornstein, Morris, ed. (1981) *The Soviet Economy: Continuity and Change.* Boulder, CO, & London: Westview Press.

Brus, Wlodzimierz (1972) *The Market in a Socialist Economy.* London: Routledge & Kegan Paul (1961).

Chikán, Attila (1981) 'Market Disequilibrium and the Volume of Stocks', in *The Economics and Management of Inventories.* Ed.: Attila Chikán. Amsterdam: Elsevier, pp. 73–85.

Csáki, Csaba (1983) 'Economic Management and Organization of Hungarian Agriculture', *Journal of Comparative Economics*, September 7, pp. 318–328.

Dániel, Zsuzsa (1985) 'The Effect of Housing Allocation on Social Inequality in Hungary', *Journal of Comparative Economics*, December 9, pp. 391–409.

Donáth, Ferenc (1980) *Reform and Revolution: Transformation of Hungary's Agriculture 1945–1975.* Budapest: Corvina.

Ehrlich, Éva (1985a) 'The Size Structure of Manufacturing Establishments and Enterprises: An International Comparison', *Journal of Comparative Economics*, 9, pp. 267–295.

Fábri, Ervin (1982) 'Superficial Changes and Deep Tendencies in Inventory Process in Hungary', *Acta Oeconomica, 28,* pp. 133–146.

Falus–Szikra, Katalin (1986) 'Wage and Income Disparities Between the First and Second Economies in Hungary', *Acta Oeconomica, 36,* pp. 99–103.

Fazekas, Károly and Köllő, János (1985) 'Fluctuations of Labour Shortage and State Intervention after 1968', in Péter Galasi and György Sziráczky, 1985, pp. 42–69.

Fehér, Ferenc, Heller, Ágnes and Márkus György, (1983a) *Dictatorship over Needs.* Oxford: Blackwell.

Gábor, R. István (1979) 'The Second (Secondary) Economy. Earning Activity and Regrouping of Income Outside the Socially Organized Production and Distribution', *Acta Oeconomica, 22,* pp. 291–311.

Gábor, István (1985) 'The Major Domains of the Second Economy', in Péter Galasi and György Sziráczky, 1985, pp. 133–178.

Gács, János (1982) 'Passive Purchasing Behaviour and Possibilities of Adjustment in the Hungarian Industry', *Acta Oeconomica, 28,* pp. 337–349.

Galsai, Péter and Sziráczky, György (1985a) *Labour Market and Second. Economy in Hungary.* Frankfurt & NY: Campus.

Galbraith, John Kenneth (1967a) *The New Industrial State.*Boston: Houghton–Mifflin.

Galbraith, John Kenneth (1967b) *American Capitalism.* Boston: Houghton–Mifflin (1952)

Gomulka, Stanislaw (1985) 'Kornai's Soft Budget Constraint and the Shortage, Phenomenon: A Criticism and Restatement', *Economics of Planning, 19,* pp. 1–11.

Granick, David (1954) *Management of the Industrial Firm in the USSR.* NY: Columbia U. Press.

Granick, David (1984) 'Central Physical Planning, Incentives and Job Rights *Comparative Economic Systems: Present Views.* Ed.: Andres Zimbalist. Boston, The Hague: Kluwer–Nijhoff.

Gregory, Paul R. and Stuart, Robert C. (1980) *Comparative Economic System.* Boston: Houghton–Mifflin.

Gregory, Paul R. and Stuart, Robert C. (1981) *Soviet Economic Structure and Performance.* NY: Harper and Row.

Grossman, Gregory (1966) 'Gold and the Sword: Money in the Soviet Command Economy', in *Industrialization in Two Systems.* Ed.: Henry Rosovsky, NY; John Wiley, pp. 204–36.

Grossman, Gregory (1977) 'The Second Economy of the USSR', *Problems of Communism, 26* (5), pp. 25–40.

Grossman, Gregory (1985) *The Second Economy in the USSR and Eastern Europe: A Bibliography,* Mimeo. Berkeley & Durham: U. of California and Duke U.

Halpern, László and Molnár, György (1985) 'Income Formation, Accumulation and Price Trends in Hungary in the 1970s', *Acta Oeconomica, 35,* pp. 105–131.

Hare, Paul, Radice, Hugo K. and Swain, Nigel, eds. (1981) *Hungary: A Decade of Economic Reform.* London & Boston: Allen & Unwin.

Hayek, Friedrich A., ed: (1935) *Collectivist Economic Planning.* London: Routledge & Kegan Paul.

Hewett, Edward A. (1981) 'Lessons of the 1970's and Prospects for the 1980's', in *East European Economic Assessment. Part I, Country Studies.* A Compendium of Papers Submitted to the U. S. Congress: Joint Economic Committee, Washington, DC: U. S. GPO.

Holzman, Franklyn D (1986) 'Soviet Inflationary Pressures 1928–1957: Causes and Cures', *Quarterly Journal of Economics,* May, *74* (2), pp. 167–88.

Hunter, Holland (1961) 'Optimal Tautness in Developmental Planning', *Economic Development and Cultural Change,* July, *9* (2), pp. 561–572.

International Currency Review (1981) May, *13* (2), p. 31.

Kapitány, Zsuzsa, Kornai, János and Szabó, Judit (1984) 'Reproduction of Shortage on the Hungarian Car Market', *Soviet Studies, 36* (2), pp. 236–256.

Keren, Michael (1972) 'On the Tautness of Plans', *Review of Economic Studies,* October *39* (4), pp. 469–486.

Keren, Michael, Miller, Jeffrey and Thornton, James R. (1983) 'The Ratchet:

A Dynamic Managerial Incentive Model of the Soviet Enterprise', *Journal of Comparative Economics*, December, 7 (4), pp. 347–367.

Konrád, Görgy and Szelényi, Iván (1979) *The Intellectuals on the Road to Class Power*. NY: Harcourt Brace Jovanovich.

Kornai, János (1959) *Overcentralization in Economic Administration*. London: Oxford U. Press, (1959).

Kornai, János (1979) 'Resource-Constrained Versus Demand-Constrained Systems', *Econometrica*, July, 47 (4), pp. 801–19.

Kornai, János (1980) *Economics of Shortage*. Amsterdam: North-Holland.

Kornai, János (1982) *Growth, Shortage and Efficiency*. Oxford: Blackwell.

Kornai, János (1984) 'Bureaucratic and Market Coordination', *Osteuropa Wirtschaft*, Dec. 29 (4), pp. 306–319.

Kornai, János (1985a) 'On the Explanatory Theory of Shortage. Comments on Two Articles by K. A. Soós', *Acta Oeconomica, 34* (1–2), pp. 145–164.

Kornai, János (1985b) 'Gomulka on the Soft Budget Constraint: A Reply', *Economics of Planning, 19* (2), pp. 49–55.

Kornai, János (1986) 'The Soft Budget Constraint', in this volume, pp. 20.

Kornai, János and Matits, Ágnes (1984) 'Softness of the Budget Constraint — An Analysis Relying on Data of Firms', *Acta Oeconomica, 32*, pp. 223–249.

Köves, András and Obláth, Gábor (1983) 'Hungarian Foreign Trade in the 1970s', *Acta Oeconomica, 30* (1), pp. 89–109.

Kowalik, Tadeusz (1984) 'Review on the Economics of Feasible Socialism Written by Alec Nove 1983', *Contribution to Political Economy*, March 3 (1), pp. 91–97.

Lackó, Mária (1980) 'Cumulating and Easing of Tensions', *Acta Oeconomica, 24* (3), pp. 357–77.

Lackó, Mária (1984) 'Behavioural Rules in the Distribution of Sectorial Investments in Hungary, 1951–1980', *Journal of Comparative Economics*, September 8 (3), pp. 290–300.

Laki, Mihály (1982) 'Liquidation and Merger in the Hungarian Industry', *Acta Oeconomica 28*, pp. 87–108.

Laki, Mihály (1984) 'The Enterprise Crisis', *Acta Oeconomica, 32* pp. 113–124.

Laky, Teréz (1980) 'The Hidden Mechanism of Recentralization in Hungary', *Acta Oeconomica, 24* (1–2), pp. 95–109.

Laky, Teréz (1985) 'Enterprise Business Work Partnership and Enterprise Interests', *Acta Oeconomica 34*, pp. 27–49.

Lange, Oscar (1936, 1937) 'On the Economic Theory of Socialism', *Review of Economic Studies* October 1936 & February 1937, 4 (1–2), pp. 53–71, 123–142.

Lavoie, Don (1985) *Rivalry and Central Planning. The Socialist Calculation Debate Reconsidered*. Cambridge: Cambridge U. Press.

Levine, Herbert (1966) 'Pressure and Planning in the Soviet Economy', in *Industrialization in Two Systems*. Ed.: Henry Rosovsky. Ny: John Wiley, pp. 266–85.

Liberman, Evsey G. (1972) 'The Plan, Profits and Bonuses', in *Socialist Economics: Selected Readings*. Eds.: Alec Nove and D. M. Nuti. Middlesex: Penguin Books, (1962), pp. 309–318.

Lindblom, Charles (1977) *Politics and Markets. The World's Political Economic Systems*. NY: Basic Books.

Macrae, Norman (1983) 'Into Entrepreneurial Socialism', *The Economist*, 19–25. March 286 (1281), pp. 23–29.

Marer, Paul (1981) 'The Mechanism and Performance of Hungary's Foreign Trade, 1968–79', in P. Hare et al., pp. 161–204.

Marer, Paul (1986a) *East-West Technology Transfer. Study of Hungary 1968–1984*. Paris: OECD.

Marer, Paul (1986b) 'Economic Reform in Hungary: From Central Planning to Regulated Market', *East European Economics: Slow Growth in the 1980's. Country studies on Eastern Europe and Yugoslavia*. Vol. 3, Joint Economic Committee, Congress of the United States, Washington, DC: U. S. GPO.

Marrese, Michael (1983) 'Agricultural Policy and Performance in Hungary', *Journal of Comparative Economics*, Sept. 7 (3), pp. 329–45.

Mises, Ludwig von (1935) 'Economic Calculation in the Socialist Commonwealth' in *Collectivist Economic Planning*. Ed.: Friedrich A. Hayek. London: Routledge & Kegan Paul, pp. 87–130.

Montias, John M. (1976) *The Structure of Economic System*. London & New Haven, CT: Yale U. Press.

Neuberger, Egon and Duffy, Wiliam (1976) *Comparative Economic Systems: A Decision-Making Approach*. Boston & London: Allyn & Bacon.

Nove, Alec (1983a) *The Economics of Feasible Socialism*. London: Allen & Unwin.

Nove, Alec (1983b) *The Soviet Economic System*. London: Allen & Unwin.

Nuti, Domenico Mario (1985) 'Hidden and Represented Inflation in Soviet-Type Economics: Definitions. Measurement and Stabilisation', *EUI Working Paper*, No. 85/200, October.

Nyers, Rezső, Bagota, Béla and Garam, József (1969) *Economic Reform in Hungary. Twenty-five Questions and Twenty-five Answers. An Interview with Rezső Nyers*. Budapest: Pannónia.

Nyers, Rezső and Tardos, Márton (1978) 'Enterprises in Hungary Before and After the Economic Reform' *Acta Oeconomica*, 20, pp. 21–44.

Nyers, Rezső and Tardos, Márton (1979) 'What Economic Development Policy Should We Adopt?' *Acta Oeconomica*, 22, pp. 11–31.

Nyers, Rezső and Tardos, Márton (1984) 'The Necessity for Consolidation of the Economy and the Possibility of Development in Hungary', *Acta Oeconomica*, 32, pp. 1–19.

Péter, György (1967) 'On the Planned Central Control and Management of the Economy', *Acta Oeconomica*, 2, pp. 23–45.

Polányi, Karl (1944) *The Great Transformation*. NY: Farrar & Rinehart.

Portes, Richard (1970) 'Economic Reforms in Hungary', *American Economic Review*, May, 60 (2), pp. 307–313.

Portes, Richard (1972) 'The Tactics and Strategy of Economic Decentralization', *Soviet Studies*, April 23 (4), pp. 629–658.

Portes, Richard (1977) 'Hungary: Economic Performance, Policy and Prospects', in *East European Economics post Helsinki*. Joint Economic Committee, Congress of the United States, Washington, DC: U. S. GPO.

Portes, Richard (1984) *The Theory and Measurement of Macroeconomic Disequilibrium in Centrally Planned Economies*, MS. U. of London: Birkbeck Coll.

Portes, Richard, Quandt, Richard, Winter, David and Yeo, S. (1986) *Macro-Economic Planning and Disequilibrium: Estimates for Poland'*, London: Centre for Economic Policy Research Discussion Paper No. 91.

Portes, Richard and Winter, David (1977) 'The Supply of Consumption Goods in Centrally Planned Economies', *Journal of Comparative Economics*, December, *1* (4), pp. 351–365.

Portes, Richard and Winter, David (1978) 'The Demand for Money and for Consumption Goods in Centrally Planned Economies', *Review of Economic Statistics*, Feb. *60* (1), pp. 8–18.

Portes, Richard and Winter, David (1980) 'Disequilibrium Estimates for Consumption Goods Markets in Centrally Planned Economies', *Review of Economic Studies*, January, *47* (1), pp. 137–159.

Révész, Gábor (1979) 'Enterprise and Plant Size: Structure of the Hungarian Economy', *Acta Oeconomica, 22*, pp. 47–68.

Román, Zoltán (1985) 'The Conditions of Market Competition in Hungarian Industry', *Acta Oeconomica, 34*, pp. 79–97.

Rupp, Kálmán (1983) *Entrepreneurs in Red*. Albany: State University of New York Press.

Sárközy, Tamás (1982) 'Problems of Social Ownership and of the Proprietory Organization', *Acta Oeconomica, 29*, pp. 225–258.

Sík, Ota (1967) 'Socialist Market Relations and Planning', in *Socialism, Capitalism and Economic Growth. Essays Presented to Maurice Dobb. Ed.*: C. H. Feinstein. Cambridge: Cambridge U. Press, pp. 133–157.

Sipos, Aladár (1983) 'Relations Between Enterprises in the Agro-Industrial Sphere in Hungary', *Acta Oeconomica, 31*, pp. 53–69.

Soós, Károly Attila (1975–76) 'Causes of Investment Fluctuations in the Hungarian Economy', *Eastern European Economics*, Winter *14* (2), pp. 25–36.

Soós, Károly Attila (1984) 'A Propos the Explanation of Shortage Phenomena: Volume of Demand and Structural Inelasticity', *Acta Oeconomica, 33*, pp. 305–320.

Stark, David (1985) 'The Micropolitics of the Firm and the Macropolitics of Reform: New Forms of Workplace Bargaining Hungarian Enterprises', in *State Versus Markets in the World–System*. Eds.: Peter Evans, Dietrich Rueschmeyer, and Evelyne Humber Stephens. Beverly Hills, CA: Sage, pp. 247–269.

Swain, Nigel (1981) 'The Evolution of Hungary's Agricultural System Since 1967', in P. Hare et al., pp. 225–251.

Szabó, Judit and Tarafás, Imre (1985). 'Hungary's Exchange Rate Policy in the 1980's' *Acta Oeconomica, 35*, pp. 53–79.

Szalai, Erzsébet (1982) 'The New Stage of the Reform Process in Hungary and the Large Enterprise', *Acta Oeconomica, 29*, pp. 25–46.

Szamuely, László (1982) 'The First Wave of the Mechanism Debate in Hungary 1954–57', *Acta Oeconomica, 29*, pp. 1–24.

Szamuely, László (1984) 'The Second Wave of the Economic Mechanism Debate and the 1968 Reform in Hungary', *Acta Oeconomica, 33*, pp. 43–67.

Szelényi, Iván (1983) *Urban Inequalities under State Socialism*. Oxford: Oxford U. Press.

Tardos, Márton (1980) 'The Role of Money: Economic Relations Between the State and the Enterprises in Hungary", *Acta Oeconomica, 25,* pp. 19–35.

Tardos, Márton (1982) 'Development Program for Economic Control and Organization in Hungary', *Acta Oeconomica, 28,* pp. 295–315.

Tardos, Márton (1986) 'The Conditions of Developing a Regulated Market', *Acta Oeconomica, 36,* pp. 67–89.

Taylor, Fred M. (1964) 'The Guidance of Production in a Socialist State', *American Economic Review,* March, 1929, *19* (1), pp. 1–80. Reprinted in Ed.: *On the Economic Theory of Socialism.* Benjamin E. Lippincott. NY: McGraw–Hill (1938)

United Nations (1970) *Statistical Yearbook 1969.* NY.

United Nations (1979) *Statistical Yearbook 1981.* NY.

United Nations (1983a) *Monthly Bulletin of Statistics,* Jan. (37) 1.

United Nations (1985a) *Statistical Yearbook 1982.* NY.

United Nations (1985b) *Monthly Bulletin of Statistics.* Oct. (39) 10.

Weber, Max (1947) *The Theory of Social and Economic Organization.* Oxford: Oxford U. Press, (1922)

Williamson, Oliver (1975) *Markets and Hierarchies: Analysis and Antitrust Implications.* NY: The Free Press.

HUNGARIAN REFERENCES

Agonács, Gábor, Bak, József, Domokos, József, Juhász Pál, Szénay, László and Tellér, Gyula (1984) 'A szövetkezeti mozgalom a gazdasági folyamatban' (The Cooperative Movement in the Process of the Economic Reform). *Valóság,* February, *27* (2), pp. 17–27.

Antal, László (1985a) *Gazdaságirányítási és pénzügyi rendszerünk a reform útján* (The Hungarian System of Economic Control and Finance on the Way of Reform). Budapest: Közgazdasági és Jogi Könyvkiadó.

Balázsy, Sándor (1954) 'Javítsuk meg tervezési módszereinket' (Let Us Improve Our Planning Methods). *Többtermelés,* November *8* (11), pp. 2–12.

Bauer, Tamás (1981) *Tervgazdaság, beruházás, ciklusok* (Planned Economy, Investment, Cycles). Budapest: Közgazdasági és Jogi Könyvkiadó.

Belyó, Pál and Drexler Béla (1985) *'Nem szervezett (elsősorban illegális) keretek között végzett szolgáltatások'* (Services Supplied Within Non-Organized, Mainly Illegal, Framework). Mimeo. Budapest, Szolgáltatási Kutatóintézet-KSH.

Berend, T. Iván (1983) *Gazdasági útkeresés (1956–65). A szocialista gazdaság magyarországi modelljének története* (Searching for New Ways in Economy). Budapest: Magvető.

Breitner, Miklós (1985) 'Milliárdok egy százalékpontból' (Billions out of One Percentage Point). *Figyelő,* August 22, *29* (34) p. 5.

Central Statistical Office (1957) *Statisztikai Évkönyv 1956* (Statistical Yearbook 1956). Budapest: Központi Statisztikai Hivatal.

Central Statistical Office (1967) *Statisztikai Évkönyv 1966* (Statistical Yearbook 1966). Budapest: Központi Statisztikai Hivatal.

178   *Vision and Reality*

Central Statistical Office (1972) *Magánkisipari adattár 1938–1971* (Reference Book of Private Small-scale Industry (1938–1971). Budapest: Központi Statisztikai Hivatal.

Central Statistical Office (1975) *A családi jövedelmek színvonala és szóródása 1972-ben* (Level and Dispersion of Family Incomes in 1972). Budapest: Központi Statisztikai Hivatal.

Central Statistical Office (1976) *Statisztikai Évkönyv 1975* (Statistical Yearbook 1975). Budapest: Központi Statisztikai Hivatal.

Central Statistical Office (1979) *Statisztikai Évkönyv 1978* (Statistical Yearbook 1978). Budapest: Központi Statisztikai Hivatal.

Central Statistical Office (1980) *Statisztikai Évkönyv 1979* (Statistical Yearbook, 1979). Budapest: Központi Statisztikai Hivatal.

Central Statistical Office (1981) *Statisztikai Évkönyv 1980* (Statistical Yearbook 1980). Budapest: Központi Statisztikai Hivatal.

Central Statistical Office (1982) *Statisztikai Évkönyv 1981* (Statistical Yearbook 1982). Budapest: Központi Statisztikai Hivatal.

Central Statistical Office (1983a) *Statisztikai Évkönyv 1982* (Statistical Yearbook 1982). Budapest: Központi Statisztikai Hivatal.

Central Statistical Office (1983b) *Mezőgazdasági adattár V.* (Reference Book of Agriculture V.). Budapest: Központi Statisztikai Hivatal.

Central Statistical Office (1984) *Statisztikai Évkönyv 1983* (Statistical Yearbook 1983.) Budapest: Központi Statisztikai Hivatal.

Central Statistical Office (1984) *Az 1980. évi népszámlálás adatai. 36. kötet. Öszszefoglaló adatok.* (1980 Census. Vol. 36. Summary data). Budapest: Központi Statisztikai Hivatal.

Central Statistical Office (1985a) *Statisztikai Évkönyv 1984.* (Statistical Yearbook 1984). Budapest: Központi Statisztikai Hivatal.

Central Statistical Office (1985b) *Lakásstatisztikai Évkönyv 1984* (Yearbook of Housing Statistics 1984). Budapest: Központi Statisztikai Hivatal.

Central Statistical Office (1985c) *Mezőgazdasági Évkönyv 1984* (Agricultural Statistical Yearbook 1984). Budapest: Központi Statisztikai Hivatal.

Central Statistical Office (1985d) *A családi jövedelmek színvonala és szóródása.* (Level and Dispersion of Family Incomes). Budapest: Központi Statisztikai Hivatal.

Chikán, Attila (1984) *A vállalati készletezési politika* (Firms' Inventory Policy). Budapest: Közgazdasági és Jogi Könyvkiadó.

Csanádi, Mária (1979) 'A vállalatnagyság, a jövedelmezőség és a preferenciák néhány összefüggése' (A Few Aspects of the Size, and Profitability of Firms and Preferences). *Pénzügyi Szemle,* February *23* (2), pp. 105–120.

Csanádi, Mária (1980) *A differenciált erőforráselosztás és támogatások újratermelődésének néhány összefüggése* (A Few Aspects of the Differentiated Resource Allocation and the Reproduction of Subsidies). Mimeo. Budapest. Pénzügykutatási Intézet.

Csanádi, Mária (1983) *Beavatkozás, szelekció, kölcsönös alkalmazkodás* (Invention, Selection, Mutual Adjustment). Mimeo. Budapest: Pénzügykutatási Intézet.

Csikós-Nagy, Béla (1985) *Árpolitikánk időszerű kérdései* (The Topical Questions of the Hungarian Price Policy). Budapest: Közgazdasági és Jogi Könyvkiadó.

Csillag, István (1983) 'Az új vállalati szervezet alapvonásai' (The Main Features of the Firms' New Organization). *Valóság*, July, *26* (7), pp. 45–59.

Csoór, Klára and Mohácsi, Piroska (1985) "Az infláció fő tényezői, 1980–84" (The Main Factors of Inflation (1980–84). *Gazdaság*, April *19* (2), pp. 21–39.

Dudás, János (1985) 'A beruházások alakulása, 1945–1984'. (Changes of Investments (1945–1984). *Statisztikai Szemle*, April/May *63* (4–5), pp. 389–411.

Ehrlich, Éva (1985b) 'A termelőegységek méretstruktúrája 18 ország feldolgozóiparában' (Production Units' Size Structure in the Manufacturing Industries of 18 Countries). *Gazdaság, 19* (3), pp. 81–114.

Erdős, Péter (1956) 'A tervgazdálkodás néhány elméleti kérdéséről' (On a Few Theoretical Problems of Planned Economy). *Közgazdasági Szemle*, June, *3* (6), pp. 676–694.

Falubíró, Vilmos (1983) 'Szabályozás és vállalati magatartás 1968-tól napjainkig' (Regulation and Firms' Behaviour from 1968 up to Now). *Gazdaság, 18* (4), pp. 31–49.

Fazekas, Károly and Köllő, János (1985b) *Munkaerőpiac és munkaerőpolitika a hetvenes években* (Labour Market and Labour Policy in the Seventies). Mimeo. Budapest: Institute of Economics.

Ferge Zsuzsa (1984) 'Szociálpolitika a gazdaságban és társadalomban' (Social Policy in Economy and in Society). *Társadalomkutatás*, April *2* (2), pp. 54–70.

Gábor, R. István and Galasi Péter (1981) *A "második" gazdaság. Tények és hipotézisek* (The "Second" Economy. Facts and Hypotheses). Budapest: Közgazdasági és Jogi Könyvkiadó.

Gábor, R. István and Kővári, György (1985) 'Keresetszabályozás és munkahelyi ösztönzés. Kísérlet egy tévhit eloszlatására' (Income Regulation and Incentive: An Attempt to Dispel a Fallacy). *Közgazdasági Szemle*, June, *32*, pp. 724–742.

Grósz, Tivadar (1986) 'A kamat közgazdasági funkcióinak érvényesülése' (The Economic Impact of the Interest Rate). *Bankszemle*, February *30* (2), pp. 26–30.

Heti Világgazdaság (1986) (Weekly World Economy), May 17, p. 55.

Hoch, Róbert (1980) 'A világpiaci árak és az árcentrum' (World Market Prices and the Price Centre). *Közgazdasági Szemle*, October *27* (10) pp. 1153–1158.

Horváth, László (1976) 'Az ágazati irányítás elvei és gyakorlati problémái' (Principles and Practical Problems of Sectoral Control). *Gazdaság, 10* (4), pp. 7–26.

Hulyák, Katalin (1983) 'Egyensúlyhiányok a lakossági fogyasztásban I–II.' (Imbalance in Household Consumption I–II). *Statisztikai Szemle*, March, *61* (3), pp. 229–243. and April, *61* (4), pp. 369–380.

Hulyák, Katalin 'A külső és belső egyensúly ökonometriai elemzése (1965–1981). (Econometric Analysis of External and Internal Equilibrium 1965–1981). *Tervgazdasági Fórum, 1* (2), pp. 41–52.

Kolosi, Tamás (1979) *Második gazdaság és társadalomszerkezet* (Second Economy and Social Structure). Mimeo. Budapest: Országos Tervhivatal.

Kolosi, Tamás (1980) "A társadalmi egyenlőtlenségről" (Social Unequelities). *Társadalmi Szemle*, June, *35* (6), pp. 45–58.

Kornai, János and Matits, Ágnes (1983) '*Az állami vállalatok jövedelmének redisztribúciója* (Redistribution of the Income of State-Owned Firms). Mimeo. Budapest: Ipari Minisztérium.

Kovács, János Mátyás (1983) "A reformalku sűrűjében" (In the Depths of the Reform Bargain). *Valóság*, March, *27* (3), pp. 30–55.

Kozma, Ferenc (1983a) 'A vállalkozó szocialista állam' (The Enterprising Socialist State). *Gazdaság, 17*, (2), pp. 56–75.

Kozma, Ferenc (1983b) 'Gazdaságirányítási rendszerünk továbbfejlesztése a szocialista építés szolgálatában' (The Further Development of the Economic Control and Management System of Hungary with a View to the Building of Socialism). *Társadalmi Szemle*, Nov. *38* (11), pp. 11–29.

Kupa, Mihály (1980) *Jövedelemelosztás—költségvetés—gazdasági folyamatok* (Income Distribution—Budget—Economic Processes). Budapest: Közgazdasági és Jogi Könyvkiadó.

Lamberger, Galina, Matolcsy, György, Szalai, Erzsébet and Voszka, Éva (1986) *Vállalatmegszűnés. Hét eset a nyolcvanas évekből: tapasztalatok és következtetések* (Exit of Enterprises. Seven Cases from the Eighties: Experiences and Conclusions). Mimeo, Budapest: MTA Ipargazdaságtani Kutatócsoport.

Liska, Tibor (1963) 'Kritika és koncepció. Tézisek a gazdasági mechanizmus reformjához' (Criticism and Conception. Theses for the Reform of the Economic Mechanism). *Közgazdasági Szemle*, September *10* (9), pp. 1058–1076.

Liska, Tibor (1969) 'A bérlakás kereskedelmi koncepciója' (The Conception of the Trade of State-Owned Flats). *Valóság*, January *12* (1), pp. 22–35.

Matits, Ágnes (1984a) *A redisztribúció szerepe az állami vállalatok jövedelmezőségének alakulásában: 1981–1982* (The Role of Redistribution in Determining the Profitability of State-Owned Firms: 1981–1982). Mimeo. Budapest: Economix.

Matits, Ágnes (1984b) *Az egyéni jövedelmek és a vállalati jövedelmezőség* (Personal Incomes and the Firms' Profitability). Mimeo. Budapest: Economix.

Matits, Ágnes (1984c) *A vállalatnagyság szerepe a redisztribúcióban megnyilvánuló részrehajlásban* (The Role of Firms' Size in the Bias of Redistribution). Mimeo. Budapest: Economix.

Matits, Ágnes and Temesi, József (1985) *A vállalati jövedelmezőség és a beruházási tevékenység kapcsolata* (Firms' Profitability and Investment Activity). Mimeo. Budapest: Economix.

Muraközy, László (1985) 'Hazánk költségvetéséről — nemzetközi összehasonlításban' (The Hungarian Budget — An International Comparison). *Pénzügyi Szemle*, October *29* (10), pp. 745–754.

Nagy, Tamás (1956) 'A politikai gazdaságtan néhány kérdéséről' (A Few Problems of Political Economy). *Közgazdasági Szemle*, June, *3* (6), pp. 657–675.

Papanek, Gábor, Sárkány, Péter and Viszt, Erzsébet (1986) *A nehéz pénzügyi helyzet rendezése iparvállalatainknál* (Settling Financial Difficulties of Hungarian Industrial Enterprises). Mimeo. Budapest: MTA Ipargazdaságtani Kutatócsoport.

Péter, György (1954a) 'A gazdaságosság jelentőségéről és szerepéről a népgazdaság tervszerű irányításában' (On the Importance and Role of Economic Efficiency in the Planned Control of the National Economy). *Közgazdasági Szemle*, December *1* (3), pp. 300–324.

Péter, György (1954b) 'Az egyszemélyi felelős vezetésről' (On Management Based on One-Man Responsibility). *Társadalmi Szemle*, August/September *9* (8–9), pp. 109–124.

Péter, György (1956) 'A gazdaságosság és a jövedelmezőség jelentősége a tervgazdálkodásban I–II.' (The Importance of Economic Efficiency and Profitability in Planned Economy (I–II.). *Közgazdasági Szemle*, June, *3* (6), pp. 695–711 and July/August *3* (7–8), pp. 851–869.

Pető, Iván and Szakács, Sándor (1985) *A hazai gazdaság négy évtizedének története 1945–1985.* I. (Forty-years' History of the Hungarian Economy 1945–1985. I.). Budapest: Közgazdasági és Jogi Könyvkiadó.

Petschnig, Mária (1985a) *Fogyasztói árindexünk — A kritika tükrében* (The Hungarian Consumer Price Index — In the Mirror of Criticism). Mimeo. Pécs–Budapest: Institute of Economics.

Petschnig, Mária (1985b) 'Mennyi az annyi?' (How Much is so Much?) *Heti Világgazdaság*, 1 June, *6* (22), p. 7.

Schweitzer, Iván (1982) *Vállalatméret* (The Firm's Size). Budapest: Közgazdasági és Jogi Könyvkiadó.

Siklaky, István (1985) *Koncepció és kritika: vita Liska Tibor 'szocialista vállalkozási szektor' javaslatáról* (Conception and Criticism: Discussion of T. Liska's Proposal of a 'Socialist Enterprising Sector'). Budapest: Magvető.

Sugár, Tamás (1984) 'A piac és a látható kéz' (The Market and the Visible Hand). *Társadalmi Szemle*, March, *29* (3), pp. 89–99.

Szabó, Judit (1985) 'Kínálati rugalmasság, elszakadó kereslet, készletek és hiány' (Inelasticity of Supply, Runaway Demand, Stocks and Shortage). *Közgazdasági Szemle*, July/August *32* (7–8), pp. 951–960.

Szabó, Kálmán (1967) 'A szocialista gazdaságirányítási rendszer' (The Socialist System of Economic Control and Management), in *A szocializmus politikai gazdaságtana. Tankönyv* (The Political Economics of Socialism. Text-book). Eds.: Berei, Andor *et al.*. Budapest: Kossuth Könyvkiadó, pp. 248–294.

Szegő, Andrea (1983b) 'Gazdaság és politika — Érdek és struktúra' (Economy and Politics — Interest and Structure). *Medvetánc*, *3* (2–3), pp. 49–92.

Tallós, György (1976) *A bankhitel szerepe gazdaságirányítási rendszerünkben* (The Role of Bank Credit in the Hungarian System of Economic Control and Management). Budapest: Kossuth.

Tardos, Róbert (1983) 'Magatartástípusok a családi gazdálkodásban' (Behavioural Types in Family Economy). *Közgazdasági Szemle*, January *30* (1), pp. 63–76.

Tellér, Gyula (1984–85) 'Ómechanizmus, új mechanizmus, ipari szövetkezetek' (Old Mechanism, New Mechanism, Industrial Cooperatives). *Medvetánc*, *4–5*, (4–1), pp. 143–165.

Tibor, Ágnes (1984) 'Statikus automobilizmus' (Static Automobilism). *Heti Világgazdaság*, April 28, 6 (18), pp. 53–55.

Tímár, János (1985a) *A társadalmi újratermelés időalapja* (The Total of Man-hours Available for Social Reproduction). Mimeo. Budapest: U. of Economics.

Tímár, János (1985b) 'Idő és munkaidő. A munkaidő és a társadalmi újratermelés időalapjának néhány problémája Magyarországon' (Time and Working Time. Some Problems of Working Time and of the Total of Man-Hours Available for Social Reproduction). *Közgazdasági Szemle*, No. 32, pp. 1299–1313.

Varga, István (1957) 'A Közgazdasági Szakértő Bizottság elgondolásai' (Conceptions of the Economic Expert Committee). *Közgazdasági Szemle*, October 4 (10), pp. 997–1008 and December 4 (12), pp. 1231–1248.

Várhegyi, Éva (1986) *A hitelrendszer hatása a vállalati költségvetési korlátra* (Impact of the Credit System on the Firm's Budget Constraint). Mimeo. Budapest: Economix.

Vass, Henrik ed. (1968) *A Magyar Szocialista Munkáspárt határozatai és dokumentumai 1963–1966* (Decrees and Documents of the Hungarian Socialist Workers' Party 1963–1966). Budapest: Kossuth.

Zelkó, Lajos (1981) 'A versenyárrendszer' elméleti és gyakorlati problémáihoz' (On the Theoretical and Practical Problems of the Competitive Price System). *Közgazdasági Szemle*, July/Aug. 27 pp. 927–940.

6. The Chinese Economic Reform — as Seen by Hungarian Economists*
(Marginal notes to our travel diary)
Co-author: Zsuzsa Dániel

On the invitation of the Chinese Academy of Sciences, we spent four weeks in China in 1985. Although we have read a great many studies about China, we do not claim to be experts on the subject by any means. We have been studying the economy of Hungary, our own country, with a population of ten million inhabitants for decades, and we still feel we do not know it well enough. How could we understand China, with a population a hundred times as large as Hungary's, with a desirable degree of thoroughness relying only on a few books, several conversations, and a visit of four weeks? All we can undertake is to record first impressions.

Several interesting books and articles have been published concerning the recent changes in China. (Lim–Wood, 1985, Perry–Wong, 1985, Solinger, 1984.) We shall not try to make a summary review of this rich literature. Such a review may perhaps provide the reader with more information than personal im-

---

* This chapter first reviews the successes of China in agriculture. The so-called 'responsibility system' entailing a strong and direct interest of peasant families has lent a great impetus to production. In the state sector there exists a 'double regulation': the old one, based on directive planning and the new one relying on enterprise autonomy. The symbiosis of the two involves several kinds of inconsistency. The budget constraint of state enterprises is soft: the profit to be retained, the survival and growth of the enterprise all depend on negotiations with superior authorities. Finally, the article discusses the problems of disharmony accompanying shortage, inflation and forced growth. In spite of these contradictions and tensions there is an atmosphere of optimism in the wake of the first successes of the reform.

pressions can do. In the present chapter, however, we shall content ourselves with reporting what we personally saw, or what Chinese economic managers or researchers said in our presence, and all this as reflected by our own way of thinking (obviously biased by economic prejudices). We met many people. We attended two scientific conferences, one discussing the reform, the other state-owned enterprise. In the company of the participants of the first conference we met and talked for two hours with Zhao Ziyang, Prime Minister of the People's Republic of China and, together with the participants of the second conference, we had a several hours' talk with Zhang Jinfu, State Councillor, a top leader of the Chinese economy. We had talks with members of the Reform Committee, university professors, enterprise managers, journalists, mayors of big cities and villages, with peasants and workers. We had long conversations, continuing late into the night, with young economists. We made visits organized by our hosts to factories, villages, and markets, and there were also opportunities for improvised, spontaneous encounters: we could enter homes, or talk to a young man who spoke English and came over to our table in a restaurant. On the basis of the above, we must make it clear in advance that, though we did our best to check the correctness of our statements against the available literature, we are aware of the subjective nature of the picture we are painting of China.

6.1 THE FACTORS SHAPING THE CHINESE ECONOMY

The large number of factors shaping the Chinese economy can be divided into four major groups.

6.1.1. In China, a *socialist political, social and economic system* exists. The character of the political structure is determined by the fact that power is held by the Chinese Communist Party and it does not share this power with any other organized body. Numerous key positions in the economy are held by the state; economic regulation is largely centralized.

In this respect, China belongs to the 'system-family' as do the Soviet Union, and the Eastern European, Asian, African and Latin-American socialist countries. True, for a long period China had political, strategic and ideological controversies, in some cases growing into veritable conflicts, with other socialist countries. This fact, however, does not change the essential similarities between the members of this system-family; quite a number of their essential features are identical. Consequently, similarities are also found in their economic mechanism, as well as in the behaviour of the economic units. It is our conviction that one of the keys to understanding China is the recognition of these system-specific identical or at least closely similar features.

6.1.2. After Mao's death, a *reform process* began in China. Before discussing it, let us say a few words about pre-reform China. Notwithstanding numerous differences, the mechanism of Eastern Europe under the Stalinist era and Mao's Chinese mechanism display essentially similar features. Both are specific historical manifestations of a general type: the 'traditional' or 'classical' socialist economic mechanism. The major characteristics of this type are generally known: preponderance of state and collective ownership, strongly centralized bureaucratic-hierarchic regulation, the decisive role of instructions, repression of price signals in the state-owned and collective sectors, chronic shortage, etc.

The word 'reform' is used in different senses. We wish to make a distinction between more or less important modifications of the traditional old mechanism, and the radical changes which deeply affect social conditions, property rights, and the power relations between economic actors, and which considerably diminish the scope of bureaucracy, while essentially increasing that of the market. We only apply the word 'reform' to the latter thorough changes. In this sense, a genuine reform process is taking place in China. After Yugoslavia and Hungary, China is the third country to step on the road of reform. The analysis of the reform is another key to understanding China today.

6.1.3. China is a *developing* country. This is in fact a euphemism to say it is underdeveloped and poor. Per capita output in advanced industrial countries was 10 to 30-fold of that of China in the 1980s.[1] A number of characteristics of the Chinese economy are not system-specific but follow from the circumstance that, its fast growth notwithstanding, it is still a country on a low development level.

6.1.4. Finally, Chinese economy is shaped by a number of factors which are *unique* and make this country different from others. This uniqueness is in fact a broad, collective category which could be further divided according to several viewpoints. Among other things, the following conditions can be listed: the huge dimensions of the country and its immense population; a cultural heritage going back many thousands of years; the historical tradition of centralization; etc. And, of course, it is not only the distant past that shapes the present, but also the recent past of almost four decades of socialism. The specific features of the latter, different from those of all other socialist countries, are well known, they are the dramatically changing phases of the Maoist era: 'let all flowers bloom', the 'big leap' and, finally, the 'cultural revolution'. And then today's political situation must be taken into account: the effect of the existing political and social power.

Certain anthropological-sociological and historical schools hold that the history of a nation and its culture can only understood in its uniqueness, while it is futile to look for common regularities connecting it with other nations. This approach would start in its examination of China from the analysis of factors mentioned under paragraph 4, or from similar ones. Others, especially some economists studying developing countries, would be disposed towards viewing China as just one of many developing countries.

Our philosophy, however, differs from the two somewhat one-sided approaches mentioned above. We hold all four viewpoints to be equally important. We would not even attempt to 'weight' them (the numbering does not imply any order of importance). It is impossible to determine any general 'weight' for the explanatory power of the four different groups.

At the same time we willingly admit that we delimited the subject of our article with a certain arbitrariness. We are Hungarian economists with our interest focused on the cause of the Hungarian reform, or, putting it more broadly, on the question of to what extent the socialist system can reform itself. Therefore, in China, those phenomena which come into the categories 1 and 2 caught our attention first. As tourists we admired the several thousand-year-old statues and the Beijing Opera: as sympathetic human beings we were shocked by the miserable housing conditions in big cities. As researcher-economists, however, what intrigued us most was the question of what respects China resembles the socialist systems we have known so far. Wherein is the Chinese reform similar to the Hungarian one? How far do the two reforms deviate and why? Many thousand miles away from our own country, in a civilization built on different historical origins, we encountered strikingly familiar phenomena again and again. In our article, we shall discuss these familiar phenomena in the first place, the common problems of *all* socialist countries, or at least of all those that *stepped on the road of reform*. First we shall treat the reform in villages and cities, agricultural and industrial production, and then problems of shortage, inflation, and forced growth. Finally, we shall examine certain contradictions in Chinese economy and society.

6.2 REFORM IN VILLAGES: THE PEASANT FARM

Although the international press and scientific works have dealt with the Chinese agricultural reform,[2] it may still be necessary to sum up the major characteristics of the changes.

In pre-reform China, a collective agricultural organization was functioning which, as for the degree of collectivization, outvied even the Soviet form of agriculture. The 'commune' united the functions of state authority ('council') and those of economic organization ('agricultural cooperative'). All kinds of commodity producing activities attempted outside the communal framework were prosecuted.[3]

After the reform, legally the land has remained the property of the communes, but in practice it has been handed over to the peasant families. They do not cultivate just a small portion of the land as 'household farming plots', but have had the *entire* land transferred to them — except for a small part kept for state-owned farms and collective cultivation. The official term for the current position is *production responsibility system*. As for the reality of social conditions, this means that the peasant is a permanent leaseholder of the land which he cultivates individually. The term of the leasehold is ever longer: today 10–15 year contracts are the most typical ones, while some are made out for 30–35 years. The farming lease is heritable. Although legally it is possible to take back the land from the leaseholding family, the change practically amounted to distributing the land among the peasant families.

Mandatory product delivery was abolished. The forms of sale

are not uniform. As a rule, the peasant pays the rent in kind and freely disposes of the rest. He can sell it by contract to central procurement agencies, to cooperative or private food traders, or he can sell it directly on the urban free market.

This change was not implemented on the basis of a well-prepared plan. At the beginning of the reform process a number of different forms appeared, some of which were less radical in abolishing the role of the communes in agricultural production. Finally, the system outlined above has become general. It was not a reform devised 'at the top', but the peasants' will manifested itself with an elementary force 'from below', to achieve the form they wanted. The political and state apparatus did not stand in the way but, on the contrary, used every means to promote the spreading of the new form.

The same massive energy with which the peasants brought about this form is apparent in the production yields. Let us firstly revert to the pre-reform situation. For a long time, agricultural production grew by 2–3 per cent on a yearly average, which was hardly keeping pace with the population increase. China's food supply was stagnating. The world then believed that this huge country, where people had hungered so much, had finally overcome its grave problems and was able to feed everyone. The tragedy has been revealed recently; in the 1960s horrible famines swept over the country demanding millions of lives.

As a result of the reform, production suddenly increased: it has been growing by about 8 per cent a year, far exceeding the population increase which has slowed down. In the years between 1978–1983 the per head income of peasants doubled. We saw the signs of increasing prosperity ourselves: the rows of new buildings, the one-storey peasant houses, and many other signs of rising living standards in villages. Ten years ago, the foreign visitor would certainly have been taken to the village worker who best knew Mao's red book. Today, however, visitors have been taken to see the peasant family who has the best house and finest furniture, and whose farm has the greatest number of animals.

The only secret of the agricultural 'miracle' is that the Chinese peasant families worked with all their energy. (We could add that nature was kind, too: the weather was favourable for many years.) The direct tangible material incentive greatly increased the zest for production. Investments or technological developments made in these years, though not unimportant, do not account for the fast growth. The source of most of the growth is more diligent, as well as more careful work. The result does not show only in the suddenly increased peasant incomes, but also in the food supply of the cities. Food is available in large quantities and there is a wide range of choice, free markets are crammed with goods.

It is no exaggeration to say that these changes are *of importance on the scale of world history*. Eight hundred million Chinese peasants switched over voluntary, with the approval and support of the socialist state, to the production form of 'family farm'. It is an event that must draw attention from all parts of the world, especially from those developing countries where the socialist transformation of society and the economy is beginning now or will begin soon. The events in China urge an overall reconsideration of the theory and practice of peasant policy and agricultural development.

Of course, the issue is still unresolved as to what the future of Chinese agriculture will be. Will it be millions of small-holdings producing for the market, and small capitalist farms, employing a few labourers permanently or occasionally, developing from them that will constitute the backbone of agriculture? Today, they are at a low level of technological development. Will the family farm become increasingly capital-intensive, and will production grow with the aid of improved technical equipment? Or will the role of the large-scale farm increase — be it state-owned, or cooperative, or privately owned —, or will certain combinations of different forms of ownership emerge?

The fast increasing productivity of agricultural work is a welcome process, though mass unemployment may appear as an accompanying phenomenon. In the pre-reform collective economy the over-population of villages remained a hidden fact. The commune provided employment for all the adult population of the villages; true, at a low productivity level and low living standards. As the Chinese put it: everybody could eat from the common iron bowl. The strong financial interest of the family farm, and the free marketing will bring redundant labour to the surface. It is worth making careful calculations comparing costs with receipts. More intensive production will finally release labour that will seek employment. It is an open question, whether the growth of industry and of the other sectors will be sufficient to continuously absorb the masses that become unemployed in the villages.

One of the important means of overcoming difficulties is the 'industrialization' of villages. This phenomenom is somewhat similar to the development of the ancillary workshops of Hungarian agricultural cooperatives. In China, non-agricultural establishments collectively owned by the villages are proliferating: they pursue industrial, building, service or commercial activities. Production is prepared by the cheapest possible investment: for example, second-hand machinery is purchased from city plants. Although they work at relatively low technological standards, these non-agricultural establishments do contribute to the national income and provide employment for labour released from agriculture. The number of families who earn a 'dual income' is growing: part of it coming from agriculture, another part from another sector.

6.3 REFORM IN THE CITY; STATE-OWNED INDUSTRY

The enormous success the reform had in the villages encouraged the Chinese leadership to launch it in the cities too. In terms of population, it is a much smaller sphere, yet its economic and political importance is obviously extremely great. One of the elements of the reform is obvious; private enterprise gains ground. Large numbers of private tradesmen and artisans appear, some at the low technical standards characteristic of the country. A family carries a sewing-machine out into the street, accepts and fulfils orders on the spot. Shoemakers lay out their tools in the street; another family appears with a kitchen stove, kettles, a few tables and chairs: a 'restaurant' business is set up. Many pursue private retail trading or handicraft activities on the free markets under the supervision of the city administration. Within trading activities, an important role is played by vendors selling their merchandise from small handcarts. All this is the usual Asian picture of bustling private activity. But it must be added that this sector had almost totally been eradicated in the Maoist era. In the reform period, it was enough to allow the existence of these activities so that masses of private merchants and artisans could start their work and contribute to supplying the population.

To reform the state-owned sector is a much more difficult problem. We shall discuss the state-owned industrial enterprise first underlining some of its characteristic features, while making it clear that the state-owned enterprises of other sectors (the building industry, services, trade) may be described in the same way.

6.3.1. A large-scale decentralization is taking place on a *regional* scale. Just conceive of 800 thousand state-owned enterprises functioning in the country! It is impossible, even geographically, to direct them from a single centre. China has twenty-one provinces and three cities of provincial right, and in some of its provinces the population is greater than in the most highly populated European country (apart from the Soviet Union). Within the framework of the reform, the central government transfers some of its decision-making rights to the provincial governments, or to lower-level local authorities subordinated to the provincial governments.

This is an important and necessary change, while we must be aware that in itself this is not a move from bureaucratic to market coordination. Each provincial government can continue to function under the old command mechanism. What is more, this regional decentralization calls into being some tendencies which may counter the emergence of a unified national market, and the free flow of commodities, capital and labour. Parallel to regional autonomy, the spirit of regional autarky is emerging. The provincial government applies protectionist rules to protect its 'own' enterprises against competition of 'imports' from other provinces. It also impedes 'exports' to other provinces, fearing that they may cause shortage on its own markets.

6.3.2. The Chinese state-owned enterprise is subject to a *dual regulation*. A part of its capacity is engaged by production prescribed by a mandatory plan target, as a continuation of the pre-reform mechanism. The material and semi-finished products' wanted for the mandatory production are ensured through bureaucratic official rationing. For this part of production, fixed official prices are set. The enterprise is free to sell what it can produce above the mandatory requirements, and to agree to price with the customer without restriction. For this free output, however, it has to acquire the necessary inputs from the free output of other enterprises. The ratios of mandatory and free production are different for each enterprise; for some, the mandatory element only amounts to 50–80 per cent, while with others the mandatory production may still practically engage the available capacity up to 100 per cent.

Chinese economists engage in lively debates among themselves about the advantages and drawbacks of this dual system. Its backers say it allows the central authority to keep in hand a large part of production of vital importance. Besides, it permits a gradual enlargement of the free sphere. Opponents of the dual system point out that a number of the well-known harmful consequences of the old command mechanism have remained: the plan bargaining, concealment of some of the resources, false information given to superior authorities in order to receive the lowest possible mandatory output and the highest possible amount of input. Enterprise managers who have so far only tried trickeries in the implementation of the mandatory plan targets, now can manipulate connections between the two (mandatory and free) spheres as well. Relying on our Hungarian experience, we agree with the critics. One thing the Hungarian reform certainly testifies to is that the system of centrally prescribed mandatory plan targets is possible to abolish by one stroke. *This* is no risk to the functioning of economy; it does not even hinder state authorities to exert a great (sometimes too great and unnecessary) influence on enterprise economy. As bold as the Chinese leadership was in transforming agriculture, it is cautious in changing anything in the mechanism of industry and, in general, in that of the state-owned sector.

6.3.3. Various measures are taken in China to make state-owned enterprise interested in increasing its profit. At the same time, the phenomenon of *'soft budget constraint'*[4] is prevailing there, too. In the course of our talks with Chinese economists they used this expression, which they had learnt from the Hungarian literature, repeatedly. The enterprise's activity is not strictly limited by its financial resources; the coercion of profitability is not predominant. The permanently loss-making enterprise can survive and even expand. The final amount of profit is not decided by the market but through bargaining between the enterprise and its superior authorities. This profit-bargaining has developed in various forms. At first, a 'profit contract' was signed between the authority and the enterprise — this is a veritable caricature of the profit motive. They agreed, after some bargaining, on the amount of profit to be delivered and the amount to be retained. Later, it was a step towards a real profit motive when enterprise taxes were introduced. The idea was that the enterprise would pay the taxes and retain the remaining profit.

Fine, but one of the taxes, the so-called 'adjustment tax' was apt to become a subject of bargaining again. Those who invented this kind of tax intended it to level out those differences between the various enterprises' profitability which cannot be explained with the good or bad performance of enterprises.

But who can determine where good or bad performance ends and where good or bad luck begins? In our view, it is already bad performance, if an enterprise is unable to adequately adjust itself to unlucky external circumstances. The problem is familiar to the Hungarian economist. After the Yugoslav and the Hungarian experience, Chinese experience also seems to confirm that wherever an attempt is made to expose the socially owned enterprise to the market, the immediate reaction is to try to obtain exemption; yes, there should be some kind of competition, but not a 'real' one in which there are winners and losers.

It also sounded familiar to the Hungarian economist's ears when Chinese enterprise managers cited examples of tendencies levelling out profits. It is the very irony of history that in the country where once the extreme egalitarian slogans of Maoism were born, egalitarianism is today asserted with respect to profit, i.e. with the profitability of state-owned enterprises. The net income the superior authorities consider to be 'too much' is taxed away from the enterprise making high profit and transferred to the loss-making enterprise. One of the managers quoted a Chinese proverb saying that 'always the buffalo that pulls most is beaten'. Another one told the following story to illustrate the practical assertion of the principle according to which an enterprise earning more profit can make more investments. 'Let us assume that enterprise No. 1 could start two new investment projects from its own savings, while enterprise No. 2 has no money even for one. In such a case, half of the money of No. 1 is taken away and handed over to No. 2, so that each can launch one investment project. And, in appreciation of its good work, No. 1 is rewarded with a red flag.'

6.3.4. The Chinese state-owned enterprise plays a *peculiar paternalistic role* in relation to its workers. This role of the Chinese enterprise has developed under the influence of several factors. One of them certainly is East-Asian tradition, as slightly similar phenomena are also found in the privately owned Japanese firms. This Asian tradition is then further enhanced by the old economic and political mechanism, the system of mandatory targets, elimination of the market, and shortage economy.

Prior to the reform, a worker of a state-owned enterprise enjoyed many advantages over the members of communes. It was a privilege to be employed by a state-owned enterprise. Now, with living standards rising fast in villages, the question is already emerging as to what extent this still is an advantageous position in comparison with the economic situation of the individually farming peasant. However, as we have mentioned, unemployment threatens today and will do so increasingly in the future, so that in a certain sense it will remain a privilege to be working for a state-owned enterprise.

Certainly, it is not easy to find employment with a state-owned enterprise, but once there, it is practically impossible to leave. The position held in a state-owned enterprise is inherited within the family. The enterprise manager cannot dismiss the worker, and the latter cannot give up his position; they are almost tied to one another.[5] One can speak of a market homogeneously integrating the economy only if there is also a smoothly functioning labour market (Tardos 1985) — but China is far from it as yet.

The enterprise did not only act as employer, but fulfilled certain functions of provisioning as well. For example, it distributed food cards, or food in kind; or it allotted dwellings. The former function is on the wane as a consequence of the 'marketization' of trade in food, while the latter still exists amid a depressing housing situation. The Chinese population has, in general, no social insurance, it receives no health services by civic rights; workers of the state-owned sector enjoy these exceptional benefits through the enterprise. The role of the enterprise extends to asserting the central demographic policy: it has a positive say in which family, when, and how many children are to be born.

In the preceding paragraphs only four questions of the state-owned sector have been examined. Yet even this much is enough to show that, in comparison with the villages (and especially the non-state-owned sectors in them) which moved far away from the conditions of the Maoist period, changes in the cities (and especially in the state-owned sectors) are of a much smaller scale. Eighteen years after the 1968 regulations, we are somewhat further advanced along this road in Hungary, even though quite a number of economists, among them the two authors of the present article, find the reform process too slow. It would be difficult now to forecast the further speed of the reform process taking place in the state-owned sector in China, or to tell at all, how far they will go in the changes, and wherein they will conserve the previous mechanism.

6.4 SHORTAGE, INFLATION, EXPANSION DRIVE

Pre-reform China was, like all the other socialist countries, a *'classic' shortage economy*. There were grave shortages in the supply of consumer goods and services to the population, and in the supply of intermediate goods and investment resources to the producers as well. As a result of the reform process, the situation is no longer uniform, in the trade of certain products and services a 'sellers' market' is still prevailing, while in that of others a 'buyers' market' has already emerged.

As we have mentioned, the food market is well supplied with goods. As for the supply of manufactures, it is difficult to make a general statement. With a lot of items, supply covers demand to a sufficient extent; the latter is strongly constrained by high and fast rising prices. As for other items, such as certain consumer durables, there is high excess demand, and they can only be had after long waiting.

Another phenomenon familiar to us was the intertwining, i.e. simultaneous presence of shortage and slack (i.e. surplus or un-utilized capacity). In front of the hotels, long rows of empty taxi cabs were waiting. At first we thought that the shortage in taxis, characteristic of most of the socialist countries, had been eliminated. Later on, however, it turned out that indeed there was a bad shortage of taxis. Exactly for this reason, institutions and enterprises hire taxis for whole days and let them wait for hours in front of their office or the hotel, because they want them to be available when their own executives or their foreign guests need them. Shortage breeds slack — in this case, unused capacity of taxis — and thereby further shortage.

The shortage harassing the consumer is most conspicuous in the non-market sphere. In the first place, urban housing shortage must be mentioned. It is already one of the gravest social and economic problems of China and, with the rising general level of consumption, it will grow even worse. The Hungarian society also struggles with the problem. It is, however, our impression, that the problem is many times worse in the overpopulated Chinese cities (several of them giant metropolises with millions of inhabitants).

In Hungary, on the present level of development, the shortage of telephone lines is one of the most tormenting shortage phenomena. China is, however, just beginning to establish a telephone network. In private homes, there are practically no telephones, except for a few 'service lines' installed in the homes of some top executives. Enterprises, institutions, and authorities also have very few telephone lines. In this country of huge dimensions it is extremely difficult, even in the most urgent official matters, to get through to another city or province.

Transportation is one of the bottlenecks of growth. To use airlines, one must have an official assignment. On one occasion, we had to change our programme: from Shanghai, instead of going to the originally planned destination, we wished to return to Beijing. A few days prior to the journey, it was impossible to have our itinerary changed in the 'commercial way' i.e. through the office of the airline. We were compelled to seek 'patronage'; our guides appealed to higher and still higher organs. At the same time, we had to prolong our stay at the hotel in Shanghai, and this could not be settled with the hotel, either. Finally, the deputy mayor helped in solving both problems. This, in a city which has 13 million inhabitants, more than the entire Hungarian population. The scope of authority of the deputy mayor is comparable to that of a Hungarian deputy prime minister – a huge responsibility and millions of tasks, and yet he himself had to deal with the hotel reservation and air-tickets of two foreign visitors. We were informed of the fact and were not surprised that decisions of small importance such as these are often made on such a high level. We felt grateful for the obliging assistance, and sorry for those in charge of administrative and economic tasks of high importance that shortage phenomena force them to engage in such 'dispatcher' activities.

It is quite obvious that other branches of transportation put a brake on development and will increasingly do so in the future. Busy highways are quite blocked up with lorries, buses, and the few cars of various institutions. What will happen if private cars appear (which is quite inevitable on a higher level of development)? Similar shortage phenomena and bottlenecks are expected to appear in other fields of infrastructure, such as water supply and drainage.

As for the enterprise supply of materials, parts, semi-finished products, and energy supply, the situation is not uniform. It differs by product, period, and region whether or not there is shortage or a balanced market. Standstills, jolts and forced substitutions in the choice of technology are rather frequent, but we have no adequate information on the subject.

Reverting now to the consumer market, some of the tensions find outlet through *open inflation*. Official reports speak of a 14–15 per cent rate, though quite a number of economists estimate it to be higher. The question is debated among academic economists of several socialist countries whether or not there is excess demand on the consumer market. In China, there is no such debate: excess demand exists without a doubt. The only thing to be debated is how to avoid that inflation getting out of control.

The almost boundless outflow of purchasing power took place mainly in two forms. One was unbridled *wage increase* in state-owned enterprises. Old administrative prohibitions freezing wages and setting strict upper limits to wage funds became much looser. Wage rise is *no longer* placed within bounds by the old mechanism, and *not yet* by a real enterprise profit motive. The enterprise manager is not particularly frightened of wage rises which are well tolerated by the 'soft budget constraint' and which can be passed on either to the superior financial authorities or to the customers. Not caring for the cost consequences, what the enterprise manager does perceive is that wage increases are popular. They are useful means to ease tensions or dissatisfaction that may occur within the enterprise. Not infrequently, wages paid out in cash are completed by extra grants in kind, for example, carpets or cameras are distributed among workers and are accounted as production costs.

The other source of the unrestrained outflow of purchasing power is *investment hunger*. The situation is similar to the Hungarian (and even more, the Polish) investment boom. Every enterprise, authority, regional organ, and ministry wants to invest more and more. The most important thing is to launch the project and when this is done, the money needed for completion can certainly be obtained in one way or another, if not now, then later. The projects started hastily and then delayed for lack of financial resources or on account of technical difficulties are termed in Chinese as 'bearded' investments.

The uninhibited outflow of purchasing power is a monetary reflexion of the *forced expansion drive*. It is another phenomenon well known from the Eastern European economic history. Success (in this case, suddenly increased agricultural production) gives the impression to economic policy makers that the system is capable of even more. And this impression dictates unrealistically high targets of growth rates. The dramatic and drastic closing down of the Maoist period and the launching of the reform released hidden energies, which enabled a suddenly accelerated growth. True, but this acceleration was a unique and non-recurring event. The high growth rate cannot be made permanent and, if it is attempted, it may lead to the well-known disastrous consequences of overtaut plans. It is remarkable that, after the Maoist era had forced the 'big leap' and failed, the reform policy breaking away from Maoism is now attempting again a 'big leap'. It seems that the temptation of organizing 'big leaps' is rooted in the deepest-lying layers of the system, which the reform has left untouched.

It is not only the aggregate targets of the national economy that present a serious problem, but the *structure* of the growth process as well. It is to be feared that the one-sidedness, distortion, and disharmony weighing on Chinese development so far will continue to exist and may even grow. We did not conceal our worry from our Chinese colleagues seeing that they envisaged the great national programme of quadrupling industrial and agricultural production. It would be much more reasonable to campaign for increasing some aggregate indicator (for example, GDP) which would include other sectors beside industry and agriculture. The narrow formulation of the programme already carries the risk that infrastructure, the service sector and, in general, all sectors other than industry and agriculture, which have long been neglected, will be pushed further into the background. Harmony has been one of the fundamental principles of Chinese culture, art, and architecture for many thousands of years. When will the idea of harmony inspire at last the plans of growth?

In connection with the expansion drive, we have yet to mention the problem of *foreign trade and foreign credits*. This country turning inwards for years has at last decided to 'open' in this respect, too, thus creating the condition for benefiting from the well-known advantages offered by the international division of labour. This is a sound change. However, with the given economic mechanism in which no self-limitation of enterprises stimulated by the profit motive has as yet emerged, an almost insatiable *import hunger* has developed. Every enterprise, every organization, every authority wants imports. The main thing is to have the foreign goods as soon as possible: consumer goods sought by the households, and modern machinery for the production units. It is not difficult to raise domestic currency in payment for these. And it is not their worry where the state can find the convertible currency needed. Foreign firms, especially the Japanese ones, eagerly rush at the seemingly boundless Chinese market. Momentarily, they also brush off the question by what means China will pay. Imports are already growing three or four times as fast as exports. It is true that China still disposes of a certain amount of foreign exchange reserves, but they are quickly melting away. There is a danger that reserves will change into a deficit and China, with its gigantic dimensions, will step on the road to indebtedness.

Yet another problem is that of *price and wage reform*. A great many Chinese economists agree in that relative prices are badly distorted; certain products and services are overvalued, while others have relatively too low prices. Similar distortions are found in the wage-system. The market is unable to function properly with such distorted price and wage-systems; it is imperative to make adjustments. It is, however, an open issue how to set to the task. Some suggest a gradual solution, i.e. a series of partial adjustments, fearing that an overall reform might cause too great a shock. Whereas others — and we find their arguments more convincing — oppose the gradual solution on the grounds that it would speed up the inflationary price-wage-cost spiral. Any partial price or wage increase would immediately increase costs, spilling over into other parts of the economy, generating price increases elsewhere, which again would lead to further price and wage increases. Later on also inflationary expectations exert their influence to this effect: every producer calculates future cost rises into his prices. It must be remembered that inflation is a *dynamic* process; this dynamics is generated and accelerated by an endless series of price and wage increases.

6.5 CONTRADICTIONS: OPENING AND REMAINING CLOSED

In the foregoing chapter, various forms of economic disequilibrium have been discussed: shortage phenomena, inflation, foreign trade deficit. Chinese economic managers and economist-researchers have recognized the harmful and dangerous nature of these phenomena, they face the facts and discuss widely what can be done to overcome the difficulties. The view is wide-spread, though not generally accepted, that further reform measures must be put off as long as the economic equilibrium is not restored. Those who hold this view suggest a clearly defined sequence: *first* macro-equilibrium, and *afterwards* further measures to reform institutions and let market forces increasingly assert themselves. Quite a number of foreign advisers are also disposed towards this view. Whereas others think, more conclusively for us, that the two spheres of efforts must not be separated in time, either. Definite steps must be taken *simultaneously* to create macro-equilibrium and to carry on with the reform of institutions. It is to be feared that a priority of macro-equilibrium would be concomitant with a *recentralization* of the mechanism, proliferation of bureaucratic regulation and interventions, and the weakening of market effects.

In China, disequilibrium has come about not only in certain economic relations, but in people's *system of values* as well. Respect for the values proclaimed by the cultural revolution has collapsed. We had conversations with several Chinese colleagues who said that at first they had believed the slogans of that period and even participated in the red guard's movement, but later on became disillusioned. Others bitterly related their ordeals. In the radical movements of the West the opinion still exists that China had followed the proper socialist way at the time of the cultural revolution, but left it with the reforms after the Maoist era.[6] Perhaps French or American authors, lacking personal experience, can less understand and interpret the Chinese events of the last decades. With Hungarians, empathy comes much more naturally.

Under the pretext of 'fighting against bureaucracy', a wild wave of terror swept over China, intellectuals were persecuted and humiliated in the name of the new culture, economic activities were deprived of sound incentives under the banner of equality. All this would have led to strengthening the basically unaffected bureaucratic institutional system had it not been disrupted by the anarchical accompanying phenomena and the disturbances of economic development.

Though the old order of values collapsed, a new one has not been established yet. As far as we could make it out from our conversations and from studying different analyses, a rather large-scale depolitization has taken place in China. Political slogans are no longer painted on the walls. As a rule, arguments are practical and pragmatic.

The artificially suppressed spirit of consumption awoke in hundreds of millions of people. Those who dislike it scornfully speak of 'consumerism', just as in the Hungary of the 1960s 'refrigerator socialism' and 'goulash communism' were the frequently coined terms. Indeed, the Chinese women forced to wear grey or green uniforms for years happily put on colourful dresses today. Shops and department stores are crammed with shoppers looking for electric fans, refrigerators, hi-fi radios. The colour TV-set is the most demanded shortage article. As for us, we do not find any condemnable, 'anti-socialist' tendency in this. It is another question, and an important and justified one, when and to what extent other values — such as commitment to great ideals — join the just claim to decent material living standards. Perhaps a longer time is needed for it and more personal experiences of success to confirm that social responsibility and activity undertaken in the transformation of the country do in fact *influence* public affairs.

The key word of the Chinese reform: 'opening', has already been mentioned in this chapter. One of its most conspicuous manifestations is opening towards the world's science and culture. In this country insulated for a long time, in which leaders flatly denied all community with the great literary, artistic, and scientific values of humanity, cultural hunger now bursts forth with an elementary force. To limit ourselves to our own trade: among the tens of thousands of young people studying abroad there are a great number of students who want to learn modern economics at the best universities of the world. Delegations of economists pay visits to different foreign countries and foreign experts are invited to hold lectures and to take part in consultations in China. They want to become acquainted with the Hungarian and the Yugoslav reforms, French planning, industrial management in the German Democratic Republic and the functioning of banks in the USA and the Federal Republic of

Germany. Of course, all this greedily devoured, fresh knowledge needs time to be digested. The acquisition of knowledge is an organic process; it does not go from one day to the next. And in China, entire generations fell out. The knowledge of the elderly generation has grown obsolete; those who were imprisoned or sent to the country to tend pigs were not in a position to read the latest professional literature. Entire cohorts of young people missed education altogether. It may be a long time before the lag can be recovered.

'Opening' is not an uncontested tendency. As a matter of fact, China is today a peculiar combination of insulation and openness, of conservation of the pre-reform *status quo* and its changing. We met several top leaders who had been themselves victims of the cultural revolution; they had been dismissed from their jobs, or tortured, and put to prison, or sent to the country where, without regard to their professional knowledge and state of health, they had been forced for many years to do hard unskilled physical work. At the same time, however, a lot of people kept their position who had held power also during the Maoist era; now one-time persecutors and persecuted live in peaceful coexistence. Economic policy is tolerant: between certain limits, it gives way to individual initiative and private property, whereas demographic policy is extremely intolerant. One can understand that the rapid population increase, which is almost unbearable from the economic point of view, must be curbed. For our part, however, we do not regard as morally acceptable the forcible means which are used in trying to assert this policy, and the list of contradictory phenomena, incompatible in the long term, could be continued.

It is impossible to foretell what the future holds in store for China. We do not think we are the only ones who cannot see it, knowing little about China, not even the most highly competent experts of Chinese matters would venture any prophesying. Recent Chinese history has been full of sharp turns, of alternating periods of 'opening' and 'insulation', of 'let all flowers bloom' and ruthless force, of 'big leap' and cautious slowdown. The possibility of a halt to or reversal of the reform process remains. This much is certain, however, that *today* no palpable signs in such a direction are apparent. Again an analogy can be drawn with Hungary. In our country, one often feels a depressed atmosphere: many people are exasperated, sceptical and pessimistic. The reform process, now coming to a halt, now moving ahead hardly has an inspiring pathos. Whereas

China is now in the midst of the first euphoria of changes. Life has returned to a society which had grown rigid, consumption has suddenly increased, life has become on the whole more pleasant and all this raises hope and confidence in almost all groups of society. We sincerely wish that their hopes and plans come true.

NOTES

1. Measured at current prices and exchange rates the ratio is about 1 to 30. Certain careful comparative analyses attempt, however, to circumvent as well as to correct exchange rates and prices to a certain degree, and they demonstrate a much lower ratio: 1 to 10. See World product (1982).
2. An excellent review can be found in Solinger (1984).
3. In the wave of literature after the Maoist era a soul-stirring short story was published about a peasant who undertook, after finishing his daily toils in the fields, to skin dead animals and prepare leather for a small fee. This man, who did a heavy and dirty, and certainly socially useful, work was qualified a 'capitalist' at a public meeting, humiliated and even physically maltreated for his sin.
4. This term was introduced by the author in his book: Kornai (1980). In economics, budget constraint is the upper bound on expenses of economic unit (household, enterprise, or any other institution) set by available financial resources. This constraint can temporarily be lifted with the aid of credit, but credit has to be repaid sooner or later; it is receipts that in the long-run constrain expenses. The budget constraint of state-owned enterprises will 'soften' if the state is willing to cover permanent losses, for example, by tax exemptions, or by granting 'soft' credits, the repayment of which at expiration is not enforced, by administrative prices passively adjusted to costs, etc. With a soft budget constraint, the profit motive becomes illusory. The survival and growth of the enterprise do not depend on market success, but on the superior authorities' benevolence.
5. On the other hand, the village worker is also 'soil-bound'; if he wants to contract for a job outside his own area, he needs the permit of his local authority. The enforcement of this constraint is all the easier, as he also needs the written permit of the same authority if he wants to buy a ticket for the train, long-distance bus, or airplane.
6. The radical 'New Left' positions of North America and Western Europe — disagreeing, among others, on the Chinese questions — are discussed in detail in Griffin–Gurley (1985).

REFERENCES

China: Socialist Economic Development (1983) World Bank: Washington.
Griffin, K.—Gurley, J. (1985) 'Radical Analyses of Imperialism, the Third World and the Transition to Socialism', *Journal of Economic Literature*, Vol. 23, September. The section on China on pp. 1134–1436.

Jordán, Gy. (1985) 'Kína mezőgazdasága ma — változások és tendenciák' (Chinese Agriculture Today — Changes and Tendencies). *Közgazdasági Szemle*, 10. pp. 1249–1260.

Kornai, J. (1980) *Economics of Shortage*. Amsterdam: North–Holland.

Lim, E.—Wood, A. (eds.) (1985) *China — Long-term Development Issues and Options*. World Bank — John Hopkins University Press: Baltimore–London.

Perry, E. J.–Wong, C. (1985) *The Political Economy of Reform in Post-Mao China*. Harvard University Press: Cambridge.

Solinger, J. D. (1984) *Three Versions of Chinese Socialism*. Boulder.

Tardos, M. (1985) "A szabályozott piac kialakításának feltételei" (Conditions of Developing a Regulated Market). *Közgazdasági Szemle*, 11, pp. 1281–1298.

World Product and Income, (1982) World Bank: Washington.

7 Preface to the Soviet Edition of *Economics of Shortage*
On the responsibility of the researcher, the adviser and the politician

It is a great pleasure and honour for me to have my book *Economics of Shortage* published in the Soviet Union.

The phenomenon discussed in the book is well-known to the reader. The Hungarians and the Soviets, the Chinese and the Romanians, the Cubans and the Poles are all equally aware of what it means to queue for meat and shoes, to be on the receiving end of rude remarks from the shop-assistant instead of the goods requested; to wait for years for a flat from the council or to find production stopped in the factory because there is a lack of raw materials and components. Shortage results in a diversity of losses: it reduces the consumer's satisfaction, hinders well-balanced production and takes away important incentives for technical development. What is, perhaps, the heaviest loss of all is that the seller has the advantage over the buyer; the individual's autonomy and freedom are violated. The seller's domination of the buyer frequently places the latter in a humiliating position, either as a customer in the shop, or as a worker in the factory. As we can see, we have here the most specific field of political economy under examination: we are not studying the relationship between man and things but are analysing the social relationships among people when trying to clarify the causes and consequences of chronic shortage.

Soviet economic science recognized this problem early. The present book also refers to works written by L. N. Kristman in 1925 and V. V. Novozhilov in 1926. Later on, however, for decades people only talked about shortage in the family, perhaps when queuing up, but shortage did not figure as a topic of scholarly research in political economy. Here it is worth stopping for a moment to consider what the actual task of the economist investigating the problems of socialism is.

In the long historical period when economists in the socialist countries carefully avoided investigating the phenomenon of shortage and other, similarly 'delicate' questions, their philosophy was determined along the following lines: socialism is a system which satisfies the old desires of mankind. All of its laws, by definition, exert a favourable influence. Consequently, all the unfavourable, harmful phenomena, which cause human suffering or economic loss, are merely passing inconveniences, resulting from negligence or bad work on the part of individuals. It is also possible that the harmful phenomena are brought about by errors on the part of this or that leader who acquired extraordinary power — a Stalin or a Mao Tse-tung — and since such individuals exert enormous influence, the losses caused can be very grave. This much is certain, however — to follow this thinking — that the problems are independent of the fundamental social relationships of the existing system. In socialism all the laws are 'good'. Problems, if they exist at all, come into being only because individuals did not recognize the 'good' laws, implemented them improperly, or acted against them.

In the works that resulted from this way of thinking the duties of the economist, namely, observation, description, and explanation of reality, appraisal of the given situation and the drawing of practical tasks and programmes are mixed up. This collection of roles is described in the international literature under different denominations, contrasting the 'positive' (descriptive-explanatory) theory with the 'normative' theory (evaluating and making recommendations). In the works that were inspired by the thinking outlined above, the answers to be given to two questions, which ought to be sharply distinct from one other, are confused: what is it that *exists* and what is it that *should exist*? What is *reality* and what should the *desired* situation be like? The imagined properties of the ideal perfect society are referred to by these works as 'objective laws', while the real internal contradictions of the real society do not even appear in their analysis. The most important requirement of scholarship, the contrasting of statements with observation, experience and facts, remains unsatisfied.

Similarly to works by a number of other authors, the present book is based upon a way of thinking and approach different from that outlined above. Its primary starting-point is that we must face reality, whether we like what we have observed or not. The first question a conscientious researcher must pose himself is not whether what he sees is 'good' but whether what he has stated is *true* or not. Is the description supplied by the researcher in accordance with the facts? And if the researcher, following his own conscience, meets this, the only possible scientific criterion, then he has the right to commit to paper what he has stated, whether the truth which thus comes to light is pleasant or unpleasant.

The word 'law' has been abused frequently and this has given rise to so much misunderstanding that the writer is reluctant to use it. Let us use more modest expressions of the system and its behavioural patterns. The basic precept of the book is that the economic system which was typical of the socialist economy prior to decentralizing reforms inevitably creates shortage. This, then, is a regularity which necessarily comes into being under certain social circumstances.

The phenomenon is *general*. No one states that in this system there is always shortage and of everything. The statement is more qualified than that: namely that none of the important spheres in the market for consumer goods and services, in production, in the allocation of labour, in investment, in foreign trade and in international currencies. The phenomenon is *chronic:* it manifests itself in every period; it always reappears following the occasional temporary success of the efforts made to defeat it. The system ensures the reproduction of shortage. The phenomenon is of a *self-generating* character: shortage breeds shortage. The phenomenon is *intensive:* it prevails, in great strength and exerts a strong influence on the behaviour of all members of society. When that is manifested in a general, chronic, self-generating and intensive shortage — in the sense described and defined here — then this system may be referred to as a *shortage economy*.

The book attempts to present a causal analysis. If a phenomenon is very frequent, permanent, and intensive, it cannot be accounted for by the occasional, accidental errors of individuals. The argument that shortage is created by errors of calculation in planning, or the selfishness and carelessness of certain factories, or the lack of care on the part of some sellers, does not seem to be convincing. We have to seek causes lying deeper than that.

The analysis presented by this book tries to proceed backwards from the phenomena observable by everyone to the more superficial and then the more general causes of a more fundamental character, delving into deeper and deeper layers of cause and effect. It discusses the extent to which shortage phenomena may be explained by the various frictions in the economy, that is by conflicts and weakness in information, decision-making and decision implementation. The next layer is the connections between chronic shortage and the different social effect mechanism: expansion drive, quantity drive, investment hunger, the hoarding tendency, the almost insatiable demand of the state sector for production inputs and especially investment resources. To go deeper again: how can the tendencies above be accounted for by the weak responsiveness of the state companies to prices and profit, the lack of compulsion towards profit, the set of phenomena which is referred to by the book as the soft budget constraint of the enterprises? This is related to the fact that state-owned companies are much more dependent upon the bureaucracy which they are subordinate to than their customers. Their life or death, their contraction or expansion does not depend on their success in competition but on what the authorities, their commanders and paternalistic foster parents wish to do with them. This causal analysis could probably be continued and the question 'why' may be raised after each answer. However, it appears even from the analysis in this work that shortage will be constantly reproduced as long as the vertical dependence of the company remains the dominating relationship in production.

Since my book has been published it has been subject to much discussion both in Hungary and abroad. In ten to twenty years' time, following a great deal more discussion and, hopefully, after extensive empirical research based upon as many facts as possible, economics will probably have understood the set of problems related to shortage better than was possible when this book was written. I expect the analysis of the book to be the subject of discussion among my Soviet colleagues as well. However, I would be very happy if, more important than this or that economic proposition of the book, the philosophy and ethics of science, upon which this work is based, met with as great understanding as possible. I would be glad to see wide agreement that we have to face facts even if they induced negative feelings in us. We do not have the right to avoid delicate truths. We cannot be satisfied with superficial answers but must try to find the deep roots of problems and maladies. We have to reveal the true regularities of the economic reality around us, the genuine explanation of mass phenomena and of the lasting implications.

Even among those who share these views there will probably be some who will put down the book in disappointment for the author presents no guidelines on how to remedy the existing disease. What is the value of a diagnosis without therapy?

Let us stay with the simile taken from health care. A few years ago I wrote a study on the analogy between the medical and economic sciences (*Contradictions and Dilemmas*. Budapest, Corvina, 1985, and Cambridge, MIT Press, 1986). Not long ago a Russian translation of it was published by the Soviet journal *Eko*. At this point I would like to return to the line of thought outlined in this work. There is no doubt that the most important thing for the sick man is to survive, and, if possible, recuperate. But this cannot be achieved by commanding the doctor to prescribe some medicine because the patient *must* recover. 'Lung disease', 'illness of the chest' or 'consumption' (later known as tuberculosis) afflicted people for thousands of years. They implored, at times threatened, first sorcerers and later the cultivators of the profession called medicine. All kinds of treatment were administered to the patients: prayer, exorcism, hot and cold baths, all varieties of medical herbs and chemicals. Finally, in 1890, modern bacteriology discovered that tuberculosis is caused by a bacillus. When Robert Koch arrived at this conclusion, he was unable to indicate how to fight the bacillus. More than half a century elapsed before a really effective medicine, streptomycin, was discovered and tuberculosis ceased to be a widespread killer. True, understanding the cause of the disease made it possible to make use of sensible forms of treatment prior to the discovery of a really effective medicine: the patients were taken care of tenderly, and sent to fresh air, their fever was alleviated, perhaps a part of their lungs was removed. The Hippocratic oath of the medical profession was respected: at least harm should not be caused to the patient.

Let us return to our own profession. The complicated regularities of the operation of the socialist system have not yet been revealed. In this respect we are in a much weaker position than the economists in the capitalist countries attempting to understand the operation of their own system. It is almost as if we were just getting down to this enormous task. Some economists are very sure of themselves: they just look around and know already what must be done. The author does not belong to this class. We do not know exactly what causes the malady of our 'patient', the socialist economy. We are not faced by a single disease but a whole complex of negative symptoms. What is the connection between them? Do they have separate causes or are they the consequences of common causes? Are they properties that are inherent to the system, *any kind* of socialist system, no matter which particular mechanism they might operate with, or do they follow exclusively from one version of socialism, an overcentralized command economy? Can all the maladies be completely remedied or may some be impossible to overcome and only an alleviation of the symptoms be possible? There is a host of questions which have not been answered convincingly yet.

The questions raised above in general terms can be made more specific with regard to the subject of the present book, namely, shortage. Although I have been studying this topic for several years, I have to confess that I am unable to provide a definite answer to a number of questions. Earlier, I stated that shortage is a necessary concomitant of a command economy, the old overcentralized mechanism. From this, however, it does not follow automatically that the statement may be used simply for normative purposes: it is sufficient to eliminate the command economy and grant a greater autonomy to the state-owned firms and this in itself will end shortages. It seems to me that this is a necessary but not sufficient condition to put an end to the shortage economy nature of the system and reverse the present situation where buyers compete for sellers and replace it by a competition between producers and sellers for buyers. It has not been fully clarified yet which are the sufficient and necessary conditions for eliminating shortage.

Scholarly examination cannot give finite answers to these open questions because the practical reforms carried out so far have not led to unambiguous results. I am a long-standing, sincere and enthusiastic advocate of reforms. However, those engaged in a scientific discipline — and this I wish to stress again most emphatically — must take as a starting-point not desires but observed facts. The reform process has a forty-year history in Yugoslavia, twenty in Hungary, and almost a whole decade in China. All three countries represent specific mixtures of amazing results and disastrous failures. It would be dishonest to notice only the results for reform propaganda purposes, or point merely to the failures for those of counter-propaganda. Among other things, from the point of view of the topic of the present book, namely shortage (and the other interrelated serious trouble, inflation) the experience of these three countries does not indicate unequivocally the solution to the problems. It is not the task of this preface to strike a balance among the reforms carried out so far and clarify why the situation is lop-sided and why progress is not more rapid. Here I merely wish to point out one idea. It is understandable that we are not in possession of an action plan aiming at the elimination of the shortage economy which would have a strong scientific foundation in the strict sense of this term.

The reform measures carried out in any of the socialist countries so far can be looked upon as 'experiments'. One might take the risk of drawing strong conclusions even from a few experiments if the results of the experiments are unequivocal. Unfortunately, the experiments of the reform processes carried out so far were not conclusive; they did not provide sufficient information to draw valid scientific inference from them.

From all the above it does *not* follow that we should stop and hold all practical steps until science has explored the problem in a finite and irrefutable manner and placed in our hands a programme of action. Here we must break away from the analogy taken from medical science and emphasize that history will not wait for the men of science to clarify the problems. There is a division of labour not only within the economy, in production, but also in social action. First, there is division of labour between the politician and the scientist. The politician, the statesman, who undertakes the responsibility of leading society, works under the compulsion of the necessity of action. He is aware that he *must* take steps even if he does not know exactly what will be the consequences of these steps and what the hidden connections are that move the complicated social medium in which he is taking political action. In most cases, it is internal conviction and beliefs rather than strict and objective scientific analysis which prompt him to decide on the steps to take.

As far as those active in science are concerned, there is a division of labour there too; not everyone is ready to undertake the same task. Some feel that they are able to make quick and resolute decisions in practical matters, following the results of research revealed so far and — which is actually far more realistic — their own common sense. At the same time other economists feel the vocation to perform basic research and analyse the deeper problems and do not consider themselves suitable for the role of practical advisers who contribute to the preparation of current decisions.

Full respect is due to those among our economist colleagues who concentrate their intellectual power on drawing up operative proposals and practical action programmes suitable of being implemented immediately. Their work is necessary; the reform policy requires their participation. They can help in making use of international experience more fully and successfully. But while sincerely feeling justification for this respect, I claim the same for those who have assigned themselves different duties. A Robert Koch was needed, a man who spent so much time over his microscope even though he did not heal one tuberculosis patient in his own lifetime. Some perform operations, bravely cutting into the flesh of the patient; others, shrinking from taking a lancet in their hands, try to discover the secrets of the human organism in the laboratory. Perhaps the work performed by the theoretical experts engaged in basic research also yields some immediate practical use: if nothing else, their analysis may prevent rash, spectacular but actually useless or even harmful actions, or cool the illusions and exaggerated expectations which may later result in disappointment. Beyond this unrewarding but useful role of helping people to see clearly, basic research and theoretical investigations may, sooner or later, indirectly and with great delay, render assistance in the thorough understanding of the situation and of the tasks to be done and, ultimately, of the practical development of society.

Mutual respect, understanding and tolerance in relation to opinions, philosophies and commitments different from our own are very much needed in our world of science. No institution, organization, movement, scientist or politician can consider themselves infallible. This book, with its insights and mistakes, is meant to help strengthen this spirit and the fruitful evolution of scholarly discussion.

Finally, I wish to end on a personal note. I wrote my first academic paper, my Ph.D. dissertation, 'Overcentralization in Economic Administration' in 1955–56. Soon after it appeared in book form in Hungarian and in 1959 it was published by Oxford University Press in English. Thirty years have elapsed since my first work was published in foreign language. Frankly, I noted with regret that while my books were translated into several languages in the socialist and in the capitalist countries, not one of them was published in the Soviet Union. True, some articles of mine appeared there, but this — I felt — could not make up for the books in which I elaborated my views and ideas far more comprehensively. All the greater, therefore, is the gratitude I feel towards those who stood up for the publication of my book. First of all, I have to name the late R. Karagedov, who presented an excellent and concise summary of the ideas of this book and recommended it for publication in the Soviet Union many years ago. But mention should also be made here of the names of other economists who repeatedly argued for the publication of the book in the Soviet Union. Let me mention at least those whose efforts to this effect are known to me: T. I. Zaslavskaya, A. G. Aganbegian and O. T. Bogomolov.

I am grateful to D. Markov and M. Usievich, the translators of the book, as well as to the editors for their enormous and strenuous work, and to the Nauka Publishing House which took on the publication. May I take the opportunity to extend my heartfelt gratitude to all those who promoted the publication of my book in the Soviet Union through their initiative and participation.

8 Individual Freedom and Reform of the Socialist Economy*

8.1 INTRODUCTION

There is a vast and constantly growing literature on the reform of socialist economies. World-wide interest has increased rapidly now that the two giants, first China and more recently the Soviet Union have followed the two pioneering, smaller countries — Yugoslavia and Hungary — in taking the first steps along the road of reform. Most analyses of the reform process adopt a narrow economic or techno-logical point of view, and concern themselves solely with issues such as efficiency, growth, material welfare, and adjustment to the world market.

This chapter discusses something quite different. The questions it raises are prompted by moral and political philosophy, and they revolve around the issue of individual freedom. The basic question is: what is the relationship between the reform of a socialist system and the liberty of the individual?

The topics chosen reflect a value judgement. I am not presenting a

* Several people were kind enough to offer valuable suggestions for improving the chapter, including T. Bauer, J. S. Berliner, Zs. Dániel, M. Ellman, R. I. Gábor, D. Hausman, Z. Kapitány, M. Laki, R. Nozick, A. Sen, A. Simono-vits and J. W. Weibull, in particular. Special thanks are due to M. Kovács for her devoted research assistance and to B. McLean and S. Mehta for help in improving the English of the chapter. The support of the Hungarian Academy of Sciences' Institute of Economics, and of Harvard University is gratefully acknowledged. Of course, responsibility for the views expressed in this chapter is entirely the author's.

normative theory here; most of the chapter in fact, will offer positive, descriptive observations. Nevertheless, let me state my credo at the beginning. I have a deep regard for individual liberty, and for the right to self fulfilment and the right to choose one's own way of life. In my value system, individual liberty is one of the fundamental, primary goods.[1] I regard the significant expansion of economic freedom as one of the major achievements of the Hungarian reform. By the same token, I consider its failure to go far enough in this direction as one of the gravest shortcomings of the Hungarian reform. One of the purposes of this chapter is to establish a new standard for the measurement of the progress of the reform movement, to be applied in conjunction with the usual measures of efficiency. Applying this standard, the chapter will report both on the successes and on the failures of the Hungarian reform.

The choice of Hungary is quite natural; it is the country I know best. But I am confident that the issues, problems, concepts and relationships discussed in this chapter can be applied to the study of other socialist countries as well. Therefore, while Hungary will be used as a demonstrative example, the discussion of observations and propositions must be construed to have a more general validity.

The larger part of the audience at the Copenhagen Congress, and also the larger part of the readership of *European Economic Review,* consists of Western economists. This audience and readership cannot expect much novelty in this chapter concerning the general discussion of individual freedom. Nevertheless, it might be interested in what is going on in this respect in the socialist system.

I hope, however, that the message will be heard in socialist countries as well. The discussion of individual freedom was an ideological taboo for decades; notions such as 'individualism' or 'liberalism' had strong pejorative connotations. But, I am convinced that respect for individual freedom is not only compatible with the original aims of many socialist thinkers but should become a fundamental ingredient of the socialist programme everywhere.

Freedom is a recurring topic in philosophy, in economics and in political theory, and not a single issue relating to it escapes being the subject of wide, and often heated, controversy. I am not embarking on any enquiry that touches upon the intricacies of modern analytical philosophy. These thoughts will remain at a modest, pragmatic, down-to-earth level and will try to keep close to the realities of life under socialist systems today.

8.2 CLARIFYING THE CONCEPTS

Even an ordinary dictionary lists several meanings under the entries for 'liberty' and 'freedom', and it is small wonder, then, that every school of philosophy applies different interpretations to them. We do not aspire to provide a comprehensive, all-encompassing characterization. All we need here is a partial interpretation that embraces the elements in the composite category 'freedom' relevant to our context. We hope no one will dispute that the attributes we are going to examine are indeed components of freedom.

This chapter is concerned only with *individual* freedom. Important though the freedom of communities (and we have in mind the freedom of firms, of associations, of towns, and of nations) may be, they will not be discussed in this chapter. We shall concentrate on *economic* freedom, in other words, on the right of the individual to dispose freely of wealth, of income, of time and of effort. Political or intellectual freedom will not be studied here, and the discussion will be confined to the economic aspects of liberty even though we are fully aware of the strong links between political, intellectual and economic freedoms.[2]

Freedom has an instrumental value; it helps the individual in his choice between alternative actions. In addition, the author joins all those who attribute an important *intrinsic value* to individual economic freedom, as a value in its own right.

This judgement must be made clear especially in the context of the discussion of socialist economies. Even if the paternalistic state were to allot me the same bundle of commodities which I would have chosen freely from a set of alternative bundles, it does not have the same meaning for me. It gives me some additional value, to make the choice myself, freely and without interference. In addition, in most cases the outcome of paternalistic interventions leads to large deviations from the bench-mark autonomous choice of the individual.[3] As for paternalism, I agree with I. Berlin's (1969) words: 'For if the essence of men is that they are autonomous beings — authors of values, of ends in themselves, the authority of which consists precisely in the fact that they are willed freely — then nothing is worse than to treat them as if they were not autonomous, but natural objects,... whose choices can be manipulated by their rulers... 'Nobody may compel me to be happy in his own way', said Kant, 'Paternalism is the greatest despotism imaginable...

paternalism is despotic, not because it is more oppressive than naked, brutal, unenlightened tyranny,... but because it is an insult to my conception of myself as a human being.'

Since we attribute an intrinsic value to individual economic freedom, we do not regard it simply as an instrument to achieve welfare or utility. I am aware that methodological objections can be raised by those who espouse a strictly monistic approach. I prefer a pluralistic framework, to separately handle incommensurables like ultimate moral principles, because this framework spells out potential conflicts and trade-offs.[4] *Hamlet* could have been a very short story indeed, and hesitation would have been ruled out if only the protagonist had formulated and solved in a straightforward way a simple problem of maximizing utility. This chapter will discuss conflicting ethical values later. Notwithstanding the methodological distinction, the ideas in it can, of course, be transposed into a monistic framework. But whoever wants to do so must decide and adequately defend his *single,* ultimate, primary good. It might be liberty interpreted in the most general way. In that case welfare must be just one of its components. Or it might be utility. In that case freedom ought to be an argument in the utility function itself.[5]

We shall not aim for a complete analysis covering all aspects of individual economic freedom in a socialist economy. Rather, we shall single out two classes of constraints of free choice, and disregard many other constraints whatever their relevance might be.

To the first class to be discussed in more detail belong the *bureaucratic constraints.* In this category we include both formal legislative orders or prohibitions and informal imperatives enforced by pressures or threats imposed upon the individual by the bureaucracy. To sharpen our sense of the nature of bureaucratic constraints it seems convenient to examine the effect of a change in the constraints. How might the constraint change to allow an increase in freedom? Here are a few illustrative situations; the list of situations is, of course, not exhaustive.

- Freedom increases when the right to make certain kinds of decision passes from the bureaucracy to the individual; for example when mandatory posting to a job after graduation gives way to the graduate choosing his first job himself.
- Freedom increases when a bureaucratic constraint on an individual's decision is lifted. For example, suppose an employee

has the right to set about leaving his job and looking for another one, but needs the consent of his superiors before he actually leaves; he becomes freer when he no longer needs that consent.

• Freedom increases when an existing bureaucratic constraint becomes quantitatively less stringent, for example if the maximum number of employees in a private firm allowable under an administrative order is raised from three to nine.

Freedom in the sense of not being constrained by another individual or by a group of individuals or by the state is often called 'negative freedom'. (In shorthand this is called freedom *from.*)[6] According to this interpretation the loosening or lifting of bureaucratic constraints undoubtedly enhances negative freedom.

It is an odd tradition of the socialist movement to belittle the relevance of negative freedom. This tradition points out the emptiness of the formal, bourgeois rights, for example by citing the freedom of the rich and the poor alike to sleep under the bridge. In this view only 'positive freedom' matters, i.e., one must have the power to do what one wants to do. (In shorthand this is called 'freedom *to*'.) However great the relevance of positive freedom, the issue of negative freedom cannot be ignored with a wave of the hand, since it plays an extremely important role in the life of the individual. Incidentally, the right to decide freely where one wants to spend the night, is not universally accepted, and we should not take it as self-evident. There have been times when the citizens of some socialist countries could not travel without written permission from the state, they had to report to the police immediately when they decided to spend more than one or two nights away from their place of permanent residence. We shall return to this issue and to other aspects of negative freedom in our subsequent discussion of the Hungarian situation.

The other class of constraints we want to focus on comprises of *limitations on choice imposed by shortages.* It is probably fair to say that we are dealing with an issue concerning 'positive freedom'. The usual concept of positive freedom refers to the individual's capabilities: his freedom increases, when his means to achieve his goals increase. This general concept leads to certain more specific ideas in our thinking. Imagine an hypothetical experiment in the free association of ideas. The first words which would come to the mind of a Western economist responding to the concept of positive freedom would probably be notions such as income, wealth, capital both physical and human. These are undoubtedly components of an individual's capabilities and limits in their availability constrain his freedom of choice. If we use the metaphor of a shop window displaying a variety of goods, then this shop window is useless if one does not have the resources of income or wealth to buy what is available there.

If a similar experiment in the free association of ideas were to be carried out in Eastern Europe, the response of an Eastern economist would be a little different. Of course, he will think of poverty and the low level of development, and of resources such as income appropriate to his situation. But surely, another association would also cross his mind. Despite a well articulated demand and money income to back it up, the individual might not be able to get the goods that he wants at the prevailing price, or indeed at any price. That is no less an obstacle in the fulfilment of his goals, than the limits of his budget.

The first type of constraint on positive freedom is general; we can find it in all systems, including socialist systems (though, of course the parameters of *distribution* vary from country to country for many reasons). The second type of constraint is more system-specific, and that is the motive for the special attention given to it in this chapter. We are talking not about sporadic and occasional excess demand, but about an economy where shortages are chronic and caused by systemic factors.[7] Shortage phenomena do occur here and there in all systems but in a 'shortage economy' they are very frequent, they appear in all segments of the economy, and they are intensive and tormenting.

I have coined the term 'forced substitution' to describe a typical situation common in a shortage economy in order to contrast it with voluntary substitution. The latter provides a free choice: the individual substituted good B for good *A*, because his tastes or the relative prices have changed. In a case of forced substitution he would have preferred good *A* to good *B* at prevailing prices, but he has no choice other than to substitute *B* for *A*, because *A* is in short supply. In some cases forced substitution causes only a minor inconvenience. In others it leads to grave and lasting suffering, for example to people forced to share an apartment for decades or even a lifetime against their will, or unable to have a telephone installed for years even though they are sick, immobilized or need a phone badly for some other reason. The victims of shortage suffer humiliation; they are at the mercy of the seller and of the bureaucrat.[8]

It might be surmised that the individual is not indifferent even towards the availability of goods which he actually does not choose at present. The wider the assortment of goods supplied, the larger the number of alternatives, and consequently the safer the availability of goods demanded, the stronger is the buyer's conviction that there is genuine free choice.

It follows from the intrinsic value of freedom, that the situation in which one chooses C while both C and D are at hand, is not identical with the situation in which one chooses C because it is the only possibility. In the latter case one is deprived of the elementary right of free choice; there was a loss of something valuable — although it was not a loss of 'welfare' or 'utility' since C would have been preferred to D anyway.

We might, therefore, conclude that an individual's economic freedom increases as the intensity and frequency of shortage phenomena decreases and the consumer is provided with greater opportunities for choice. The relationship is all the more immediate, and stronger, if the change for the better is not just provisional, but if it becomes permanent as a result of a reform of the economic mechanism.

The two sets of constraints on freedom, which will be at the heart of our discussion, namely bureaucratic constraints and curtailment of choice due to chronic shortages, are interrelated. Bureaucratic control is among the factors which explain why shortages occur; shortages induce bureaucratic rationing. Yet the two sets overlap only partially, and so it is analytically useful to consider them separately.

It follows that in our conceptual framework we regard freedom as a *multidimensional* category. All the restrictions on the individual's economic freedom mentioned so far can be observed. They can be represented either by a binary indicator (reflecting the presence or the absence of a certain constraint), or they can be represented by a scale ranging, e.g., from zero to one (reflecting the stringency of the restriction in question)[9]. Each indicator represents a specific well-defined dimension of freedom, which is not, when approached in this way, an intangible metaphysical entity. Are Hungarian individuals free with regard to their economic actions? One cannot give a simple 'yes' or 'no' answer. But one can give meaningful answers for each type of constraint which is relevant to our enquiry and consider the degree of freedom or lack of freedom in each particular dimension.

8.3 YARDSTICKS: THE MINIMAL AND THE MAXIMAL STATE

To appraise the changes in the degree of individual freedom one needs yardsticks. To consider the restriction on freedom in a private market economy, the point of departure might be taken to be 'Locke's state of nature', i.e., the state of individuals living in *complete anarchy*[10]. In the scheme presented in Fig. 8.1 there is a vertical axis, resrepresenting the degree of state control over the economic spheres No. 1, 2, 3,....

Degree 0, or complete anarchy, is not sustainable. Going upwards from 0 one arrives at the points (denoted by Δ on the scheme) representing what political philosophers have called the 'minimal'

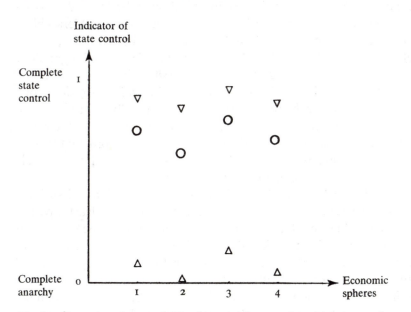

Fig. 8.1: Illustration of the yardsticks: from complete anarchy to complete state control. *Legend:* ∇ maximal state, O actual state, Δ minimal state. (*Note:* The figure is used only as a simple schematic illustration of the points made in the text. Our train of thought does not require the assumption of cardinal comparability between different spheres of the economy.)

or the 'night-watchman' state. The role of the state is limited to the protection of the citizen against violence and theft and to the enforcement of voluntary contracts.[11] (Here we disregard for the sake of brevity the role of the state in external affairs.) Any additional state activity, including measures designed for redistributive justice and the supply of public goods, goes beyond the minimal state.

Turning to the upper end of the axis, degree i represents complete state control of all spheres of the economy, with nothing left to private initiative or choice.[12] This Orwellian situation is entirely hypothetical and without any historical precedent; it has never existed at any time. Let us introduce by way of contrast to the notion of the minimal state, a new notion, that of the *maximal* state (represented by the symbols Δ on the scheme)[13]. This is a lower degree of 'etatization'[14] than the terminal point of the scale, i.e., the point of complete state control. The maximal state is not an abstract theoretical notion, but an historical concept; this is the highest *feasible* degree of bureaucratic power, where feasibility depends on the practical conditions for enforcing centralization. Among such conditions are the technology of information gathering and processing and of communication between the officials in the hierarchical bureaucracy; the organizational abilities of the bureaucracy; the art of mass-manipulation; the ultimate limits of tolerance of repression, and so on. So the maximal state, of necessity, allows certain minor concessions to be made with regard to individual freedom, one typical concession being a limited degree of individual choice on the market for consumer goods. Such arrangements are tolerated, but only provisionally, and the proviso always remains that further steps in the direction of complete state control would be desirable should they ever become feasible.

Looking at the actual historical record we find that all socialist countries have come close to the maximal state for at least a period of time in their evolution — the Soviet Union after the collectivization of agriculture under Stalin, China after the establishment of the communes under Mao, and Eastern Europe during the period 1949–1953. There are substantial differences among the different spheres of the economy in terms of how close they have come to the maximal state in each country during the peak periods of etatization. We have no space here to elaborate in detail; with a degree of simplification needed for a general analysis one can, however, say the maximal state has been the historical point of departure for the reform process in socialist countries. As a consequence of the reform, the degree of central control in the *actual* state (represented by symbols o on the scheme) is lower than in the maximal state.

It is quite understandable for scholars and politicians discussing the problems of a welfare state to think in terms of how close to or how far from the minimal state are they and how close should they be. It is no less understandable for scholars and politicians considering the problems of reform in socialist countries to think in diametrically opposite terms: how close to or how far from the maximal state are they and how close should they be.

8.4 CHANGES IN HUNGARY

We now turn to a survey of the changes in Hungary. It would take much too long to follow the whole historical course of the reform process. Therefore we shall contrast two specific periods instead: the early 1950s, a period which saw the peak of bureaucratic centralization in most (although not in all) spheres, and came closest to our concept of a maximal state, and the present period which began in the mid-1980s and which we shall call the 'reformed state'.

Each observation will be presented in a concise and simplified form, and qualitative analysis will not be bolstered by statistics.[15] Besides, many qualifications could be added to each item for the sake of precision, but limitations of space do not allow to us to become immersed in details.[16]

Part of the change has taken the form of a definitive amendment of Hungarian law, and has resulted in the repeal of old legislation and in the introduction of new laws. Another and certainly no less important part has been the result, not of openly declared new rules, but simply of the relaxation in the enforcement of old laws and governmental directives. The state has not only shrunk, but has 'softened' as well, a fact which has opened new doors for private initiative and enterprise, and for voluntary, private contracts, often in the grey area between legality and illegality, in what is often called the second economy. These effects have been inseparably accompanied by such side-effects as weakening of respect for the law, and a laxity in the attitudes towards cheating and corruption. In our survey we shall endeavour to make clear which changes have occurred formally and which changes have come about informally through a 'softening' of state control, although we cannot always make a sharp distinction in every case.

8.4.1 Property and entrepreneurship

In a maximal state almost all people earning wages or salaries must be employed by the state. With a few exceptions there is only route towards upward mobility in society, and that is by making a career within the bureaucratic hierarchy.

In Hungary cooperatives have existed, mainly in agriculture and in urban services, but they have not arisen out of a genuine, voluntary cooperative movement. In their functioning they have differed little from their state-owned counterparts: managers have always been appointed by the bureaucracy *de facto* and they have had to follow mandatory plans. In addition, the number of private craftsmen has been almost negligible, and of these only a few have ever hired labour, typically one employee at most. Before the period of reform shadow-economy activities did occur, but only sporadically, since it was rather risky to pursue them.

The most visible, and in my view the most important change has been the evolution of a significant private sector. This sector operates in various forms; we shall only mention the most important:

(*i*) *Small family businesses:* Here we find craftsmen, traders, owners of car repair shops, and the like. These are now licensed by the state authorities and allowed to hire a limited number of employees.

(*ii*) *Small family farming:* In this sector we find that part of the family's working time is spent on the private farm, while one or more members of the family often work on an agricultural cooperative, or on a state farm or in other sectors of the economy.

(*iii*) *Private 'business work partnerships'.* These must be officially licensed, and they may run small or medium-sized businesses. The members are owners who have formed a partnership to which they also jointly contribute their labour.

(*iv*) *Self-employed, freelance individuals; part-time workers serving larger companies, but working at home:* A substantial proportion of these work in the 'second economy'.

It is impossible to estimate the total size of the formal and informal private sector, since much of it, by definition, is unrecorded.

According to crude guesses, it generates one-fifth to one-quarter of total national output. At least three-quarters of all Hungarian families make some contribution to the second economy. Moreover the full significance of this factor lies not in actual production but, as was alluded to in our methodological discussion earlier, in the opportunity offered by the mere existence of a substantial private sector. Before the reform there was ultimately only a single employer, the state, hence there was no meaningful economic alternative to working in the state sector. Today, even if the great majority of individuals continue to be employed by the state, they have more freedom on account of the simple fact that the exit option exists. If they wish, they can start a private business or experiment with self employment, or become an employee of a private business. That is to say, in spite of the overwhelming presence of the state, its employment *monopoly* has been broken. The individual, consequently, has become far more independent, and though subject to many restrictions he or she can still be his or her own boss. The acquisition of this feeling marks a change of historical importance.

For those who are energetic and gifted, there are now two ways to move ahead in life, instead of only one. As before, they might always choose to make a career in the bureaucratic hierarchy, but another course is now open; they might choose to become an entrepreneur. Many individuals prefer the second option because they like taking charge of their own affairs, and enjoy the independence and the opportunities for risk-taking on the market.[17] In addition, they are often able to earn far more than those in the highest government positions, provided they are efficient, and encounter a bit of luck. It is exciting to see how genuine entrepreneurs have emerged again after a period of several decades in which this personal characteristic was almost completely suppressed. There are people, who in a truly Schumpeterian way, introduce innovations, create new products, open up new markets and establish new organizations.

But private activities are still severely impeded by a range of bureaucratic curbs: administrative licensing, capricious changes in taxation and handicaps in the access to land, buildings, materials, credit and foreign currency. There are upper limits to the number of people that can be employed: the number of permanent staff may not exceed nine (in commerce it may not exceed twelve), inclusive of family members. This can be circumvented, for example, by the hiring of more casual labour rather than permanent labour, but private businessmen feel, quite rightly, that there is no way for them to become 'big capitalists'. Moreover, and this is perhaps the most important constraint, small private business has been operating in an atmosphere of uncertainty and insecurity, without adequate guarantees of property rights and without protection against un-predictable bureaucratic intervention.

In a quick digression, let us look at the problem from the angle of moral and political philosophy.[18] It is important to ensure that all the restrictions imposed by the state are not motivated by *consequentialist* considerations of ethics; not motivated for example, by keeping in mind the distributional pattern to be achieved or by keeping in mind the limits of tolerable inequality. What really matters is the permissibility or rather impermissibility of a certain *procedure,* namely the 'capitalistic relationship between a private businessman and a large number of employees', resulting in certain income *entitlements.* A rich, private businessman might, if he wishes, spend his income on luxury goods. But he is not permitted to build up a large private business, even if the entrepreneur and a large number of prospective employees are willing to enter into a voluntary labour contract. In our judgement, this constitutes a serious curtailment of individual freedom of choice in order to prohibit the evolution of procedures and institutions of a capitalist kind.

To sum up, the reformed state is a curious and inconsistent blend of the traditional 'night-watchman' state — which protects the safety of public and private property — with a 'revolutionary organization' that limits property rights or in some cases goes so far as to appropriate private property.

8.4.2 Choice of profession, job and working hours

These issues have partly been covered in the preceding section on the state-owned and private sectors, but there are quite a few other issues which deserve further enquiry. The survey is presented here (and also in the latter sections 8.4.3 and 8.4.4) in a tabulated form.

The situation has not been perfectly uniform either in time or over the various segments of the economy. To obtain a sharper contrast, we have singled out the most extreme situations (which were by no means unimportant exceptions but were, rather, situations which have prevailed for some time in at least one major sector). We shall use the same selection in the subsequent tables.

Table 8.1 covers only the state-owned sector.

This table is self-explanatory, and we comment only on row 4. Here we must keep in mind the information provided in section 8.4.1 above, on the private sector and use it in conjunction with the information provided on the state-owned sector as described in table 8.1 In the maximal state individual options in connection with the classical choice, between more work (in order to earn more) and more leisure, were severely restricted. Work, in the sense of a regular job, was mandated by law, and only precisely specified exceptions permitted for reasons of health, maternity, and the like. Those who did not conform were labelled as 'parasites' and were liable for prosecution. An employee could be compelled to work overtime, but if overtime was not required by his employer, he could not find (and in fact was not allowed to find) other ways to earn more. This situation has changed dramatically in the reformed state. On the one hand individuals are now permitted not to have a regular job. While the old law obliging people to work remains in force, it is not consistently applied and violations are largely ignored. On the other hand individuals can now choose to work far more than the prescribed legal minimum of 40 hours, and they often hold second or even third jobs. They do a variety of odd jobs, working partly in the first economy and partly in the second economy. According to some estimates, at least half the adult population works for more than 60 hours a week, not counting household work, and a smaller fraction of the population works even more, 80 or 100 hours a week. As a result, many Hungarians are physically exhausted from overwork. But as far as the freedom of the individual to choose between work and leisure is concerned, it has expanded enormously.[19]

8.4.3 Consumer choice[20]

The changes are surveyed in Table 8.2, which is not fully comprehensive, since it only covers the most representative sectors. Just a few comments on the table need to be made.

Rows 3 and 5: According to the guiding notions of socialist transformation, housing and medical care are basic needs which the state must satisfy. Every citizen is entitled to them, and thus rents are much below the market-clearing level and medical care free of charge. But the individual has no way of influencing the quantity of resources used in these sectors, since it is entirely up to the bureaucracy to decide on their allocation. In fact, special attention is not paid to these basic needs: rather, the priority goes to other sectors,

Table 8. 1: Choice of profession, job and working hours

Choice problem	Maximal state: early fifties	
	State control (at the peak of bureaucratic centralization)	Remaining scope for individual choice
(1) Choice of secondary and higher eduction	Strong bureaucratic influence on the choice regarding where to apply for admission. Number of applicants greatly exceeds capacity of educational institutions. Severe selection, priorities according to political criteria. Where composition of demand for education and manpower diverge, applicants for higher education redirected according to requirements of production	Within the bureaucratric constraint, some (but not all) individuals able to influence decision concerning their education
(2) Choice of first job after education	Mandatory posting	Some influence on posting
(3) Change of job	Not permitted without consent of superiors. Severe penalties for 'arbitrary' quitting. Mandatory transfers if considered necessary by superiors. Mandatory use of 'labour exchanges' in arranging transfers from one job to the other	Employee able to initiate own transfer and in some cases to influence decision
(4) Extension of working hours	Bureaucratic pressure on employee to work overtime if required by enterprise. Otherwise usually prohibited	Minor possibilities of seeking extension of working time for extra payment
(5) Employment abroad	None permitted	None

Reformed state: mid-eighties	
Individual freedom (at the peak of decentralization)	Remaining bureaucratic constraints
Individual freedom in the choice regarding where to apply for admission	Excess demand for secondary and particularly for higher education remains. Many applicants not admitted. Bureaucratic assignment to certain professions in vocational training not infrequent. Composition of educational services not adjusted to demand
Free choice	None
No formal administrative restriction on changing jobs	Bureaucratic pressure against changing jobs can be applied in professions where the number of jobs is small
More flexibility in overtime arrangements. 'Enterprise business work partnerships' (Hungarian abbreviation VGMK), a new institution mainly providing opportunities to do extra work within the company at higher wages	Some bureaucratic constraint on 'regular' overtime. Many restrictions on the activities of VGMKs
Possible	Work permit from Hungarian authorities, required. Mandatory repatriation of prescribed percentage of foreign earnings

Table 8.2: Consumer choice: goods and services

Good or service	Maximal state: early fifties	
	State control and constraints due to shortages (at the peak of bureaucratic centralization)	Remaining scope for individual choice
(1) Food	In certain periods basic foodstuffs rationed (coupons). Chronic, intensive shortages; whole groups of commodities almost completely lacking. Some foodstuffs directly distributed to workers within state-owned enterprises. Special, better supplied stores for the privileged groups	Purchases for money subject to constraints listed on the left. Sporadic black markets
(2) Other consumer goods	No coupons. Chronic intensive shortages. Special stores (as in 1)	As 1
(3) Housing	*Urban housing:* Apartment housing nationalized. State-owned apartments allotted by authorities. Intensive shortage waiting lists for years. Frequent forced sharing of apartments. Forced evacuations and relocations by administrative order. Subletting severely restricted. Narrow limits within which houses or flats may be privately owned	*Urban housing:* Some minor possibilities for selling or buying privately-owned family houses or condominium apartments. Exchanges of state-owned apartments between tenants allowed on a voluntary basis, but official permit required. Some scope for obtaining a subtenancy *Rural housing:* mainly private; housing can be sold and bought, subject to administrative restrictions

Reformed state: mid-eighties

Individual freedom (at the peak of decentralization)	Remaining bureaucratic constraints and shortage phenomena
Great improvement in supply. Abolition of all official rationing. Abolition of stores for privileged, with some exceptions	Shortage phenomena persist, although much less intensive: partial shortages in the range available, late deliveries, insufficient allocation for some localities, etc. Special stores selling for convertible currency
Great improvement in supply	As in 1

Urban and rural housing: Rapid expansion of private housing; majority of new buildings private. Small proportion of state-owned housing privatized. Illicit, but tacitly tolerated trading of state-owned housing tenancies. Wide-spread subletting, providing substantial rent income to individuals in cities and in resorts	*Urban housing:* Greater part of urban housing still state-owned: intensive shortage, very long waiting time, poor adjustment of the composition of supply to demand
	
	Urban and rural housing: Severe limits on home ownership: what kind and how much housing may be owned by an individual.
	    Excess demand for mortgages, tight credit rationing.
	    Recurrent shortage of building materials and capacity for private building

Table 8.2: (continued)

Good or service	Maximal state: early fifties	
	State control and constraints due to shortages (at the peak of bureaucratic centralization)	Remaining scope for individual choice
(4) Transport and communication	All transport services supplied by state-owned enterprises. Private cars allowed only to a small number of privileged. Administrative allocation of telephone lines to homes. Extremely long waiting lists for telephones	Subject to constraints listed on left, means of transportation chosen by individuals. No special permit for long-distance domestic travel required (as in some other socialist countries)
(5) Medical service	National health service; medical care free of charge. No freedom of choice – mandatory assignment of doctor and place of treatment (hospital, etc.). Intensive excess demand for medical services, overcrowded hospitals and surgeries, long waiting lists. Private practice by doctors, prohibited with few exceptions. Special hospitals for privileged	In some cases a chance to influence which doctor individuals are assigned to and to choose the place of treatment. Some exceptions to the general prohibition of private medical practice
(6) Child care	Increasing proportion of women work due to low wages and social pressures. Institutional child care: public day nurseries and kindergartens. Excess demand for and administrative allocation of institutional child care	No administrative prevention of a mother staying at home with children

Reformed state: mid-eighties

Individual freedom (at the peak of decentralization)	Remaining bureaucratic constraints and shortage phenomena
Rapid growth in number of private cars, free market for second-hand cars. Queue-jumping for a telephone line allowed if the individual buys a telephone bond	Chronic excess demand for new private cars sold by a monopoly, state-owned company, long waiting lists. Privileged individuals can jump the queue. Waiting lists for telephones lengthening, administrative allocation continues
Curious 'dual-allocation' system in health service. Nominally still free of charge, but many patients tip doctors ('gratitude money') in the hope of better treatment, a practice which is illegal, but tolerated, and has strong influence on the choice of doctor and place of treatment. Private practice greatly extended	Formal mandatory assignment of doctor and place of treatment still prevails. Free choice not legal, and so risky and inconvenient. Excess demand for medical service remains or has even increased. Special hospitals for privileged continue
Extension of maternity leave, accompanied by modest financial support. Rising proportion of mothers stay at home with children, also encouraged by availability of part-time work or home-work. Some private child care: private kindergartens, babysitters, etc.	Some excess demand for public day nurseries and kindergartens remains, accompanied by retention of administrative allocation

Table 8.2 (continued)

	Maximal state: early fifties	
	State control and constraints due to shortages (at the peak of bureaucratic centralization)	Remaining scope for individual choice
(7) Recreation and travel to foreign countries	Places in public holiday accommodation assigned by trade-union officials. Travel to foreign countries for family visits and tourism very rare, allowed only to the privileged. Usually in organized groups without family. Tourism to Western countries almost nil	Holidays could be spent at homes of relatives or friends

that is mainly to those which the planners consider as having a direct impact on economic growth. Housing and health are persistently neglected, and their share of total national investment is far lower than in market economies. Centralization of resource allocation allows a suppression of consumer priorities.

The reform has brought about beneficial changes by enhancing the influence of consumer choice, but the changes have not been smooth or painless. After decades of neglect, the bulk of the burden of provision of housing has been passed back to the households. A citizen in need of housing is in deep trouble. There is not enough credit, and there is no well-developed system of small and medium-sized contractors prepared to build private homes quickly and reliably. Many households have been forced by shortages and by high prices to build their houses in a 'do-it-yourself' fashion, with help from family, friends and the second economy, at the expense of tremendous sacrifices in terms of money and time. Some households are simply unable to cope with this cumbersome process and become lost amidst the inadequate supply of public housing and the insupportable costs of private housing. Still, many individuals feel that

Reformed state: mid-eighties	
Individual freedom (at the peak of decentralization)	Remaining bureaucratic constraints and shortage phenomena

Many families own holiday home. Commercial holiday facilities (hotels, campsites, rooms in private homes) available.
  Very large number travel individually or with family to foreign countries, East and West, for family visits and tourism
	Administrative allocation in much public holiday accommodation (Trade Union, company guest houses) remains, but several other possibilities available.
	  Administrative permission required to travel abroad, including consent of the employer (except travel to a few socialist countries). Frequency of private tourist trips restricted. (See under purchase of hard currency in section 8.4.)

the situation has improved, because they at least have a clear conception as to how to tackle their accommodation requirements.

In the health service there is a somewhat perverse combination of bureaucratic rationing and veiled commercialization. The mere fact that medical care is free of charge to every citizen does not make patients satisfied, since the quality of service is frequently substandard. Besides there is substantial disaffection amongst the doctors and the medical staff. Louder and louder public complaints have pushed the planners to allocate more resources to the health sector. The wide-spread occurrence of 'gratitude money' is a peculiar signal of many people's willingness to spend more of their own money on their health directly, hoping to get better care and attention. However, an appropriate institutional and economic framework for satisfying the citizens' demand for medical care has yet to be found.

Attention should be drawn to row 7 of table 2 and also to row 5 in table 1, that is to the right to travel to and to work in foreign countries. The number of private Hungarian tourists travelling to non-socialist countries is increasing from year to year. From 22,000 in 1958 it has increased to 655,000 in 1985[21] (out of a population of 10.6 million). The number of tourists travelling to socialist countries is several times greater. In spite of remaining restrictions, this is a tremendously important change, and after decades of severe isolation, most Hungarians now enjoy the freedom to explore the world.

8.4.4 Household saving and investment

Under the pre-reform system the decision on how much to spend and how much to save out of their income was left to households, subject to certain restrictions.

Almost annually, low-yield government 'bonds' were issued and citizens were compelled to buy them by aggressive political campaigns. This practice has now been abolished. (We shall return to the problem of other, more 'commercial' bonds.)

Involuntary saving appears when consumer goods and services that are demanded are not supplied in sufficient volume and so a proportion of household income intended for spending cannot be spent. There is controversy among students of consumer macro-markets in socialist economies over the extent to which shortage-induced saving exists, given that involuntary saving is difficult to measure. In any case, wherever it has occurred it has clearly amounted to a restriction of individual freedom. Under the reformed state, spending possibilities have certainly expanded very much, if not in the first, then in the second economy. Hence shortage-induced saving, if it ever existed at all, has certainly ceased to be prevalent.

Once saving has been decided upon, the question arises as to what form the savings should be held in. Before the reform, the number of choices was very small. Most savings were kept in cash or savings accounts at the bank which typically yielded a low nominal (and in most cases a zero or negative real) rate of interest. Only a narrowly limited set of value-retaining real assets was available. The tight restrictions on purchasing real estate have already been mentioned. There were also administrative restrictions on holding precious metals and trade in art objects was small. The reform has increased the number of options. Banks offer a wider range of savings accounts, although the real interest rates remain low or even negative. Citizens can buy various life insurance, endowment and save-as-you-earn policies, to supplement the insurance and pensions provided by the state. Companies, cooperatives and local authorities now issue bonds with impressive returns, backed by a state guarantee, and these are proving very popular. The opportunities to buy real estate, though still very restricted, have widened, and the markets for other value-retaining assets have expanded.

In spite of these achievements serious restrictions remain.

Private business is in great need of outside financing and the state banking sector is tight-fisted with the credit it will provide. Many individuals would gladly lend to private business. Others would be ready to invest in private business and become silent partners in private enterprise.[22] These kinds of private financial and capital markets, of course, require appropriate institutions, legal regulations and a machinery for the enforcement of legal contracts. But these do not exist. On the contrary, such arrangements are illegal. Nevertheless, to some extent they are entered into, in the guise of personal loans and as acts of friendship (which are not illegal), and accordingly they are based solely on individual confidence, which makes them rather risky and prevents their expansion. Here, then, is a case in which the state, otherwise certainly more than a 'minimal' state, does not fulfil some of the necessary duties of even a minimal state, duties which require it to protect property and to enforce private contracts.

The proposal to allow state-owned enterprises to issue, in some way, common stocks making them in effect companies in mixed ownership, has been raised in discussion several times, but has not been accepted so far.

The Hungarian currency is not convertible. An individual Hungarian cannot purchase foreign currency freely, particularly not convertible currency. There are a few narrow channels for obtaining hard currency legally (for example a modest travel allowance which may be applied for every third year). Otherwise, there are fairly extensive illegal markets in various shades of black and grey, but operating in them is inconvenient and risky. This presents no small problem. Availability of foreign currency is a condition of full-fledged individual freedom, since it is required for the development of all kinds of human and cultural contacts with foreign countries.

This rounds up our brief comparison of individual economic freedom in Hungary before and since the reform. To sum up, the survey demonstrates what has been said in the introduction. The reform process has increased individual economic freedom substantially. At the same time, the present state of affairs does not satisfy those who regard liberty as a fundamental value.

8.5 GROWTH AND WELFARE VERSUS FREEDOM

What is the relationship between individual freedom and welfare? (Limitations of space do not permit the considerations of the relationship between freedom and other fundamental values.) Welfare is, of course, strongly associated with the growth of production and consumption.

There are two wide-spread views. Socialist ideology assumes a negative relationship between growth and material welfare on the one hand, and freedom on the other. While not denying the moral value inherent in individual liberty, it requires that it should be subordinate to the public interest. Once the new socialist order has been established, the public interest amounts to a steady growth in production and productivity that fuels a growth in consumption. Individual liberties that impede growth must be sacrificed for public interest.

There are many arguments designed to demonstrate the existence of a trade-off. The most important is the need for a high rate of investment, since this is regarded as the main engine of fast growth. A high investment rate, the argument runs, cannot be assured if investment is mainly or exclusively financed out of individual, voluntary savings. Moreover, fine-tuning of supply to consumer demand is costly, requiring too frequent modifications of production, too wide a variety of goods, too large a level of stocks, and so on. Bureaucratic centralization and chronic shortages, therefore, save these costs of fine adjustment.[23] Perfect freedom of labour causes too high a rate of mobility which undermines discipline and the smoothness of production and causes a loss of skills and of acquired experience. The list of arguments could be extended.

The opposite view, taken by the disciples of market socialism, points to a strong positive relationship between individual freedom and growth. Free choice, free enterprise, the profit motive and competition on the market are among the strongest stimuli to efficient effort.

Unfortunately, the Hungarian experiment has not provided us with conclusive evidence. It has not provided us with unambiguous support either for the 'complementary' or the 'trade-off' point-of-view. Part of the reason is, no doubt, the fact that the reform itself has been inconsistent so far, lingering half-way along the road to individual freedom. While the discipline formerly enforced by the bureaucracy has slackened and the state has grown 'softer', a natural consequence has been that various methods of forced growth achieved mainly with the help of extremely high investment rate and large involuntary savings rate are no longer available. At the same time the tough discipline of competition has not prevailed yet and so the motivation linked to free choice is not yet strong enough in all spheres of the economy.

At this point one can follow two alternative trains of thought. The first one, that of the constructive reformer, is to work out a programme for the elimination of the inconsistencies and for the strengthening of the bonds between free choice and efficiency. Such an exercise might no doubt be fruitful, but nevertheless another line of thought will be followed which hinges on a prediction. The prediction is that the Hungarian situation will not remain exceptional. If not in exactly the same way, something comparable, probably an inconsistent 'half-way' reform, can be expected to evolve in all other socialist countries which begin a reform process of decentralization and liberalization while maintaining their existing political structure. The prediction is supported by the preliminary experiences in China and Poland.

Let us now explicitly confront a choice problem: If we have to choose between the historical reality of the 'maximal' state and the other historical reality of a semi-reformed 'less-than-maximal' state, what should we prefer?[24]

Let us be more specific, and look at the German Democratic Republic, whose leadership has distanced itself from any Yugoslav, Hungarian or Chinese-style reform. It is a country in which the non-reformed institutional framework has been preserved intact and has managed its affairs in an intelligent and effective way. To justify itself, the Hungarian reform must bear comparison with the GDR. To this end, to facilitate comparison Table 8.3 presents the conventional figures for the growth rates of production and consumption of GDR and Hungary. At first sight the figures for the GDR are more favourable.

Before appraising them, however, a few words of qualification. First there might be a bias in the measurement of growth to the disadvantage of Hungary.[25] Second, we must also take into account the fact that the GDR has a special relationship with the Federal Republic of Germany, which certainly contributes to its impressive economic results. No other socialist country enjoys similar backing, and this factor certainly explains part of the difference.

It is difficult to arrive at a numerical estimate for the correct difference between the growth rates of the GDR and Hungary. To present the choice problem in a sharper form, let us assume that there *is* a positive difference in the growth rates of production and consumption in the GDR's favour. The other side of the coin,

Table 8.3: Average annual growth rates in GDR and Hungary (per cent).*

	German Democratic Republic	Hungary
National income		
(1) 1956–68	7.4	5.7
(2) 1969–86	4.7	3.4
Personal consumption		
(3) 1954–59	7.3	3.9
(4) 1961–74	3.9	4.7
(5) 1974–80	4.0	2.7
(6) 1980–83	0.5	0.2

* 'National income' is a net output concept within the framework of the 'Material Product System' (MPS), the accounting system used in socialist countries. 'Personal Consumption' consists of all consumer goods (excluded dwellings) purchased by households, received in kind as payment for work, or produced on own account on personal plots. The arbitrariness in choosing the periods for comparison is explained by the lack of commensurable data for the whole period. The data are not available for each year, the definition of personal consumption and the choice of base year for deflating current prices was altered repeatedly by the statistical agencies. These difficulties notwithstanding, the calculation of average annual growth rates is commensurable across the two countries for each period listed in the table. On the whole it seems to be obvious that the increase of personal consumption has been faster on the average in the GDR than in Hungary for the last 30 years.

Sources: Row 1: Central Statistical Office (CSO) (1971), p. 77.
Row 2: CSO (1971), p. 77. (1975), p. 73, (1986a), p. 64, (1986b), p. 374.
Row 3: United Nations (UN) (1968). pp. 236. 293.
Row 4: UN (1977), pp. 465, 579.
Row 5: UN (1982), pp. 435, UN (1983), pp. 576, 726.
Row 6: CSO (1986a), p. 306.

however, is that individual liberties are substantially greater in Hungary than they are in the GDR. In spite of a rather high consumption per capita rate, individual economic freedom in the GDR is strongly restricted by various shortage phenomena.[26] There are no thorough comparative studies, but observers would agree that the Hungarian consumer has more opportunities to choose from, mostly on account of the additional supply resulting from the informal private sector and on account of more generous consumer good imports. As for bureaucratic constraints on individual freedom, the difference in favour of Hungary is even more tangible. Comparing the two-dimensional performance vectors for each of the two countries (including a composite indicator of growth and material welfare in the first dimension, and a composite indicator of individual economic freedom in the second dimension), neither vector *dominates* the other. Put another way, we face a fundamental value judgement: a choice between greater individual liberty coupled with slower growth of production on the one hand, and greater material welfare coupled with restrictions on individual liberty on the other.

It clearly follows from the statement in the introduction that if under a given socio-political and institutional framework there would be a negative relationship, or a trade-off between the expansion of liberty and growth, then I would, with some qualifications, opt for the increase of liberty. That is to say, in case the only choice is between a well-managed, disciplined, tough, highly centralized GDR and a more liberal — and, yes, more anarchic — Hungary, I would prefer the Hungarian situation.

This evaluation does not imply a blanket appoval of all that has happened in Hungary since the beginning of reform. But this is not the place to present my critical analysis, which can be found in my other studies. Here, my statement means only that despite all the mismanagement, the great tragedies, the thousands of mistakes, inconsistencies and repeated reverses, the Hungarian road comes closer to my system of ethical values than the GDR road does.

The second qualification is that the above choice is not based on a lexicographical ordering, which unconditionally places liberty above all other values. I do not regard liberty as a yes-no problem. I am not prepared to sacrifice liberty in general; some restrictions on some of its dimensions would be accepted if such a sacrifice were indispensable to a significant improvement in material well-being. But

I would disapprove of giving up too much for too little, since I attribute a very high value to individual freedom. There is not, of course, any *a priori* quantitative criterion, of what is 'too much' or 'too little'. The ethical dilemma can, unfortunately, only be decided case by case.

Without intending to blur the sharp moral problem, one can go on to ask if such a sacrifice is really needed, at least in the present Hungarian situation. One can be sure that Hungary is not the efficiency frontier concerning the achievement of primary goals like welfare, justice and freedom. There are many potential measures of a further reform which could improve efficiency and material well-being without being accompanied by any further restriction of individual liberty. In fact, there are many potential changes which could improve efficiency and material well-being precisely by increasing individual freedom, that is by abolishing restrictions on competition and entrepreneurship.

8.6 VALUES IN PUBLIC OPINION

Commenting on the positive description of changes, I have talked explicitly about my own value judgement, but this has little importance. What really matters is the value judgement made by the Hungarian population.

A widely accepted stereotype put forward is that there are two, antagonistic attitudes: that is to say that the bureaucracy opposes the extension of individual liberty, but the rest of the people demand it. The real situation is not quite so simple:

A bureaucracy is not a homogeneous, monolithic social group. Many members are ambivalent in this respect. Most of them do not want to surrender their personal power, but they do not mind seeing the power of other individuals eroded. As citizens, they enjoy many of the liberties recently acquired: more freedom to choose in the education of their children, to select their own doctor if they are ill, to travel, to obtain consumer goods with less difficulty, and so on. Moreover, it is worth bearing in mind that many members of the bureaucracy, some in quite high positions, have lost their blind faith in the prevailing institutions and have become more open to new ideas.

As for the Hungarians in the street, they form a still less homogeneous population. E. Hankiss and his colleagues at the Institute of Sociology of the Hungarian Academy of Sciences conducted a remarkable survey in which they asked a large sample of individuals about their values and lifestyle. One set of questions was identical to the questions put by researchers in the United States and other Western countries to a similar sample. The subjects were asked to rank a set of 18 primary values, and the findings, relevant from our point of view, are summarized in Table 8.4. Americans attach a much higher value to freedom than Hungarians. Among Americans freedom follows immediately after peace and family security. Hungarians regard the same two values of peace and family security as first and second, but then these values are followed by five other values before we counter freedom.[27] Only 25 per cent of Hungarians rank freedom among the first four values.

What can be the explanation for this striking difference in preference, for the relatively low value attached to freedom by the Hungarians?

Have Hungarians become accustomed to a situation in which others must decide for them and all that remains for them to do is to obey? There is the parable in Dostoyevsky's *Brothers Karamazov*

Table 8.4: Ranking of primary values in Hungary and in the USA[a]

Primary value	USA 1968	Hungary 1978	Hungary 1982
Peace	3.30 (1)	2.54 (1)	3.88 (1)
Family security	3.81 (2)	4.09 (2)	5.30 (2)
Freedom	5.53 (3)	8.45 (9)	8.80 (8)
Equity	8.51 (7)	9.53 (12)	9.07 (10)
Salvation	8.75 (8)	17.70 (18)	15.47 (18)

[a] The evaluation is based on a representative random sample drawn nationally. For the sake of brevity we do not present the ranking of all the 18 values, only of a few selected examples. In each entry the first number is the mean of the ranks given by the whole sample. The second number in parentheses is the rank in the ordering over the whole set of 18 primary values according to the average ranks given by the sample of individuals.
Sources: For the first column Rokeach (1979), for the second column Hankiss et al. (1982). The data for the third column were supplied directly by Hankiss and his collaborators.

about the Grand Inquisitor who explains that people are scared of freedom and want to be directed by the supreme authority.[28] Paternalism gives a reassuring feeling of security and protection.

Or perhaps the well-known psychological effect of 'sour grapes' is at work: if one does not have enough liberty, for the sake of one's peace of mind, one adjusts one's aspirations to one's possibilities, and 'devaluates' freedom.[29]

Or can it result from a bias in education, and in the mass media? For decades the value of liberty has not been placed in the foreground of moral education. Characteristically, the crucial argument in favour of a legitimization of the market, decentralization or other reform measures was efficiency — the prospect of greater material welfare for greater, more intensive labour. Liberty as a value per se has hardly even been mentioned in the argument.

Table 8.4 does not show a clear trend, over a time period of 5 years, in the value attributed to freedom. Perhaps the trend has changed since the last survey in 1982 and will change further in the future. Maybe this is indeed the case in which, to use economic terminology, supply creates its own demand, at least in the long term. Hungarians receive more individual freedom, they become more accustomed to it and — after a time lag — demand more and more of it.

The survey had raised the question in a rather abstract way, by asking for a hypothetical ranking of general, primary values. Most Hungarians probably rate specific, well-defined individual liberties highly, while not being aware of the fact that these are part and parcel of a more general primary good, namely, individual freedom.

This explanation is indirectly supported by another study; a public opinion poll which was conducted on a small sample of blue collar workers and students in 1987.[30] This time no ranking of abstract ethical values was asked for, but a series of concrete, specific questions were raised to find out how much an individual is willing to pay for more freedom of choice. The answers show a rather high regard for this value. It turned out that about one-half of the respondents were willing to pay a significantly higher price for the following liberties: (1) choosing the primary school for a child freely, instead of the school assigned by the education bureaucracy, (2) choosing a doctor freely, instead of the doctor assigned by the health care bureaucracy and (3) choosing between a larger variety of TV programmes than the present two channels. The figures do not show large differences between the response of the two groups, except on the question concerning primary education. Here students attribute a significantly higher value to the freedom of choice, perhaps because they have a more immediate experience with the impact of the quality of primary education on later success in learning.

Our earlier proposition, namely that Hungarians value well-defined individual liberties highly, can be supported by another approach. There is clearly no excess supply of liberties; all new opportunities are immediately exploited, demonstrating that there has been a concealed demand for the right of free choice. Following the pattern of the theory of revealed preference, one could speak about a 'revealed ethical system of values'. Neither the intellectual advocates of reform nor its pragmatic implementers say much about individual freedom, but the movement of the institutional system in the particular direction surveyed in section 8.4 *reveals* a relative shift of moral values in favour of individual freedom.[31]

8.7 TOWARD A 'MEDIUM STATE'

What are the prospects? Almost half a century ago, F. Hayek[32] suggested that centralization, or even slight cuts in individual freedom would place the society on a slippery downward slope to complete etatization. He did not say so directly, but the reader is inclined to draw the ultimate conclusion: that this is a one-way street. Once the society has arrived at a critical point of centralization, at whose existence Hayek has clearly hinted, there might be no return. Looking back today on his analysis, full of remarkable insights confirmed by later experience, 'the one-way street' aspect of it at least is seen to have been disproved. The road between anarchy and complete state control, or more precisely between the minimal and maximal state is clearly two-way, and a wide variety of movements can be observed: slow progress in one direction which stops at a certain point, alternating, back-and-forth movements that are almost cyclical, and so on. The 'maximal state', as has clearly been demonstrated in the reforming countries, is not irreversible or final.

Many students of the socialist economies, myself included, expect that probably a blend of state control and individual freedom will evolve somewhere midway between the maximal and the minimal state. We might call it the *medium state*.

One cannot associate with this concept any notions of 'optimality'. Let us start with some normative ideas. In discussions of the role of the state among political scientists, economists and philosophers, three functions are mentioned: (1) Active governmental macro-policy is needed for stabilization, full employment and balanced economic relations with the outside world. (2) Governmental activities are required to combat adverse externalities and ensure the appropriate supply of public goods. (3) Governmental redistribution of income is called for on the grounds of social justice and in order to support the poor and weak. Let us use the term '*justifiable* medium state' for a state in which governmental activities are restricted to those which serve at least one of these three functions to a substantial extent. As a citizen I sympathize with the idea of establishing such a state, a fact which clearly follows from the system of values indicated earlier. I regard not only liberty, but also welfare (and along with it growth in physical output, efficiency and productivity) and social justice as fundamental values. Irrespective of these personal value judgements, I am fully aware that the normative idea of a 'justifiable medium state' is highly controversial; the fulfilment of the three functions just mentioned may cause great damage to one or other of the primary values. I want to be cautious in choosing the right epithet: I am talking about the 'justifiable' activities of the state and not suggesting that a state of that kind is patently justified. The epithet merely conveys the fact that one might put reasonable arguments in favour of such a state, and that these arguments cannot be rejected out of hand.

In any case, one should not expect the end results of the reform process in socialist countries to be a 'justifiable medium state' or the realization of any well thought-out blueprint embodying the three reasonable functions mentioned earlier. It will certainly not be an embodiment of a rigorous normative theory but will be an arbitrary, *ad hoc* medium state, arising out of improvisations, myopic political struggles, pressures and counter-pressures, innovation and inertia, and compromises between a yearning for the expansion of liberty and a temptation for its restriction. On the one hand such a state will retain governmental activities not needed for the performance of the three justifiable functions. On the other, some of the three functions may remain partly or completely unperformed, just as they have been up to now. For example, the state may not be sufficiently active in pursuing a reasonable stabilization policy (Function 1), or in protecting the natural environment (Function 2) or in supporting the needy through its social policy (Function 3), and so on.

Can such an arbitrarily evolved medium state solidify itself, and can there emerge an equilibrium between conflicting pressures for and against more state control, for and against more individual liberty?[33]

Powerful forces operate in socialist economies, which attempt to revert to the maximal state and to deprive the individual of free choice in many economic spheres. Many bureaucrats who have lost power want to regain it. Besides, there are also internal consistency requirements for administrative control. When a great deal, but not all, of economic activity is regulated in a bureaucratic manner, loopholes begin to appear. It is only natural that efforts are made to close these loopholes with more central regulations, laws and orders. Finally, traditional ideology and ethics have an important influence, because they appear to legitimize trends towards re-etatization, calling for an end to a whole range of undesirables, including anarchy, selfish individualism, profiteering, unearned income based on property instead of work, and the immoral affluence of a few fortunate people while the rest of society cannot share anything like the same level of welfare.

Yet there are opposing trends towards the medium (or perhaps the less-than-medium) state. The present dividing line between the legal rights of the individual and the actions bureaucratically prohibited or discouraged, is not a 'natural border'. Pressure is applied not for 'freedom' in general, but for specific extensions of individual liberties in the various dimensions of life.

The forces that seek to enhance individual economic freedom are not homogeneous. They consist of different categories differentiated by their general political philosophies and visions of a good state. Among them are liberal-minded bureaucrats willing to relax the stringency of control, and enlightened planners able to perceive the limitations of the old-fashioned command-economy and preferring to concentrate on the determination of a few main variables and relationships, while seeking to keep these indicators tightly under control. Many reformers are enthusiastic about a Scandinavian style of welfare state, which they hope will be more just and more egali-

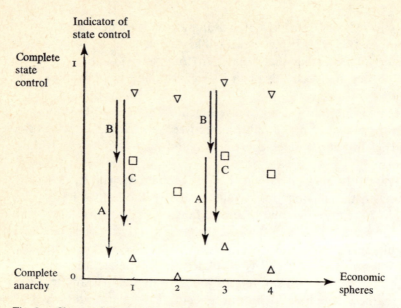

Fig. 8.2: Changes desired by Western conservatives and Eastern reformers. *Legend:* ∇ maximal state, □ medium state, △ minimal state. A: movements desired by Western conservatives, B: movements desired by Eastern 'mainstream' reformers, C: movements desired by Eastern extreme liberal reformers.

tarian than the present one. Then there are those who would like to go beyond a medium state, and closer to the minimal state, but are glad for the time being to see movement away from the maximal state, towards more individual freedom, however small that movement might be.

Here a brief digression is needed. Some Western observers view the Eastern European reformers as 'Thatcherites' in disguise. To explain what a gross misconception this is, let us use the scheme of fig. 8.1 again. In fig. 8.2 there are three arrows. *A* represents conservatives in the West, while *B* and *C* represent two groups of reformers in the East. What they have in common is that all their arrows point downwards, in other words they all want to roll back the activity of the state and increase individual freedom, a fact which explains why there is much in common in the argument and rhetoric they use. Nevertheless, the differences between the groups are extremely important. What is too much of state activity, and too little of freedom, for Group *A,* is a desirable level of state activity and an acceptable level of individual freedom for the mainstream of Eastern reformers. One finds more intellectual and ethical kinship between Groups *A* and *C,* that is between some of the Western conservatives and some of the Eastern 'extreme liberals' but perhaps even the people in Group *C* would have strong reservations about dismantling all the institutions created by the maximal and/or the medium state.

The dichotomy between Group *B* and *C* is a crude oversimplification. Even the previous, more qualified classification of the various currents among reformers is somewhat simplistic. It would be better to say that the camp of reformers includes a range of widely differing views, commitments, latent programmes and perspectives. Once a medium state is firmly in place this coalition might very well fall apart. Some groups would then want to move upwards again in certain respects, and some other groups would wish to move downwards in other respects. Controversies could become quite sharp over the precise line to be drawn in the collation of state power with individual rights. The cement holding the 'coalition' together is precisely the ever acute danger of reversal; the fear that things may take a turn for the worse. Ultimately, this cohesion may contribute to a stabilization of a 'medium' state in which the opposing political and social forces, the ideologies and the systems of ethical values are delicately balanced.

The evolution of such a 'medium state equilibrium' and its endurance is not a firm prediction. It is only one of the avenues which history might take. Complete or partial movements back to the maximal state, granted in many dimensions of life, cannot be excluded from the forecasts.

The outcome of all these trends will depend, as always in history, on the actual constellation of relative strengths of the various groups, and on many other unpredictable factors. What is certain is that all those who take an active part in the events now face an extraordinary intellectual and moral challenge and must bear great responsibility for future generations.

NOTES

1. Rawls traces the value attached to liberty back to the high value placed on self-respect, which is 'perhaps the most important primary good ... It includes a person's sense of his own value, his secure conviction that his conception of his good, his plan of life, is worth carrying out .... Self-respect implies a confidence in one's ability, so far as it is within one's power, to fulfil one's

    intentions ... Without it nothing may seem worth doing ... we sink into apathy and cynicism'. See J. Rawls (1971, p. 440).

2. There is a growing awareness of these relations among Hungarian authors; particularly among political scientists and sociologists, and recently in papers by economists advocating radical reform as well. Special attention of Hungarian scholars was drawn to the issue by the publication of the late I. Bibó's collected papers (1986), republishing his (1935) essay,[6] Coercion, Law, Freedom[9]. From the more recent literature we mention the remarkable studies by Antal et al. (1987), Bihari (1986), Bruszt (1987), Fricz (1987), Gombár (1984), Hankiss (1987). An outstanding contribution to political-moral philosophy is J. Kis (1986); his work is an analysis of the theoretical foundations of human rights. Unfortunately, most of this literature is not yet available in English.

3. In the apt phrase of Fehér, Heller and Márkus (1983): this is 'dictatorship over needs'.

4. For more detailed theoretical arguments against a simple-minded monistic approach see A. Sen (1985), especially the chapters on pluralism and incompleteness, and on pluralism, well-being and agency. Sen explains that in certain cases only a partial ordering of alternatives can be established in connection with ultimate moral principles. 'Assertive incompleteness' of the ordering may exist. 'There is — on this view — no additional moral criterion that can be used to rank the unranked pairs in terms of moral goodness ... Intelligent moral choice demands that we do not choose — explicitly or by default — an alternative that we can see is morally inferior to another feasible alternative. But this does not require that the chosen alternative be seen to be 'best' in that set of feasible alternatives, since there may be no best alternative at all, given the incompleteness of our moral ranking'. See Sen (1985, pp. 180–181).

5. For further criticism of an oversimplified 'welfarism' and for the discussion of moral theories in economics see. S.C. Kolm's (1987) paper presented at the Copenhagen meeting.

6. For the distinction between positive and negative freedom see I. Berlin (1969), G. G. MacCallum (1967), F. Oppenheim (1961, esp. pp. 109–135) and S. Gordon (1980, pp. 133–134).

7. For a more detailed analysis of the causes and consequences of the shortage syndrome see the author's book (1980) *Economics of Shortage*.

8. Assar Lindbeck in his Schumpeter Lecture (1988) talks about the loss in satisfaction when the consumer is prevented from achieving a better consumption bundle because of rationing or government decree. The term 'rationing' has a conventional narrow meaning in the sense of applying coupons or other forms of bureaucratic allotment. In recent disequilibrium analysis of any kind of allocation procedure used on the shorter side of the market is called rationing, including queuing or even a completely random selection. Shortage-imposed constraints on free choice appear in all types of rationing.

9. Perhaps it is not a hopeless task to try to devise composite indices of individual economic freedom, based on several observable, partial indicators of

freedom, in the same way that one might calculate a composite index of human intelligence or economic upswings and downswings.

10. See J. Locke (1960, 1967).

11. R. Nozick (1974) introduced the notion of an 'ultraminimal' state completely free from any redistributive function, in contradistinction to the classical definition of the minimal state which implies a certain degree of coerced redistribution; that is, even individuals who do not want protection, receive it and pay for it.

12. Imre Madách's 19th-century Hungarian drama *The Tragedy of Man* contains a prophetic anti-Utopian scene of a society called the *Phalanster*. (This name was adopted from the work of the eminent Utopian socialist, Fourier.) Here everybody has a mandatory, assigned job and must work in the collective enterprise. Plato is a shepherd. Luther a stoker, and Michelangelo a cabinet-maker carving the legs of chairs. See Madách (1861, 1953. pp. 127–145).

13. Here and in the rest of the chapter we shall not discuss the role of the Party separately. The functioning of the Party is thoroughly entwined with that of governmental agencies, the Party being the dominant force in this joint activity. Throughout the chapter, concepts like 'state', 'government' and 'bureaucracy' embrace the institutions of the Party.

14. The practice and the ideology of 'etatism' is analysed in B. Horvat (1982).

15. Data are available, but they describe the situation in minute detail, while here we shall deal with phenomena for which descriptive indicators cannot be measured by a simple process of summation.

16. The readers can find a more elaborate survey of the Hungarian reform process in this book. The study offers some statistics and a long list of references for those who seek more detail and more quantitative data.

17. On these two types of upward mobility and on entrepreneurship in the Hungarian village, see P. Juhász (1982) and I. Szelényi and R. Manchin (1986). See furthermore I. R. Gábor and T. D. Horváth (1987).

18. See R. Nozick (1974, esp. chs. 7 and 8) and also A. Sen (1981) and A. Sen and B. Williams (1982).

19. A public opinion poll in 1986 asked this question to a sample of individuals: 'What do you do when your real income declines?' The answer of 42 per cent of the respondents was, 'We cut expenses' while 41 per cent replied. 'We extend our working hours and earn more''. The source of the data and also of some more data referred to in the later parts of the paper is a memorandum compiled by K. I. Farkas and J. Pataki (1987) summarizing some findings of the Mass Communication Research Centre in Budapest. Their valuable help and the support of the Mass Communication Research Centre is gratefully acknowledged.

20. Limitations of space prevent examination of a very important aspect: the transmission mechanism between consumer choice and production response. For that purpose a close look at the operation of the price and taxation system, incentives to companies, etc. would be required. These could be topics for a separate paper.

21. *Source:* Central Statistical Office (1966, 1986b).

22. In the public opinion polls in 1983 quoted repeatedly, the following question was put to the sample: 'Assume that you inherited unexpectedly Ft 100,000 (around 1.4 year's average wage). You have two options: to place it into the usual savings account or to become a partner in a small private business. The second option is risky. Which one would you choose?' 48 per cent opted for the first and 47 per cent for the second. *Source:* K. I. Farkas and J. Pataki (1987).

23. P. Wiles, a distinguished analyst of socialist economies who was certainly not an exponent of the ideology of the socialist countries, wrote a paper entitled 'Growth versus Choice') (1956). His main line of thought was this: Socialist economies jettison the right of the individual to choose between 'more hair brush and less nail brush') or vice versa, but are able to enforce a high investment rate, and hence a high growth rate, which provides ultimately more brushes of both kind.

24. This seems to be a fair comparison. It is fair to compare either alternative utopias, or alternative historical realities. It is not permissible to compare an historically *real* Stalinism with the Utopia of an *ideal* 'market socialism'.

25. Hungarian experts on price statistics are convinced that Hungarian price indices are more accurate than those in most other socialist countries including the GDR and reflect the process of inflation better. If that is so, it will mean there is a bias in the comparison, to the disadvantage of Hungary insofar as we are concerned with real growth.

26. See Bryson (1984) about GDR consumption. Collier (1986) presents an extremely interesting study about the effect of forced substitution. He raised the following question: 'What would be the most an average East German family would be willing to pay for the 'bourgeois' right to attain its notional demand at existing prices? This sum as a percentage of original total expenditures is defined to be the gap between the effective and national purchasing power of the GDR Mark' (p. 24). Based on careful econometric analysis, Collier's estimate for the gap is 13 per cent. Since the actual number depends on the 'fineness' of accounting for forced substitution, a more disaggregated analysis would probably lead to an even larger gap. Translated into the conceptual framework of this paper: that is the surcharge the citizen would be willing to pay for the increase of individual freedom in consumer choice.

27. As for the distribution of rankings, freedom's value is higher among the younger generation than among the older generation, higher among the self-employed people or entrepreneurs than among state employees.

28. Dostoyevsky (1880, 1958, pp. 288–311).

29. On 'sour grapes', see J. Elster (1982).

30. *Source:* K. I. Farkas and J. Pataki (1987).

31. This observation does not imply that the shift in moral values has caused the institutional changes. This paper does not undertake a causal explanatory analysis of the changes in socialist countries. It only examines what values are *served* by the institutional changes. The approach leaves open the question of whether or not these values have really operated as motives.

32. F. Hayek (1944, 1976).

33. On this 'reform equilibrium' see T. Bauer's papers (1987a, b).

REFERENCES

Antal, L., Bokros, L., Csillag, I., Lengyel, L., Matolcsy G. (1987) 'Fordulat és reform' (Turn and Reform). *Közgazdasági Szemle*, 34, pp. 642–663.
Bauer, T. (1987a) 'Reforming or Perfectioning the Economic Mechanism', *European Economic* Review 31, pp. 132–138.
Bauer, T. (1987b) 'A gazdasági mechanizmus továbbfejlesztése vagy reformja?' (Reforming or Perfectioning the Economic Mechanism). *Közgazdasági Szemle* 34, pp. 527–546.
Berlin, I. (1969) 'Two Concepts of Liberty', in: Berlin, I. *Four Essays on Liberty*. Oxford: Oxford University Press, pp. 118–172.
Bibó, I. (1935) (1968). 'Kényszer, jog, szabadság' (Coercion, Law, Freedom). in: *Válogatott tanulmányok* (Selected Papers) Vol., 1. Budapest: Magvető, pp. 7–147.
Bihari, M. (1986) 'Reform és demokrácia' (Reform and Democracy), *Társadalomkutatás*, pp. 104–108.
Brust, L. (1987) 'A több szólamú politikai rendszer felé' (Toward the Polyphonic Political System), *Valóság, 30*, pp. 87–95.
Bryson, P. J. (1984) *The Consumer under Socialist Planning, The East German Case*, New York: Praeger.
Central Statistical Office (1966) *Idegenforgalmi adattár 1958–1965* (Reference Book of Tourism 1958–1965), CSO, Budapest.
Central Statistical Office (1971) *Statisztikai Évkönyv 1970* (Statistical Yearbook 1970), CSO, Budapest.
Central Statistical Office (1975) *Statisztikai Évkönyv 1974* (Statistical Yearbook 1974), CSO, Budapest.
Central Statistical Office (1986a) *Nemzetközi Statisztikai Évkönyv 1985* (International Statistical Yearbook 1985), CSO, Budapest.
Central Statistical Office (1986) *Statisztikai Évkönyv 1985* (Statistical Yearbook 1985), CSO, Budapest.
Collier, I. L. (1986) 'Effective Power in a Quantity Constrained Economy: An Estimate for the German Democratic Republic'. *Review of Economic Studies*, 54, pp. 24–32.
Dostoyevsky, F. (1880, 1958) *The Brothers Karamazov*, Harmondsworth: Penguin.
Elster, J. (1982) 'Sour grapes — Utilization and the Genesis of Wants', in: A. Sen, B. Williams (eds.): *Utilitarianism and Beyond*, Cambridge: Cambridge University Press, pp. 219–238.
Farkas, K. I, Pataki, J. (1987) 'Feljegyzés az 1980–86. évi gazdasági közvéleménykutatásokról' (Memorandum on Economic Public Opinion Researches in 1980–86). Unpublished manuscript, Budapest: Mass Communication Research Center.
Fehér, F., Heller, Á., Márkus, G. (1983) *Dictatorship over Needs*. Oxford: Blackwell.
Fricz, T. (1987) 'Az individualizáció esélyei' (Chances of Individualism), *Valóság, 30*, pp. 77–86.
Gábor, R. I. T. D. Horváth (1978) 'Bukás és visszavonulás a magánkisiparban'

(Failure and Retreat in the Private Small-scale Industry), *Közgazdasági Szemle, 34,* pp. 404–419.

Gombár, C. (1984) *Egy állampolgár gondolatai* (A Citizen's Thoughts). Budapest: Kossuth.

Gordon, S. (1980) *Welfare, Justice and Freedom.* New York: Columbia University Press.

Hankiss, E. (1986) *The Black Box: Interaction and Conflict of Social Paradigm in Contemporary Societies, Mimeo.* Budapest: Institute of Sociology.

Hankiss, E., Manchin, R., Füstös L., and Szakolczai Á. (1982) *Kényszerpályán? A magyar társadalom értékrendszerének alakulása 1930 és 1980 között* (Are We on a Forced Path? The Value System of the Hungarian Society between 1930 and 1980). Budapest: Institute of Sociology.

Hayek, F. A. (1944, 1976) *The Road to Serfdom.* Chicago, IL: University of Chicago Press.

Horvat, B. (1982) *The Political Economy of Socialism.* Armonk NY: Sharpe.

Juhász, P. (1982) 'Agrárpiac, kisüzem, nagyüzem' (Agrarian Market, Small-scale Enterprise, Large-scale Enterprise). *Medvetánc, 2,* pp. 117–139.

Kis, J. (1986) *Vannak-e jogaink?* (Do We Have Human Rights?), Budapest: Független Kiadó.

Kolm, S. C. (1987) *Liberty-based Public Economics: its Foundations, Principle, Method, Application and Structural Results.* Mimeo. Paris: CERAS.

Kornai, J. (1980) *Economics of Shortage,* Amsterdam: North-Holland.

Kornai, J. (1986) 'The Hungarian Reform Process: Visions, Hopes and Reality.' in this book, pp. 99.

Lindbeck, A. (1988) 'Individual Freedom and Welfare State Policy'. *European Economic Review, 32,* 1988.

Locke, J. (1960, 1967) *Two Treaties of Government,* New York: Cambridge University Press.

MacCallum, G. G. (1967) 'Negative and Positive Freedom', *Philosophical Review,* 76.

Madách, I. (1861, 1953) *The Tragedy of Man,* Sydney: Pannónia.

Nozick, R. (1974) *Anarchy, State and Utopia.* New York: Basic Books.

Oppenheim, F. E. (1961) *Dimensions of Freedom,* New York: St. Martins Press, London: Macmillan.

Rawls, J. (1971) *A Theory of Justice, Cambridge,* MA: Harvard University Press.

Rokeach, M. (1979) *Understanding of Human Values.* New York: Free Press,

Sen, A. (1985) 'Well-being, Agency and Freedom: The Dewey Lectures 1984', *Journal Philosophy,* 82. pp. 169–221.

Sen, A. (1988) 'Freedom of Choice: Concept and Content', *European Economic Review, 32,* 1988.

Sen, A. Williams, B. (1982) 'Introduction: Utilitarianism and Beyond', in: A. Sen and B. Williams, (eds.). *Utilitarianism and Beyond,* Cambridge: Cambridge University Press, pp. 1–22.

Szelényi, I. R. Manchin (1987) *Interrupted Embourgeoisement,* Mimeo. New York: Graduate School, City University of New York.

United Nations (1968) *Yearbook of National Accounts Statistics 1967,* New York: UN.

United Nations (1977) *Yearbook of National Accounts Statistics 1975*, New York: UN.
United Nations (1982) *Yearbook of National Accounts Statistics 1980*, New York: UN.
United Nations (1983) *Yearbook of National Accounts Statistics 1982*, New York: UN.
Wiles, P. (1956) 'Growth versus Choice', *Economic Journal*, 66. pp. 244–255.

Index